A dog is...

The dog is the most ancient of all domesticated species. It has successfully adapted to life with us through its willingness to accept the human family as its pack.

...a pack animal

A dog thrives in the company of other dogs. Through trial and error, ritual display, and sometimes by physical dispute, it finds its place in the pack and is content to remain a full member of an established social hierarchy. A dog's brain is adapted to communal activity – hunting, playing, sleeping, and eating together. In any group of dogs, there is a leader who controls collective activity and, although other dominant members may challenge the "top dog", the pack unerringly follows the leader's authority.

The placing of the dog's eyes gives it a wider field of vision than that of a human, although humans have a greater degree of binocular vision – seeing with both eyes at the same time.

Binocular vision
Monocular vision

140°
20°   20°

100°
70°   70°

Human field of vision

Canine field of vision

Most humans see the world in a spectrum of colours of light from red to violet (lower bar). Dogs see these colours differently (upper bar).

Spectrum of visible light as seen by dogs and humans

...driven by its senses

A dog's success as a hunter depends upon its acute senses. Its laterally placed eyes provide accurate peripheral vision allowing it to detect the slightest movement at a distance. Its hearing is adapted to detect the high-pitched sounds of small rodents and similar prey. A dog's most remarkable sense, however, is its ability to smell. An average dog has hundreds of millions of scent receptors in its nose – laid out flat, the surface area of its nasal membranes is far greater than the surface area of its whole body.

A dog can smell biochemicals – such as butyric acid, a component of human perspiration – at one millionth the concentration at which we can detect them.

The greyhound's robust skeleton provides an ideal framework for its body, cushioning the impact with the ground as it "flies" with superb speed and grace.

...full of energy

A dog is built to endure. It can survive without water four times longer than humans before suffering irreversible kidney damage. It can live without food for days at a time without a drop in energy-giving blood sugar. It can walk, trot, canter, run, or gallop far longer than humans without building up debilitating waste chemicals in its muscles. Its natural inclination is to lope and trot rather than walk or amble. A dog thrives on physical activity and is naturally inquisitive. It wants to explore, investigate, and evaluate, continually tasting the experiences of life.

Like humans, the dog has a lifelong need for play, not just as a learning experience, but as a satisfying end in itself.

The bond between dogs and humans develops through training and the use of rewards to reinforce positive behaviour.

...our best friend

A dog is our best friend because we share so many common characteristics. People and dogs are both gregariously sociable species that enjoy the company of others. Both are territorial: while people mark their territories with physical boundaries such as fences, dogs mark theirs with scents in body waste products. People and dogs enjoy play as a recreational activity. Both share common basic emotions, such as contentment, anxiety, jealousy, anger, sympathy, and elation. People and dogs share a variety of expressions and body language that's why we understand one another so surprisingly well.

People with lifelong attachments to dogs are generally healthier than people who do not own dogs, just as dogs with enduring social structures are more reliable, content, and even perhaps healthier than those without.

Massive temporalis muscle closes the jaw with enough force to crush bone

Large, powerful, deep-rooted canines for holding prey and tearing flesh

Blade-shaped molars slide past each other to shear meat from bone

Hinged jaw opens and closes with a scissor-like action

Masseter muscle allows only limited side-to-side movement of the jaw for chewing

The design of the dog's jaw is a vestige of its origins as a hunting animal – specialized for catching, killing, and eating prey. Modern dogs have adapted to domestic life, but their instincts for finding food still remain.

...an adaptable opportunist

A dog is ever alert to opportunity. As an evolutionary scavenger, it seldom passes up the opportunity to rummage through our leftovers, be it waste in the rubbish bin or the remnants of fast food meals on the street. A dog is a natural and wholly honest thief. If it sees something, whether it is another dog's toy, a piece of wood, a bone, or a piece of cake, it is fair game. Dogs are primarily carnivorous, but can survive on virtually any type of food, whether it is of animal or vegetable origin. The dog's superb adaptability has made it the most successful canine, and perhaps numerically the most successful land carnivore, ever.

A dog is a wonderful companion because its looks and behaviour press all the right buttons in us. We are putty in the paws of pups because their high foreheads and large eyes mimic the shape of the human infant face. We love to touch them because stroking a dog reduces blood pressure, skin temperature, and heart rate – physical changes that occurred in infancy when we touched our mothers. We enjoy caring for dogs because, perhaps uniquely amongst mammals, we have a lifelong need to nurture, to care for others.

...a companion
for life

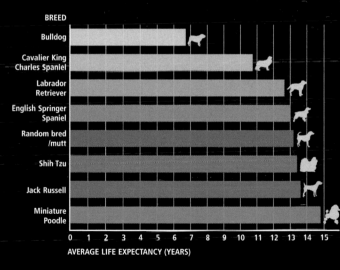

BREED

Bulldog

Cavalier King Charles Spaniel

Labrador Retriever

English Springer Spaniel

Random bred /mutt

Shih Tzu

Jack Russell

Miniature Poodle

0 1 2 3 4 5 6 7 8 9 10 11 12 13 14 15

AVERAGE LIFE EXPECTANCY (YEARS)

Dog life expectancy is different between breeds because breeding only for looks and temperament sometimes carries with it tendencies to certain life-shortening diseases as well. Size also has an influence on lifespan: giant breeds generally have a shorter life expectancy than smaller dogs.

Dog
Owner's
Manual

DR BRUCE FOGLE

LONDON, NEW YORK, MUNICH,
MELBOURNE, DELHI

FOR DORLING KINDERSLEY
Managing Editor **Deirdre Headon**
Managing Art Editor **Lee Griffiths**
Senior Art Editor **Wendy Bartlet**
Senior Editors **Heather Jones, Simon Tuite**
Senior Designer **Jo Doran**
DTP Designer **Louise Waller**
Production Manager **Lauren Britton**
Production Controller **Mandy Inness**
Picture Researcher **Sarah Duncan**
Picture Librarian **Hayley Smith**
Jacket Designer **Nathalie Godwin**

FOR COBALT ID
Editors **Kati Dye, Marek Walisiewicz**
Art Editors **Darren Bland, Paul Reid**
Illustrator **Debbie Maizels**

Produced for Dorling Kindersley by Cobalt id

The *Dog Owner's Manual* provides general information on a
wide range of animal health and veterinary topics. The book
is not a substitute for advice from a qualified veterinary
practitioner. You are advised always to consult your
veterinary surgeon or other appropriate expert if you have
specific queries in relation to your pet's health. Before
administering any medicine or any treatment to your pet,
you should ensure that you always read and follow the
instructions contained in the information leaflet. The
naming of any organization, product, or alternative therapy
in this book does not imply endorsement by the publisher
and the omission of any such names does not indicate
disapproval. The publisher regrets it cannot accept any
responsibility for acts or omissions based on the
information in this book

2 4 6 8 10 9 7 5 3 1

First published in Great Britain in 2003
by Dorling Kindersley Limited,
80 Strand, London, WC2R ORL
A Penguin Company

A CIP catalogue record for this book is available from the
British Library

ISBN 0-7513-5158-X

Colour reproduction by Colourscan
Printed and bound in Slovakia by Tlaciarne BB

See our complete catalogue at
www.dk.com

Contents

Introduction 19

CHAPTER ONE
Dog design 20

Origins 22
Skin and coat 24
Skeleton and movement 26
Brain and mind 28
Hormonal responses 30
Vision 32
Hearing, scent, and taste 34
Breathing and circulation 36
Consuming 38
Urinary and genital systems 42
Immunity 44
Communication 46
People and dogs 48

CHAPTER TWO
Breeds 50

Selective breeding 52
Showing your dog 54
Dogs with missions 56
Small dogs 58
Medium-sized dogs 82
Large dogs 93
Extra-large dogs 117
Mixed breed dogs 128

CHAPTER THREE
Behaviour 130

Natural variability 132
Pack mentality 134
Canine genetics 136
Courtship and mating 138
Expecting puppies 140
Giving birth 142
Dependent on mother 144
Early socialization 146
Joining the human pack 148
Table manners 150
Marking territory 152
The importance of play 154
Regular groomers 156
Graceful aging 158
Do dogs love us? 160

CHAPTER FOUR
Living with your dog 162

Choosing your dog 164
Dog equipment 168
Crate training 170
The first 24 hours 172
House training 174
Practical toys 176
Home and garden 178
Training essentials 180
Basic training 182
Behavioural problems 188
Body maintenance 194
Good nutrition 198
New experiences 202
Canine activities 204

CHAPTER FIVE
Health concerns 206

Choosing a vet 208
Examining your dog 210
Practical prevention 212
Parasite control 214
Responsible ownership 216
Giving medicines 218
When accidents happen 220
Life-saving first aid 222
Wounds and injuries 226
Poisoning 228
Skin and coat conditions 230
Respiratory disorders 234
Blood and circulation 238
Brain disorders 240
Hormonal disorders 242
Muscles, bones, and joints 244
Spinal disorders 250
Mouth and teeth 252
Stomach problems 254
Digestive disorders 256
Urinary tract disorders 260
The reproductive tract 264
Eye disorders 266
Hearing disorders 268
Immune-system disorders 270
Cancer 272
Emotional disorders 274
Geriatric conditions 276
The end of a dog's life 278

Glossary of medical terms 280
Useful contacts 283
Index 284
Acknowledgments 288

Introduction

The dog is one of the animal world's greatest success stories. It is found on every continent, in every type of habitat, and often in great numbers – more than 150 million in Europe and North America alone. The dog's transition from wild wolf to pampered family pet has taken just 12,000 years – a blink of the eye in evolutionary terms – largely because of its capacity to adapt to new environments shaped by humans. This book concentrates on the continuing relationship between dogs and people. It explores our influence on their shape, size, and behaviour. It examines the ways in which we interact with dogs, harnessing their natural instincts for mutual benefit. And it focuses on practical techniques for maintaining good health, setting out what to do when problems happen. Living with a dog can be challenging, tiring, exhilarating, and immensely rewarding – often all in the course of one day. This book gives you the means to make the most of this special relationship.

DR BRUCE FOGLE
DVM, MRCVS

CHAPTER ONE

Dog design

The dog is perhaps the most versatile and the most extreme of all mammals – a product of its great genetic malleability. In no other species is there such overwhelming variety in size, shape, colour, and coat length and texture. Internally, the dog's heart, lungs, and muscles are designed for endurance; its digestive system is able to cope with animal or vegetable sources of nutrition; and its body wastes are adapted for use in communication with other dogs. The dog has the ability to learn throughout life and its sensory abilities are outstanding. In particular, its ability to use scent, both to hunt and to communicate with other dogs, is so much more sophisticated than ours that it is beyond our comprehension.

Origins

- Dogs evolved from meat-eating mammals
- The wolf is the domestic dog's closest relative
- Human intervention created today's breeds

The domestic dog, and all other members of the canine family, or Canidae, evolved to pursue and capture prey in open grasslands. The dog (Canis familiaris) belongs to the genus Canis, along with its closest relatives – the wolf, the coyote, and several species of jackal. Other members of the canine family include 21 species of fox, hyenas, the African Wild Dog, and the Raccoon Dog. All of these animals share a common evolutionary past and a large variety of similar behaviours.

STRIPED HYENA
(HYAENA HYAENA)

RED FOX
(VULPES VULPES)

The wolf family

The parentage of the domestic dog has been meticulously investigated by anatomists and behaviourists for over 100 years, and it is now a commonly held belief that the wolf is its direct ancestor. Of all the members of the Canidae family, wolves (Canis lupus) are the most sociable, and vary most in their social organization and size, and even in their coat colour. Until its numbers were decimated by human hunters, the wolf was the most widespread of all land mammals.

The first domestic dogs

It is unlikely that the domestic dog developed from the wolf as a result of intentional selective breeding. It is more probable that the dog is "self-domesticated", and that initial changes in size, physiology, and behaviour occurred through natural selection. At least 12,000 years ago, wolves were attracted to the first sites of permanent human habitation. This new environment favoured the survival of small, sociable animals. No doubt humans took wolf cubs from their dens and cared for them. The dogs that evolved guarded campsites, assisted in hunting, and provided food when wild prey was scarce.

Modern dogs

Natural environmental pressures resulted in the wolf becoming smaller, relaxed with humans, and sociable, but it was only after many generations of selective breeding by humans that the great diversity of dog breeds developed. Intensive selection increased barking, valuable as a warning signal. Drop ears and a different tail carriage were also selected for, to distinguish domesticated

Prehistoric ancestor

A mongoose-like animal that lived over 30 million years ago, *Cynodictis* is believed to be an ancestor of the wolf and the dog. This fossilized skull was found in North America, where it is possible that the dog's earliest ancestors may have evolved.

CYNODICTIS SKULL

dogs from their wilder, less predictable ancestors. The size of the frontal sinuses on the head increased, making the dog appear more intelligent. At first, dogs were bred to be smaller than wolves, with the creation of miniatures and dwarfs. Later, size was enhanced, producing today's giant breeds.

GOLDEN RETRIEVER

JAPANESE CHIN

WOLF *(CANIS LUPUS)*

Although today's dog breeds look strikingly different to their wolf ancestors, the wolf is actually a closer relation to the Golden Retriever and Japanese Chin than it is to other canines such as the fox or hyena.

Skin and coat

- Skin has protective and sensory roles
- Dogs shed and replace their coat regularly
- Coat texture varies between breeds

The dog's skin and hair provide a physical barrier, preventing harmful chemicals and microbes from entering the body. The skin is a sensory organ that controls the temperature of the dog's body – raising or lowering of the hair increases or decreases heat loss. Glands in the skin secrete or excrete substances that give the coat its shine and nourish the skin. Individual skin cells carry out surveillance for potential dangers to the dog's body, and influence the immune response when injuries occur.

The structure of the skin

The skin consists of two main sections. The surface (epidermis) is thin and not particularly strong, but preserves its protective function and integrity by continually laying down new cells.

Under the epidermis, the strong, elastic dermis provides strength, as well as the blood and nerve supply to the epidermis. Within the dermis are numerous skin glands, such as the tubular sebaceous glands: these secrete a waterproofing substance called sebum into hair follicles to protect, nourish, and lubricate the epidermis.

OLD ENGLISH SHEEPDOG

DOBERMAN

Short, hard, glossy coat

Hair growth

The dog's hair grows in cycles. There is an active growth period, followed by a transitional period, then a resting period. One hair is shed when another is ready to replace it. The growth cycle is controlled by a number of factors, including temperature, increasing or decreasing daylight hours, body hormones, nutrition, stress, and genetic influences.

Hair is shed most prolifically in spring, when the dense winter coat is no longer needed, and again in the autumn when the short summer topcoat is replaced by a long, dense coat, and new down grows. Changes in the production of pituitary, thyroid, adrenal, and sex hormones dramatically affect coat texture and density. Male hormones stimulate increased hair density, while female hormones have the opposite effect.

Paws

The nails and pads of the foot are modified skin structures. Nail is produced from a specialized extension of the epidermis. The footpads have a thick, protective, insulating epidermal layer, and are much less sensitive to heat and cold than are other parts of the dog's skin.

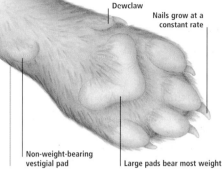

Dewclaw

Nails grow at a constant rate

Non-weight-bearing vestigial pad

Large pads bear most weight

Coats of hair vary more dramatically in dogs than in most other domestic species, because many hairs of varying texture can grow from an individual hair follicle. The robust primary hairs, often called the topcoat, may be surrounded by small secondary hairs, also known as down or undercoat.

STANDARD POODLE

Profuse, long topcoat covering a waterproof undercoat

The Poodle's coat does not shed and grows continually, so it must be clipped

Skeleton and movement

- An athletic body for an energetic lifestyle
- Powerful muscles allow agility and stamina
- A strong skeleton encases the vital organs

The dog is a natural hunter, and combines strength with resilience. The robust skeleton provides a superb framework for the dog's body. A sturdy skull, with deep, protective pockets for the eyes and ears, surrounds the brain. Folds of nasal membrane are attached to delicate bone, housed inside the muzzle. In the neck and back, the

The working skeleton

Bone is living tissue that needs constant nourishment. This is supplied via blood vessels that enter the shaft of each bone through a "nutrient foramen". If this blood supply is destroyed, the bone dies. In puppyhood, bones grow at "growth plates" near the ends of bones. These regions, profusely supplied with blood, are softer than mature bone, and more prone to damage.

If a bone breaks, its fibrous surface produces new cells to bridge the gap of the fracture. Once filled, the fracture is remodelled from the inside.

Thigh muscles give explosive energy for the chase

vertebrae have extensions to which powerful muscles are attached. As there is no collarbone, the shoulder blades are unattached to the rest of the skeleton, allowing great flexibility for running. Long ribs form a protective cage housing the heart, lungs, and liver. The shoulders and hips act as pivots, enabling the limbs to move gracefully and accurately. The skeletal system is held together by strong ligaments, elastic tendons, and powerful muscles adapted for endurance.

A healthy dog is athletic and energetic.

Powerful foreleg muscles extend the leg

Robust rib cage protects the vital organs

Joints and ligaments

Bones are joined at cartilaginous joints, which act like shock absorbers for the body, cushioning concussive forces as the dog runs and jumps. Each joint is surrounded by a joint capsule, filled with lubricating joint fluid. Fibrous ligaments anchor bones together in a different way, permitting movement only in specific directions, while preventing excessive movements that might cause injury to delicate parts of the anatomy.

Muscles and movement

Dogs are built for endurance and strength, and a healthy dog has perfectly coordinated movement and a smooth gait. The front legs bear over 60 per cent of a dog's weight, while the hind legs have massive muscles to power instant acceleration and to maintain speed. Muscles are attached to the skeleton by elastic tendons, and are supplied with oxygen carried in the blood.

Neck muscles allow head to be turned over 220 degrees

Powerful jaw muscles give strength to bite or hold

Muscles protect the delicate oesophagus

Shoulder is attached to body only by muscles

Thin muscle covers outer chest

The achilles tendon is the most prominent tendon in a dog's body

The dog has three types of muscle – smooth muscle controlling movement of organs; cardiac muscle in the heart; and skeletal muscle. Of these, only skeletal muscle is under conscious, voluntary control.

Diminished size

Although outwardly they look very different, the diminutive skeleton of the Maltese Terrier is extremely similar to that of its wolf ancestors, but for its reduced size. Smaller size first appeared naturally in dog evolution, but this trait has been accentuated through our intervention in dog breeding. Miniaturization proportionally reduces the size of every bone, from the skull, to the ribs, to the long limb bones.

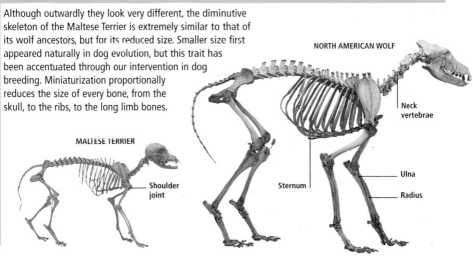

NORTH AMERICAN WOLF

MALTESE TERRIER

Shoulder joint

Neck vertebrae

Sternum

Ulna

Radius

Brain and mind

■ The brain processes information from the senses
■ The central nervous system transmits messages around the body
■ Every dog has a unique personality

The dog's brain synthesizes, interprets, and acts on all the information it receives from the senses. This vital organ needs a great deal of nourishment to function properly, and is served by a large artery bringing oxygenated blood from the heart. The brain and spinal cord, together known as the central nervous system, are protected by the robust bone of the skull and spinal column. Sensory information, transmitted from nerve receptors in the organs and tissues, travels through peripheral nerves to the spinal cord, and then to the brain.

The brain receives 20 per cent of the blood flow from the heart.

Cerebrum

Pituitary

Thalamus gland

Hypothalamus

Cerebellum

How the brain works

The brain consists of billions of cells (neurons), each of which may have up to 10,000 connections with other cells. These carry information in the form of electrical impulses. Neurons communicate with other neurons using chemicals called neurotransmitters. The speed of these transmissions depends partly upon a fatty substance called myelin. In the dog's prime, messages are transmitted at great speed, but as the brain ages, messages move more slowly. In certain diseases, myelin is not formed properly, or degenerates; this results in reduced nerve function.

Instinct and learning

Input from each sense feeds into the brain through its own set of dedicated nerves. A network of cells throughout the brain, known as the limbic system, almost certainly integrates instinct and learning. The conflict between what a dog instinctively wants to do and what we teach it to do probably takes place in the brain's limbic system. Humans can override this system by giving rewards to the dog for obeying its owners rather than following its "lower" instincts.

The central nervous system

The brain is the control centre of the central nervous system, and the spinal cord is its major highway for sending information around the body. Twelve pairs of nerves originate in the brain and supply regions of the head and neck, such as the eyes and nose. Further pairs of nerves that emerge from the spinal cord serve the rest of the body.

All complex behaviour – for example, the response of a male dog to the scent markings of another dog – involves the central nervous system. When the male dog picks up the scent, information travels to the brain via the olfactory nerve. The brain passes electrical activity down the spinal cord to the spinal nerve that serves the bladder.

These signals stimulate the sphincter muscle (which keeps the bladder shut) to relax. The feeling of imminent sphincter relaxation is sent via the spinal cord back up to the brain. Here it triggers more brain activity, which feeds back down the spinal cord to the nerves feeding the muscles of the hind leg. This instructs the dog to lift its hind leg before urinating.

Your dog's mind

All dogs behave within the constraints of the canine brain, but that does not mean that dogs only function on instinct. Far from it. Each dog has its own unique character, tolerance, trainability, and

Touch

Touch is the first sense a dog develops, and remains important throughout its life. The entire body, including the paws, is covered with touch-sensitive nerve endings. Over the eyes, on the muzzle, and below the jaws are touch-sensitive hairs (vibrissae), capable of sensing air flow.

"intelligence". Your dog's mind is that of a sociable member of an extended family – the pack. In one sense, the dog's mind is similar to our own: personality is uniquely formed both by genetic inheritance and from learning and early experiences.

Trainability varies between different dog breeds. German Shepherd Dogs are extremely quick learners and will master new tasks with ease.

Hormonal responses

- Hormones regulate body responses
- Feedback mechanisms control hormone levels
- Training influences a dog's hormonal feedback

Hormones – the body's chemical messengers – are responsible for managing and maintaining a dog's body functions in response to both internal and external changes. Most hormones are produced by the major endocrine glands: the pituitary, thyroid, parathyroid, and adrenal glands, the ovaries or testicles, and the pancreas. Hormones produced by these glands are discharged into the bloodstream, travelling to act on other parts of the body. The endocrine system is controlled by the pituitary – a "master" gland situated at the base of the brain. This is, in turn, under the control of a chemical-producing part of the brain called the hypothalamus.

Hormonal feedback

Hormone levels are maintained and adjusted by "negative feedback". This works in a similar way to the control of

Hypothalamus controls pituitary activity

Pituitary gland stimulates other glands

Thyroid gland is controlled by pituitary gland

Hormones travel in bloodstream to target cells

Adrenal glands, adjacent to kidneys, produce adrenalin and cortisone

Kidneys

Testosterone production in testes is controlled by pituitary gland

Hormonal feedback integrates and coordinates the body's responses.

a room's temperature by a thermostat and boiler system: a thermostat monitors air temperature; if the temperature falls below a set point, the thermostat switches the boiler on. Once the temperature has risen above the set point, the thermostat switches the boiler off again.

In the endocrine system, a sight, sound, or smell may stimulate production of a hormone by the pituitary gland. This hormone travels in the bloodstream to other glands, stimulating them to produce a number of new hormones that act on organs and muscles to provide a response. The new hormones also travel in the bloodstream to the pituitary, and diminish production of the original stimulating hormone. This form of reciprocal control occurs constantly to maintain and control body responses.

Pituitary gland

The pituitary gland produces a variety of hormones that control several other endocrine glands and influence a range of physiological processes in the body. Hormones produced by the pituitary stimulate the adrenal and thyroid glands, and regulate growth, egg and sperm production, sex-hormone manufacture, production of skin pigments, concentration of urine, uterine contractions, and milk letdown.

Adrenal secretions

The central portion of the adrenal glands – the adrenal medulla – is primarily under the control of the nervous system. When the dog is stressed or sexually excited, the medulla produces adrenalin, a component of the "fight or flight" mechanism.

Hormonal influences

Dog behaviour is largely influenced by hormonal body responses. These responses are not only determined by genetics, but also by early experiences and training.

A mother dog's normal "fight or flight" response is overridden during lactation, ensuring that her puppies are not put at risk. The same hormones that stimulate milk production also have a calming influence on her.

Puppy play is not just important for exercise and improving balance, but also allows the young dog to develop greater control of its emotional hormonal responses.

Training can teach dogs to overcome their natural hormonal instincts.

Vision

- Dogs have sensitive eyesight characteristic of a hunter
- Dogs have a wide angle of vision
- Colour is unimportant to dogs

Dogs are far better than humans at seeing the slightest movement far in the distance, but at close range their eyesight is not as good as ours. A dog's eye is flatter than that of a human, and although the dog can change the shape of its lenses, thereby adjusting focal length, it cannot do so as effectively as we can. A dog's eyes are more sensitive to light and movement than ours, but their resolving power is correspondingly less efficient. The consequence is that a human finds it easier than a dog to see a lost tennis ball lying in the grass, whereas a dog can more easily see slight movements out of the corners of its eyes.

Peripheral vision varies between breeds of dog, depending on the position and slant of the eyes.

Shades of grey

Colour vision is of less importance to carnivores than it is to animals that feed on coloured berries, fruits, and seeds: the dog's eyes typify the carnivore design. The retina has a high proportion of "rod" light receptor cells; these register only in black and white, but are responsible for sensitive vision in very low levels of light. The dog's retina has far fewer "cone" cells – light receptors required for colour vision and seeing in bright light conditions.

Behind the retina is a glistening, opaque layer of cells known as the "tapetum lucidum"; this enhances vision at twilight by reflecting faint light back to the rod cells, and can be seen as a glowing reflection in your dog's eyes when you take a flash photograph. To further aid night vision, dogs can dilate their pupils widely, to capture as much light as possible.

How the eye works

The light-sensitive retina in the eye detects light and converts it into nerve impulses that are sent down the optic nerve to be interpreted by the brain. Light entering through the pupil is focused on to the retina by the transparent cornea and lens. The iris regulates the amount of light entering the eye by increasing or decreasing the size of the pupil. Behind the lens is a large, fluid-filled posterior chamber. Glands in the eye produce tears to keep the cornea moist, and a third eyelid, hidden by the lower lid, sweeps the eye clean.

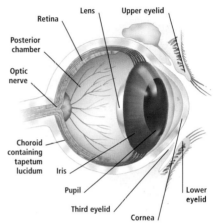

Retina
Lens
Upper eyelid
Posterior chamber
Optic nerve
Choroid containing tapetum lucidum
Iris
Pupil
Third eyelid
Cornea
Lower eyelid

Sighthounds were bred to hunt by sight – to detect, and then chase, capture, and kill prey. These special breeds, such as the elegant Borzoi, are alert and athletic, with keen eyesight to detect the slightest movement at distance.

Hearing

- A dog's hearing is four times better than ours
- Dogs can hear sounds too high-pitched for our ears
- A dog's acute hearing helps us with training

Mobile ears scan the environment for sound.

Both ears are used to capture and funnel the sound waves.

The location of the source of sound is pinpointed.

A dog can locate a source of sound in six-hundredths of a second, and it can hear sounds four times further away than a human can. Dogs are also better at hearing high-pitched sounds, and can detect sounds in the ultrasonic frequency range that are inaudible to humans. This requirement evolved in the dog's wolf ancestors, whose diet of large herbivores was supplemented with small animals, such as mice, that make high-pitched calls. For the domestic dog, however, acute hearing can be a disadvantage: some dogs have extremely sensitive hearing and develop a fear of certain sounds, such as the rumble of distant thunder.

Humans have exploited the keen hearing of dogs to make training and communication easier. Dogs respond quickly to the sound of a whistle or a clicker. For example, shepherds just need a whistle to communicate with their sheepdogs over great distances.

Ear structure

The cartilaginous outer ear (pinna) captures sound, and funnels it down the external ear canal to the eardrum (tympanic membrane). Vibrations in the eardrum are passed on to structures in the middle ear – the hammer, anvil, and stirrup. Known as the ossicles, these bony structures amplify and transmit sound, and protect the inner ear from excessive vibration. The cochlea (part of the inner ear) captures these sounds and converts them to nerve signals, which are sent to the brain for decoding.

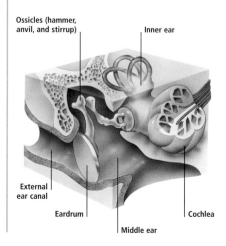

Ossicles (hammer, anvil, and stirrup)

Inner ear

External ear canal

Eardrum

Middle ear

Cochlea

Scent and taste

- Smell is a dog's most important sense
- Sensory cells in a dog's nose transmit scent information to the brain
- Dogs have an uncomplicated sense of taste

Dogs have far fewer taste buds than do humans. Although their limited number of taste buds register a range of tastes, it is probably more realistic to think of the dog's response to taste as pleasant, indifferent, or unpleasant.

Smell is the dog's most advanced sense, and a large part of a dog's brain is devoted to interpreting scent. The scenting ability of some dogs is so acute they can detect odours diluted to one-millionth the concentration at which humans can detect them. Dogs have a sex scent-detecting vomeronasal organ in the roof of the mouth; this scenting apparatus transmits information directly to the limbic system – the part of the brain most intimately involved in emotional behaviour.

How these senses work

Taste receptors on a dog's tongue are sensitive to sweet, sour, bitter, and salty tastes. Dogs have a well-developed sense of smell – moisture on the nose helps to capture scent, which is then transmitted on to the lining of the nasal membranes where there are closely packed sensory cells. These convert the scent to a chemical message, which is then transmitted to the olfactory bulb region of the brain.

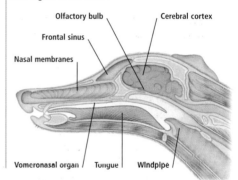

Olfactory bulb   Cerebral cortex

Frontal sinus

Nasal membranes

Vomeronasal organ / Tongue / Windpipe

Dogs use their sense of smell as an important tool for communication, gleaning a variety of different types of information about one another through careful analysis of each other's body odours.

Breathing and circulation

- The blood system transports oxygen around the body
- Red blood cells absorb oxygen in the lungs
- The liver removes waste products from the blood

Blood carries nourishment – in the form of oxygen and nutrients – around the body. If a dog exercises vigorously, a great deal of oxygen is required, and the dog's respiratory and circulatory systems respond automatically, increasing blood flow through the heart and lungs. Although the supply of blood to the brain remains constant, flow to the heart muscle quadruples, and flow to body muscles increases twentyfold. If needed, up to 90 per cent of the blood pumped out by the heart can be diverted to the muscles, providing the dog with extra stamina. At the same time, blood flow to other parts of the body diminishes.

Blood circulation

The heart pumps blood around the body through a network of blood vessels. Pressure varies within this system – it is highest in the blood vessels leaving the heart and lowest in

The heart and blood system provides oxygen to all tissues in the body, and transports waste products to the liver for detoxification.

Carotid artery carries blood to the brain

Trachea carries air to and from the lungs

Ribs protect the heart and lungs

Pulse can be felt in femoral artery in groin

Major arteries transport blood from the heart

Heart size and shape varies according to size of dog

Veins drain waste-laden blood back to liver and lungs

Feet have a profuse supply of blood

Red blood cells

Red blood cells *(below)* can carry oxygen because they contain the chemical compound haemoglobin. Iron atoms in haemoglobin combine loosely with oxygen from the lungs to form oxyhaemoglobin, which has a bright-red colour. The heart pumps the freshened blood around the body where the blood cells release oxygen to the tissues, reforming simple haemoglobin. Venous blood that has given up its oxygen has a dark, red-blue colour.

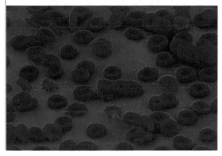

A dog's circulatory system responds to increased exercise to provide extra oxygen to the muscles and expel carbon dioxide as rapidly as possible.

the blood vessels returning to the heart. Vessels taking blood away from the heart (arteries) have strong, elastic walls that can withstand the higher pressure, and can expand and contract to alter flow. Vessels returning blood to the heart (veins) have thinner walls and contain valves; these allow blood to flow only in one direction, ensuring the circulation of blood back to the heart.

The muscles in the walls of the very smallest arteries – the arterioles – can constrict and relax under the control of the nervous and hormonal systems. This allows the body to vary the quantities of blood passing through these vessels and redirect it to where it is most needed. Any increase in muscle activity, and the corresponding increase in waste products, causes local arterioles to dilate, increasing the flow

of blood through that vessel up to 256 times the resting flow, and quickly getting blood to the required area.

At the end of the arteries and arterioles are tiny capillaries – thin-walled blood vessels that feed into all areas of the body. Here, oxygen, nutrients, and waste products are exchanged by diffusion through the capillary walls.

Gas exchange

The lungs consist of a highly branched network of tubes leading to clusters of alveoli – these are like tiny balloons that can be inflated with air. When a dog breathes in, air is drawn through the nose, down the windpipe or trachea, and inflates the lungs.

Oxygen diffuses through the walls of the alveoli into the bloodstream, where it is absorbed by red blood cells and transported for use throughout the body. Waste carbon dioxide passes in the opposite direction, and is expelled.

Consuming

- Dogs are opportunistic omnivores
- Digestion takes place primarily in the intestines
- A dog's teeth are ideal for a mixed diet

Unlike other predators, dogs are omnivores, eating more than just meat. They have far fewer taste buds on their tongues than humans, and are willing to consume almost anything that might offer nourishment. This lack of fussiness is combined with a sensitive vomiting reflex, which permits them to reject foods after eating if they are unpalatable or dangerous.

The dog has a large stomach and a relatively short intestinal tract, an ideal arrangement for the opportunistic hunter and scavenger. Food breakdown starts in the stomach, but most of the digestion takes place in the intestines.

Natural gorgers

In the wild, dogs gorge themselves when any kind of food is available, and then live off that nourishment for several days. The food sits in the stomach where it remains largely undigested, and only a small amount at a time is passed into the intestines. In well-fed domestic dogs, and especially in larger breeds, this natural gorging behaviour, combined with insufficient exercise, can lead to serious weight problems.

The dog's diet

A nutritious, well-balanced diet produces a well-muscled, strong-boned, healthy-coated canine. Part of the daily diet of a healthy dog should consist of meat: this is a good source of protein, and also provides fat that contains the essential fatty acids needed for a variety of body functions, including good skin and coat condition.

The remainder of a dog's diet should consist of soluble and insoluble fibre, and a balanced diet will also provide all of a dog's daily vitamin requirements. Some dogs like to eat grass and other vegetation. Grass, roots, berries, and uncooked vegetables are poor sources of nourishment – being hard to digest – but they can provide roughage.

The dog's dentition

The dog's mouth is ideally constructed for a scavenger's diet. It is long and deep, with large canine teeth for stabbing, catching, and holding prey, small incisors for nibbling meat off bones, and for grooming its skin and coat, and premolars and molars adapted both for shearing and cutting meat, and also for grinding and chewing foods such as roots and grass. Saliva lubricates food after it is chewed to ease its entry into the digestive system. Canine teeth are sturdy and strong, although they may chip or fracture when bones are chewed. A more common

Dogs evolved to eat whatever is available, and to eat it quickly before someone else can.

Canine teeth

The dog's set of teeth is specialized for an omnivorous diet, with 12 small incisors for cutting and biting, four large canine teeth with extremely deep roots for holding and tearing meat, 16 premolars for shearing, cutting, and holding, and 10 molars to chew and grind meat and other food.

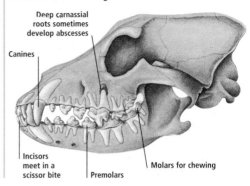

Deep carnassial roots sometimes develop abscesses

Canines

Incisors meet in a scissor bite

Premolars

Molars for chewing

problem, however, is periodontal disease, a bacterial disease of the soft and hard tissues that surround and support the teeth. This condition is often seen in companion dogs; it affects 70 per cent of dogs over four years of age, but can be prevented through routine dental hygiene.

As humans, we suffer from tooth cavities because of the large amount of sugar we consume; food also catches between our teeth, which have pits and fissures in their biting surfaces. Dogs are much less susceptible to cavities because the teeth are not so tightly packed, and food does not get trapped. There are also few pits and fissures where food can stagnate.

The gastrointestinal system

The alimentary canal – the path by which food enters the body, is converted into nourishment and absorbed, and waste is expelled – is structurally simple, but its function is complex. The process of digestion starts in the mouth, where the action of the teeth begins to break food down. Saliva in the mouth binds it together and lubricates it for passage through the oesophagus; production of saliva also keeps the mouth "clean" and taste buds sensitive. The oesophagus is very elastic, and allows large lumps of meat to pass through; unfortunately, this also permits undigestible objects such as bones and toys to be swallowed.

Food passes through the oesophagus to the stomach. Acid and enzymes produced by the stomach begin to break down protein, connective tissue, and muscle fibres in the food. Secretion of these digestive "juices" is controlled by gastrointestinal hormones. Glands in the stomach produce mucus to prevent the gastric acid from damaging the walls of the stomach or intestines.

Waves of muscle contraction in the stomach mix the food and move it towards a tight valve – the pyloric sphincter – which opens to allow portions of food to enter the small intestine.

The intestines

The common bile duct delivers bile produced by the liver, and digestive juices from the pancreas, into the top of the small intestine, or duodenum. These secretions contain bicarbonate, to neutralize the stomach acid, and enzymes that break food down into simple molecules that can be absorbed through the walls of the small intestine. The absorbed nutrients pass into the bloodstream and are transported for use by the body's cells. The walls of the small intestine are lined with finger-like

The dog's gastrointestinal system permits it to gorge on food infrequently but copiously.

Oesophagus dilates to allow food to pass

The pyloric sphincter, hidden behind tip of spleen, relaxes to permit food to enter intestines

Nutrients are absorbed into the bloodstream in the small intestine

Stomach acts as a large holding tank

The role of bile

The liver produces a digestive liquid known as bile. This acts on food in the small intestine, breaking down fat into a suspension of tiny droplets, and helping to dissolve fat-soluble vitamins. Bile contains bile pigments – the product of the breakdown, by the liver, of haemoglobin from red blood cells; these pigments give bile its characteristic yellow colour. The pear-shaped gall bladder receives and stores bile produced by the liver, and concentrates it by removing water. When food enters the duodenum, hormones are released that stimulate the gall bladder to deliver its payload of bile, through the common bile duct, into the small intestine.

Gall bladder

Common bile duct

Pancreas

Small intestine

projections called villi, increasing the surface area available for absorption of nutrients. Waves of muscle contraction in the small intestine mix the food and move it along.

Once digestion is complete, the residue passes to the large intestine, or colon, where water and salts are absorbed. The colon is inhabited by vast numbers of bacteria – these decrease the body's susceptibility to infection, synthesize vitamins, and break down waste material. Within 36 hours of eating, waste food is converted to faeces, and is expelled.

Increased thirst can indicate a medical problem, and should be investigated by a vet.

The role of the liver

The liver has a central role in digestion: it produces bile acids to break down food, and also carries out a wide range of metabolic functions. Nutrients carried in the bloodstream travel to the liver, where they are modified into different forms, stored for later use, or distributed to the rest of the body. For example, excess carbohydrate is converted by the liver into glycogen, and stored until needed; when required the liver converts it back into glucose. The liver also neutralizes harmful substances, such as drugs and poisons.

Daily water requirements

A dog loses water daily in urine and faeces, through panting, and to some extent through sweating from the pads. Dogs are as dependent on water as humans, and can suffer irreversible body dehydration and damage if it is unavailable for over 48 hours. Although canned dog food is usually 75 per cent liquid, this is not enough to satisfy a dog's needs. Dogs should be provided with a clean bowl of water every day to drink from when thirsty.

Urinary and genital systems

- The kidneys filter the blood of potentially harmful waste
- Male dogs are constantly sexually active
- Female dogs have two reproductive cycles per year

The dog's urinary and reproductive systems are integrated in a typically mammalian fashion. Two kidneys filter the blood of unwanted or potentially toxic substances, and clear waste is passed to the bladder. A single urethra discharges urine from the penis, or through the vulva of the female. The reproductive system integrates itself into the latter part of the urinary system. Spermatic cords from the male dog's testes carry sperm through to the urethra. In the female, the vagina leads to the vulva, where the urethra empties.

How the urinary system works

Each kidney consists of around 400,000 individual filtration units called nephrons. Each nephron is enveloped in a symmetrical rosette of microscopic blood vessels called a glomerulus. This is where blood is cleansed of waste.

As a dog ages, the number of nephrons diminishes, to be replaced by scar tissue. However, it is only after the majority of nephrons have been destroyed that a dog shows typical signs of kidney disease, such as increased thirst and increased urinating.

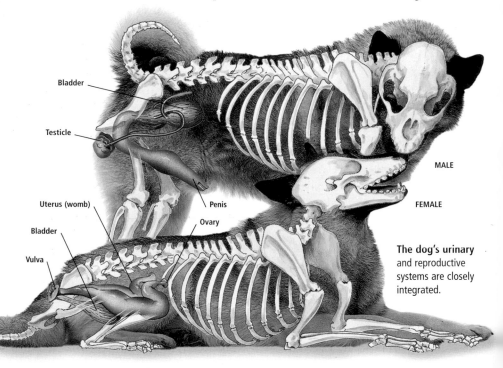

Bladder

Testicle

MALE

Uterus (womb)

Penis

Ovary

FEMALE

Bladder

Vulva

The dog's urinary and reproductive systems are closely integrated.

Urine from the nephrons collects in the hollow middle of each kidney, and travels down the urethra to the bladder, where it is stored and intermittently released. The sphincter muscle controls the exit from the bladder.

Any condition that affects the sphincter muscle, whether physical, hormonal, or psychological, can cause it to relax, triggering the release of urine. When diagnosing a urogenital problem *(see also pp.260–63)*, a veterinary surgeon may analyse a dog's urine for content such as protein, blood cells, glucose, mineral crystals, or bacteria, and also may test for acidity or alkalinity (pH) and concentration.

Hormonal influences

The male dog mates opportunistically and is always sexually active. From puberty onwards, sperm cells are produced in coiled masses of tubes in the dog's testes. The male is attracted to the scent of hormonally active females, and this stimulates the pituitary or "master gland" at the base of the brain to instruct his testes to produce more testosterone and sperm cells.

The female will usually have two hormonally active reproductive cycles (oestrous cycles) each year. For about 12 days before oestrus, her vulva swells and she produces a discharge. During oestrus, lasting five days, this discharge stops and her ovaries release eggs into the fallopian tubes. Only then does she choose a mate. If mating is successful, the resulting pregnancy lasts for about 63 days *(see pp.140–41)*.

However, even if mating does not occur, the female will still experience a hormonal pregnancy (or metoestrus stage) lasting eight weeks, followed by a

Mating

Sperm cells *(below)* are stored in the epididymis and, during mating, travel through two spermatic cords to the prostate gland. Here they are mixed in a transport medium with a high sugar content. This provides nourishment to keep the sperm cells healthy. Sperm is passed to the bitch during mating, and meets released eggs in the fallopian tube, where union occurs. The fertilized eggs develop in the uterus over the next two months.

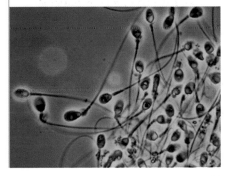

15-week period of reproductive rest (anoestrus stage) until the next season.

When to mate

A bitch is sexually mature by 10 months of age, and willingly mates during her first oestrus. However, at this early stage in her life, she has not yet reached emotional and physical maturity; this often leads to small litters and poor mothering. Mating is usually more productive during subsequent oestrus cycles.

Most bitches ovulate between 10 and 12 days after the cycle begins, but this pattern can vary between individuals, so most breeders mate their bitches twice, on the 10th and 12th, or 11th and 13th days. Examining vaginal smears under a microscope gives a reasonable indication of when a bitch has ovulated, but a more accurate assessment can be made by monitoring hormone levels in the blood.

Immunity

- The body has many lines of defence against invaders
- Defences may be innate or specific
- Full immunity takes time to develop

The job of a dog's immune system is to recognize, stop, and destroy disease-causing viruses, bacteria, fungi, and mycoplasms (pathogens), and to deal with internal dangers, such as cancer. Some parts of the immune system offer a general, innate, form of protection, while others are highly specific – like magic bullets designed to deal with specific invaders.

Innate defences

The largest component of the immune system is the skin, which is an effective barrier against most pathogens, as long as it remains unbroken. Any invaders trying to gain access through the body openings and internal passages are met with a variety of enzymes contained in mucous secretions; and pathogens that reach the digestive tract are faced with a very hostile chemical environment –

the stomach, for example, contains deadly hydrochloric acid as well as protein-digesting enzymes, and many bacteria are killed by the bile salts secreted into the small intestine.

Pathogens that manage to penetrate these outer and inner surfaces encounter a further barrage of innate defences. Blood chemicals called complement proteins attach to and burst invading bacteria; specialized white blood cells called phagocytes swallow up and digest foreign molecules, cells, and viruses; while chemicals called interferons increase the resistance of neighbouring cells to infection by the same or other viruses.

Early immunity derives from antibodies passed to pups in the mother's first milk.

Specific defences

A single millilitre of blood contains about five million oxygen-carrying red cells, and some 100,000 white cells. These white cells are involved in the body's targeted responses to invaders. Two different types of white blood cell, known as B and T cells, mediate two different kinds of immune response, which operate simultaneously to destroy invading pathogens.

Immune responses

B cells work by recognizing proteins (antigens) on the surface of an invader, such as a bacterium. Each B cell can "recognize" only one antigen, but the body of a mature dog contains a vast number of different B cells. Between them, the B cells are capable of dealing with almost any invader the dog encounters. When a B cell recognizes "its" antigen, it quickly divides and its clones begin to produce antibodies – proteins that bind specifically to the particular antigen. The antibodies seek out and lock on to the bacterium, destroying it in the process. T cells work in a slightly different way (see right), detecting and destroying mutated or virus-infected cells.

Immunity and maturity

Immunity takes time to develop, but temporary immunity is passed by a mother to her pups in her first milk. At birth, a pup's intestinal tract is permeable enough for these maternal antibodies to be absorbed into the bloodstream and so give protection from infectious agents. Maternal antibodies drop to low levels when a pup is about 10–12 weeks old, which is when it needs its final inoculation.

T cells and immunity

A form of immune response based on cells called T cells targets virus-infected parasites, and cancer cells. Rather than antibodies to attack invaders, T cells engage directly with the enemy.

1 Cells infected with virus are first engulfed by phagocytes. They are then brought into contact with T cells, some of which match up to the invader's antigens.

Virus-infected cell | Viral antigen | Phagocyte | Non-matching T cells | Matching T cell

2 The matching T cell divides and multiplies. It produces killer T cells, which contain toxic proteins, and memory T cells, which "remember" the viral antigen in case of future reinfection.

Memory T cell | Killer T cell | Toxic proteins

3 Killer T cells lock on to the infected cell and release their cargo of toxic poisons, which destroy the invader. The killer T cells can then go on to seek out further infected cells.

Released toxin | Infected cell | Antigen

Inflammation and healing

Injury often causes redness, pain, and swelling. This happens because cells around the injury site release the chemical histamine. This in turn triggers local blood vessels to become "leaky" and allow phagocytes to escape into the tissue – these engulf and dispose of foreign cells (below).

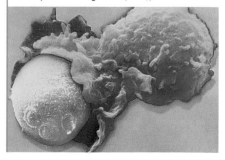

Communication

■ Dogs use an effective language of sounds
■ Scents and odours impart a wealth of information
■ Body language can convey status

Dogs have a rich vocabulary of sounds, scents, and postures through which they convey remarkably subtle messages to other members of their species. Their voices can communicate alarm, warning, or pleasure, and a range of canine emotions. Scent in their urine and faeces marks out their territory and establishes the sexual status quo. Body language, including subtle shifts in the position of ears and tail, can express a vivid panoply of feelings and instructions.

A howl can mean loneliness, alarm, or even celebration.

Vocal expression

Canine vocal communication is surprisingly effective. A mother quickly learns the different voices of each of her puppies, and understands their sounds of hunger, pain, and pleasure.

Dogs express themselves vocally with a variety of sounds – infant cries, whimpers, and whines; warning growls and sharp barks; attention-seeking, plaintive barks and howls; painful yips; yelps and screams; and pleasurable moans. For the wolf, the howl is the most important vocal method of communication, but dogs bark more than they howl, a trait intentionally enhanced through domestication. The dog's alarm bark was perhaps one of the first canine traits selected for by our ancestors.

Scent marking

Dogs cock their legs to leave their urine scent marks as close as possible to the nose level of other dogs. Males attempt to leave as much information about themselves as possible – it is not unusual for a male dog to mark 80 distinct sites with his urine in a four-hour period.

A male urinates to cover smells of other dogs

Using body scents

Smell is the most important sense for a dog. To mark their territory, dogs leave scent markers to act as "business cards" – these give information about the status of the depositor.

Dogs produce chemicals called pheromones, which are present in saliva, faeces, and urine, and in secretions from the vagina and penis. By mixing or coating body waste products with these chemicals, dogs use their waste to distribute information.

As well as the scents in body waste products, the dog produces body odours in virtually all other body discharges and secretions, including saliva and ear wax. All these odours transmit information, and dogs sniff each other to pick up this

Body language is instinctive in dogs. This puppy has dropped into a "play bow", a distinctive and vivid gesture that simply, eloquently, and silently asks another dog to join in play.

data. For example, the ear odour of a female dog may contain substances that indicate her sexual status.

Body language

A dog displays its emotions, thoughts, and demands through detailed body language. Subtle changes in the positions of the ears, tail, mouth, face, hair, or posture convey a wealth of facts. Eye contact is particularly potent. The dominant dog stares, while the submissive dog avoids direct eye contact by averting its gaze. Body posture is equally explicit. The dominant dog stands erect; the submissive dog grovels. We can understand and interpret the dog's body language because we communicate with each other and with dogs in similar ways.

Body postures are not static; they reflect the dog's changing emotions. The calm dog has relaxed tail and ears, but as it becomes alert, both are raised. If the dog then feels aggressive, it raises its hackles, lifts its tail higher, and pulls back its lips to display its teeth. It displays further aggression by leaning forward and snarling.

People and dogs

- There is a breed of dog to suit everyone
- Human intervention has had positive and negative effects
- There is no justification for tail docking and ear cropping

All of us have personalities, aspirations, and values that we consider to be uniquely our own. The joy of dogs is that there are so many different temperaments, looks, sizes, and abilities within the species, we can satisfy our own needs by carefully selecting a dog that fits us like a glove. Consider your choice carefully: if you love dogs, but the idea of wiping drool off the walls does not appeal, a St. Bernard may not be your ideal choice. If you are a control freak and like everything done your way, you would probably be better off with a small Poodle on which you can carry out canine topiary, rather than a sleek Basenji. If you want to be surrounded by those who love, honour, and obey, there is nothing better than a female Golden or Labrador Retriever.

Remember that appearance is not all that matters. A breed may look good, but the way it looks probably reflects the original job for which it was developed. Its other characteristics – its instincts, behaviours, and habits – may well make it unsuitable as a pet for you.

Improving the dog

Selective breeding has brought about enormous changes in dog design over the millennia. We have reduced and enlarged the dog's body, flattened its face, and shortened its legs. Certainly we have shrunk its brain

Selective breeding has enhanced the features in dogs that we find appealing or useful.

Genetic interference

Perhaps the greatest imminent threat to dogs comes from genetic engineering. We will soon be able to modify breeds in previously unimaginable ways, by inserting new genes from dogs and other species. The uses of genetic engineering may have apparent value – for example, producing a dog that does not make the canine skin allergen, Can F1, which provokes allergy in people – but they may also be frivolous or insidious. Engineering for shapes or behaviours that are not part of the dog's natural repertoire is one possible outcome. Our relationship with dogs has, until now, been mutually beneficial. Only time will tell whether that mutuality continues.

and greatly truncated its intestinal tract. We have increased the incidence of inherited disease in some dogs while dramatically extending the natural life expectancy of others.

Going to extremes

For much of the 20th century, breed standards favoured extremes: a head as big as possible, skin as wrinkly as possible, eyes as prominent as possible, size as small as possible. Fortunately this is no longer the case, and virtually all breed standards have been rewritten. However, this does not mean that all breeders now aim for these physically healthier shapes; some will still breed for extremes because it is, unfortunately, good for sales.

Surgical "improvements"

It was once believed that cutting off a dog's tail would prevent it from getting rabies. This procedure is called docking, and it developed into a traditional practice with working dogs, especially terriers and

spaniels, to prevent tail injuries. Today, many companion dogs still have their tails amputated, but only to satisfy the vanity of their owners. Tails are usually removed within three days of birth; puppies feel pain when this is done, but as their nerves are not fully developed, the sensation of pain is often delayed.

Other dogs have their ears partly amputated – "cropped" is the benign word people like to use – for no other reason than to make them look fierce. This is primarily a German tradition, born out of the military origins and uses of breeds like Great Danes, Boxers, Dobermans, and Schnauzers. This mutilation is banned in its country of origin, and also in most other places. North America remains the only significant region in the world where ear and tail amputations are still routinely performed.

There is no medical or work-related justification for any of these procedures to be performed on companion dogs. Many dedicated, dog-loving veterinary surgeons will no longer carry out tail docking or ear cropping for ethical reasons.

Tail docking should only be performed for medical reasons.

CHAPTER TWO

Breeds

It is tempting to think of breeds as discrete categories – like apples and pears. In reality, there are no fixed boundaries: any group of dogs in which the pups are physically and behaviourally similar to their parents is a "breed", and unrecognized "breeds" still exist throughout Asia, Africa, and parts of South America. However, what we conventionally call a breed is a group of dogs selectively bred to conform to a "breed standard" – a set of ideal characteristics written by a breed club. While there are over 400 recognized breeds worldwide, the 20 most popular constitute almost half of all pedigree dogs, and the top 50 make up over 90 per cent of all dogs.

Selective breeding

- Dogs were originally bred for a specific function
- Today they are bred more for form and temperament
- Breed standards have exaggerated some features

From the earliest days of the species, the evolutionary fate of the dog has been in human hands. People have always selected dogs from which to breed to produce the best working animals – herders, guards, and eaters. But it was only when people developed "leisure time" that selective breeding of dogs for their looks really took off.

Royal influence

Hunting has been a priviledged pastime of royal courts from China to western Europe for thousands of years, and many dogs were selectively bred for their hunting abilities. For example, small dogs were bred to spring birds from cover; these evolved into today's spaniels. Larger dogs were bred to find animals that had taken cover; these are the forbears of today's pointers.

Breeding for looks

Royalty bred their hunting dogs to impress – a pack of colour-coordinated lemon and white hounds looked better than a mixed pack. Selective breeding for looks had begun, and it accelerated as wealthy women in many countries began to keep small companion dogs as living fashion accessories. These dogs were bred for their coat texture, colour, and affectionate personality, as well as their diminutive size.

The first dog shows

By the mid-1800s, ownership of dogs bred for their looks was common amongst the affluent of Europe. The first dog shows were social events organized by aristocrats, and in 1860 the first Dog Show Society, the primary purpose of which was to show dogs, came into existence in Birmingham,

Spaniels retain their hunting skills, although the breed has now diverged along separate work and show lines.

England. Within three years, the Acclimation Societé held the first dog show on the European continent in Paris, France, exhibiting continental and British breeds as well as an array of North American and Nordic breeds and dogs described as coming from "the Bazaars in the East". At this time the definition of a "breed" remained open to very loose interpretation.

Today's Bulldog is a gentle companion, very different in disposition to its ancestors.

The kennel clubs

In 1873, a club for dog breeders and enthusiasts was formed in England. One of the first acts of this Kennel Club was to produce a stud book that contained the pedigrees of more than 4,000 dogs divided into 40 breeds. Then, in 1880, the Club decreed that no dog could be exhibited at a show held under Club rules unless it had first been registered with the Kennel Club.

Similar clubs were soon established in France (Societé Centrale Canine), the USA (American Kennel Club), and internationally (for example, the International Cynological Federation). The influence of the kennel clubs cannot be underestimated; by setting formal "standards" for different breeds, they effectively set parameters for the selective breeding of dogs, and so shaped the course of dog evolution.

Breeding to standards

The English Bulldog exemplifies how breeding to written standards can have

drawbacks. The English Bulldog was once bred to attack and hold on to the neck of a bull. By the mid-1800s this offensive "sport" was banned, but bulldogs retained their working antecedents, including body shape, powerful jaws, and large heads. Bulldog Club standards emphasized these physical features, stating that the head should be "as big as possible". To win at shows, bulldogs were bred for larger and larger heads until they were so large that most had to be born by Caesarean section because the pup's head did not fit through the mother's birth canal.

In a similar, though less dramatic way, other breeds were bred to conform to standards for coat length or texture. Mixed colour poodles, for example, were once common, but are now extremely rare because breed standards stipulate solid colours only.

Selective breeding guarantees the familiar but diminishes genetic variability.

Showing your dog

- Confident dog personalities always shine
- Requires obedience training
- An inexpensive hobby

At a kennel club-sanctioned dog show, dogs are not judged against each other. Instead, they are measured against a breed standard – a description of the ideal dog, a list of features written and occasionally amended by the breed club. Judges look for dogs that come closest to this ideal of perfection, and dogs are penalized for departures from the breed standard.

Winning dogs are born exhibitionists, exuding an aura of confidence in the show ring.

Training is vital

Dog shows are basically beauty contests, but personality is still important. Train your dog from an early age so that it will allow itself to be handled by judges. It must be willing to allow its mouth to be opened and to let its tail and feet be examined. Train your dog to keep still while it is examined; this is usually possible with food treats, which are acceptable bribes in the show ring.

Before the show

Visit some shows alone so you know what to expect, and make sure your dog's vaccination records are current. A few days before the show, clip your dog's nails and give it a bath. This allows sufficient time for natural oils to renew the gloss of the coat. Artificial means of improving your dog's good looks are never permitted.

If you are used to taking your dog on car journeys, you will be well prepared for visiting shows; a dog crate is a safe and sensible method of transport. Be sure to take ample food, water, and bowls for your dog. A large umbrella will help protect it (and you) from the sun and rain at outdoor shows. Always take your own poop scoops and clean up your dog's waste. A bottle of water and a towel are handy in case your dog's feet or coat get muddy between the car park and the show ring.

In the ring

Take your place in the line of dogs and handlers, set your dog in its show stance, and carry out fine leg, tail, and neck adjustments. The judge, usually a respected breeder, carries out a visual and physical inspection of your dog. He or she feels the texture of the body and coat and assesses the dog's conformation to the breed standard. A judge's interpretation of the standard is subjective, so different dogs will win different shows.

Grooming certain breeds in preparation for a show is time-consuming.

Gaiting

Breed standards include descriptions of how a dog should move. The judge may ask you to trot the dog in a triangle so that he or she can watch from the front, side, and behind, penalizing any dog that moves in a stilted manner. Winning individuals are show offs who "gait" with confidence and pleasure. Although judges mainly concentrate on the dogs, the rapport between dog and handler is important too.

A sensible approach to showing your dog is to consider it an enjoyable hobby, fun for you and your canine buddy.

Final judging

The judge may make a shortlist from the entries and ask to see them move again. The winner receives a rosette for best in class and others for second, third, reserve, and highly commended. Within each breed, the winners of different classes (male, female, youngster, adult) may compete with one other for best in breed. Within groups – Terriers for example – the winners of each breed compete with one other for best in group. Finally, the winners of each group compete with one other for the Best in Show.

The costs of showing

Showing your dog can be inexpensive fun. If you take care of all your own arrangements, you pay only for entry fees, transport, and accommodation. But at higher levels, costly professional handlers are often employed. These individuals take on several dogs and work full time on the show circuit. Handlers may indeed improve a dog's chances of winning, but it is the rare dog that earns these expenses back in stud fees or puppy prices.

Dogs with missions

■ Many dogs still work in traditional roles
■ New jobs for dogs are always evolving
■ Selective breeding produces dogs suited to novel tasks

Around the world, dogs still work with humans in time-honoured ways, such as guarding property, pulling sleds, herding, and hunting. But in the last century, many new jobs have arisen for which dogs are eminently suited.

Dogs for blind people

These were the first "assistance dogs" of the 20th century. In Germany, just after World War I, German Shepherd Dogs were trained to act as the eyes of servicemen blinded during the conflict, and the idea of the "seeing eye" dog soon became widespread. While German Shepherds are still trained as guide dogs, they have been largely superseded by Labrador Retrievers and Golden Retrievers. In the UK, the charity Guide Dogs for the Blind has effectively created a new breed, the Lab/Golden cross, producing around a thousand of these pups each year. These dogs have a temperament ideally suited to the demands of the job.

Dogs for deaf people

Hearing dogs for deaf people are just regular dogs with a naturally curious and responsive disposition. A branch of the American Humane Association was the first to attempt, in the 1970s, to train dogs for this role. Unlike dogs for blind or physically disabled people, hearing dogs work 24 hours a day, responding to sounds such as the baby crying or a knock at the door or a smoke alarm going off – sounds you and I take for granted. Most hearing dogs are mixed breeds, often rescued from shelters. The world's biggest producer of hearing dogs, the UK charity Hearing Dogs for Deaf People, has found that crossbreeds with working

Service dogs, such as these guide dogs, are a lifeline for many people.

Dogs have pulled sleds and carts for centuries. Still a viable form of transport in remote areas, dog sledding has also developed into a sport.

Law enforcement and military agencies make extensive use of trained dogs as patrol partners, trackers, and detectors of drugs and contraband.

Cocker Spaniel in their bloodlines are the best to train. Poodle crosses are almost as good.

Dogs for physically disabled people

The first dogs purpose-trained to assist wheelchair users appeared in the US in the 1980s. The most popular and successful breed for this role is the Golden Retriever. Each dog is trained to the unique needs of the disabled person, but core training includes picking up any items the person has dropped and walking with the wheelchair. Some dogs open fridges, others can turn lights on and off!

Therapy dogs

Dog owners visit their doctors less often than non-owners. They use fewer prescription drugs and suffer less from minor health complaints. In short, dogs are good for us, not only because they make us exercise more, but also because they confer psychological benefits.

For some dogs, providing these benefits is a vocation. "Therapy dogs" are easy-going family pets that visit people in institutions – retirement homes, hospitals, and hospices – on a regular basis. Wherever they visit, they bring their no-nonsense honesty; they allow themselves to be touched and stroked because they enjoy it. Touch is perhaps the most underrated human sense, and one that is frequently denied to people placed in institutions, so these animals play an important role in many people's lives.

Your dog could be suitable as a therapy dog; consult your vet to find out more.

Search and rescue dogs

Earthquake, avalanche, and mountain rescue dogs do serious professional work, but most of them are, in fact, pet dogs trained to work when needed. Search and rescue is simply "hide and seek" played for serious stakes, in which a dog uses its air- and ground-scenting abilities to seek out the lost individual.

Larger dogs, especially the Border Collie, are used in professional search and rescue, although Japanese experience shows that even small dogs such as Shelties are capable of being trained in this vital job.

Chihuahua

- The ultimate toy lapdog
- Adaptable and a good traveller
- Ideal for city living

Although small and dainty, the Chihuahua is alert, swift, and bold. Both the shorthaired and the hardier longhaired Chihuahua offer comfort, constancy, and companionship. Shivering at the slightest breeze, and happiest when on the lap of its human companion, the Chihuahua is most at home indoors, and indeed is too fragile to live outside.

History The Chihuahua is named after the Mexican state from which it was first exported to the United States, and then around the world, but its origins are shrouded in mystery. Some experts speculate that small dogs arrived in the Americas with the Spanish armies of Hernando Cortes in 1519. Others believe that the Chinese voyaged to America, bringing with them miniaturized dogs before the arrival of Europeans.

Key facts

Country of origin
Mexico

Date of origin
1800s

Life expectancy
12–14 yrs

Temperament
Spirited and alert. Neither snappy nor shy with people but often wary of other dogs.

Maintenance
Requires only little exercise and light grooming.

Smooth coat is more common than long coat

Very thin bones of front legs are quite fragile

15–23 cm (6–9 in)

Weight 1–3 kg (2–6 lb)

Physical characteristics

Head	Distinctive domed skull, with a short muzzle and lean cheeks.
Eyes	Typically dark or ruby, and set well apart.
Ears	Large ears flare to the sides, and are set widely on the head.
Body	Long and compact, with a level back.
Coat	Wide range of colours. Smooth and long coats are soft and flat or slightly wavy.
Tail	Medium in length and carried over back.

Maltese

- Gentle-mannered and playful
- Aristocratic appearance
- Needs regular and thorough grooming

Once known as the Maltese Terrier, this good-tempered, sweet-natured, sometimes sensitive breed does not shed its hair and develops a long, luxurious coat. This creates a matting problem, especially at around eight months of age when the puppy coat is replaced by adult hair. The breed is good with children, but play should be supervised due to the dog's small frame. It relishes exercise, but can adapt to a more sedentary life.

History Phoenician traders probably brought the ancient "Melita" (the archaic name for Malta) breed to Malta more than 2,000 years ago. Today's Maltese may be the result of crossing spaniels with the Miniature Poodle.

Hair is white, sometimes with a hint of tan or lemon on the ears

Legs are short and straight

20–25 cm (8–10 in)

Weight 2–3 kg (4–6 lb)

Key facts

Country of origin
Mediterranean region

Date of origin
Antiquity

Life expectancy
14–15 yrs

Temperament
Trusting and affectionate, and sometimes vigorously playful despite its size.

Maintenance
Daily grooming is essential to maintain the dog's elegant appearance.

Other names
Bichon Maltais

Physical characteristics

Head	Skull slightly rounded. Muzzle is fine and tapered, with teeth that meet in an edge-to-edge bite.
Eyes	Large, round, dark, and slightly protruding.
Ears	Heavily feathered with long hair.
Body	Compact, with fairly deep chest.
Coat	Long, white, silky coat with no undercoat.
Tail	Weight of long hair causes tail to curve to one side.

Miniature Pinscher

- A fearless watchdog for the smaller home
- Highly alert and spirited
- Can be possessive of loved ones

The Miniature Pinscher was originally bred to control rodents. Today, this feisty little terrier (*pinscher* is German for terrier or biter) is kept strictly as a companion, but its ratting ability remains fully developed. Although it resembles a tiny Doberman, it is only related to that breed by country of origin, and predates it by perhaps 200 years. In spite of its size, it will quite happily challenge dogs that are ten times larger than itself, and has a tendency to snap first and ask questions later.

History Developed from the German Pinscher hundreds of years ago, the "MinPin", as it is affectionately known, was originally a bulky, efficient stable ratter. Its refined appearance today is a result of more recent selective breeding.

Ears may be erect or dropped

Muscular hindquarters

Hind legs are straight and parallel when viewed from behind

Cat-like feet

Key facts

Country of origin
Germany

Date of origin
1700s

Life expectancy
13–14 yrs

Temperament
Lively and playful well into old age.

Maintenance
Requires only light grooming and moderate exercise.

Other names
Zwergpinscher, MinPin

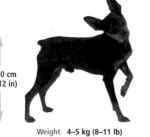

25–30 cm
(10–12 in)

Weight 4–5 kg (8–11 lb)

Physical characteristics

Head	In good proportion to body, with a short, straight, and fine muzzle.
Eyes	Dark, shining, and almond-shaped.
Ears	Large, and set high on head.
Body	Square in profile, with well-developed forequarters.
Coat	Shiny, straight, hard, and short, clinging closely to the body.
Tail	Was traditionally docked.

Pomeranian

- Strong, hearty, and active
- An excellent family pet
- Loyal and willing, but can be cocky

Queen Victoria popularized the Pomeranian in Britain when she added the breed to her kennels. In the early days, the Pomeranian was both larger and whiter than it is now. The white colour is usually associated with larger dogs up to 13 kg (30 lb) in weight, but breeders, selecting for a smaller size, also brought out the now prevalent sable and orange colours. The Pomeranian, being a naturally large breed that has been recently reduced in size, still acts like a "big dog". It will bark unchecked, making it a superb watchdog that will also challenge larger dogs. This breed makes an excellent companion.

History Today's small dog was developed in Pomerania, Germany, about 200 years ago by breeding from small varieties of the large German Spitz. Its classic spitz shape and orange coat illustrate its more distant Arctic origins.

Key facts

Country of origin
Germany

Date of origin
1800s

Life expectancy
15 yrs

Temperament
Extrovert and vivacious.

Maintenance
The thick coat needs regular brushing, but otherwise easy to care for.

Other names
Dwarf Spitz, Loulou

Topcoat has a coarse texture

Fine-boned legs

22–28 cm
(8¹⁄₂–11 in)

Weight   2–3 kg (4–6 lb)

Physical characteristics

Head	Short muzzle and a fox-like expression.
Eyes	Dark, bright, slightly oval in shape, and set well into the skull.
Ears	Small and erect.
Body	Highly compact but sturdy.
Coat	Double coat with dense undercoat and long, straight topcoat that forms a frill over the shoulders and chest.
Tail	Plumed tail lies flat on the back.

Pug

■ Pugnacious and individualistic
■ A lot of dog in a small package
■ Amongst the oldest of all breeds

Pugs are an acquired taste, but many dog owners are completely addicted to this vibrant breed. A Pug is extremely tough and opinionated – it knows what it wants and stands its ground until satisfied. Its muscular, compact body, flat face, and unblinking stare give it a strong presence and personality. Although it is strong-willed and forceful, it is rarely aggressive. Affectionate and playful with its human family, and especially with children, it makes an amusing and rewarding companion.

History Miniaturized from mastiffs in the Far East at least 2,400 years ago, the Pug's ancestors were once companions of Buddhist priests. Introduced into Holland in the 1500s via the Dutch East India Company, this dog then became the companion of aristocrats and kings.

Key facts

Country of origin
China

Date of origin
Antiquity

Life expectancy
13–15 yrs

Temperament
An independent, resolute, and charming character.

Maintenance
Relatively easy to look after, requiring only light exercise and occasional grooming.

Other names
Carlin, Mops

Short but wide back is level from the withers to the tail

Strong, straight legs

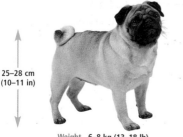

25–28 cm
(10–11 in)

Weight   6–8 kg (13–18 lb)

Physical characteristics

Head	Large in proportion to body, with a short, blunt muzzle. Well-defined wrinkles.
Eyes	Lustrous, dark, and very large.
Ears	Thin, small, and black in colour. May be folded back (rose) or forward (button).
Body	Short and square.
Coat	The short, soft, and glossy coat may be black, silver, apricot, or fawn in colour.
Tail	Tightly curled and twisted.

Yorkshire Terrier

- The world's most popular terrier
- Independent and spirited
- Compact and neat appearance

This feisty, miniature package of energy is one of the most numerous pure-bred dogs in Europe and in North America. Although often regarded as a fashion accessory, the typical Yorkshire Terrier is a dynamo, with little understanding of its small size. It plays hard, and has seemingly unlimited energy. Many Yorkies are spoiled from the moment they are acquired, and never have the opportunity to show their willingness to learn. Excessive breeding has also produced nervous and meek examples of the breed, but they are fortunately a minority. Reduction in size has brought with it a range of medical problems.

History The breed originated in the early 1800s in the West Riding area of Yorkshire, Great Britain. Miners, wanting to develop a terrier for ratting small enough to carry in a pocket, probably crossed black-and-tan terriers with the Paisley and Clydesdale Terriers.

Straight, thin legs hidden by abundant hair

Hair has been cut from ears

Long hair demands attention

Key facts

Country of origin
Great Britain

Date of origin
1800s

Life expectancy
14 yrs

Temperament
Tenacious and alert.

Maintenance
Regular grooming is required.

Other names
Broken-haired Scottish Terrier

22¹/₂–23¹/₂ cm
(9 in)

Weight 2¹/₂–3¹/₂ kg (5–7 lb)

Physical characteristics

Head	Small and flat. Short muzzle with black nose. Face is narrow but bushy whiskers give a squarer look.
Eyes	Dark and shining.
Ears	V-shaped and erect.
Body	Well-proportioned, with a short back.
Coat	Long, straight, and silky. Steely-blue on body, bright tan on head and chest.
Tail	Usually docked.

Bichon Frise

- A lively, cheerful, and attractive companion
- Highly trainable with gentle handling
- Unusual decorative appearance

Adaptable, happy, and bold, the Bichon has found a large following since its emergence from obscurity in the late 1970s. Despite its puffball appearance, this breed is game and hardy – farmers in Norway even train these dogs to round up sheep. The teeth and gums require attention, because there is a tendency for tartar formation and gum infection. Although many white-haired breeds suffer from chronic skin complaints, the Bichon is less affected by allergic skin problems.

History The exact origins of the breed are unknown. By the 14th century, sailors had introduced it to the island of Tenerife, and by the 15th century it was a royal favourite.

Dense hair exaggerates round shape of head

Broad, rounded thighs

Nails are typically white

Key facts

Country of origin
Mediterranean region

Date of origin
Middle Ages

Life expectancy
14 yrs

Temperament
Happy and active. Gets along exceptionally well with strangers, dogs, and other animals.

Maintenance
Regular grooming is essential.

Other names
Tenerife Dog

23–30 cm
(9–11 in)

Weight   3–6 kg (6–13 lb)

Physical characteristics

Head	Slightly rounded skull, with flat cheeks. Light muzzle with large, black nose.
Eyes	Forward-looking, round, and dark in colour; surrounded by rims of dark skin.
Ears	Drooping ears covered in long hair.
Body	Small but sturdy, with a deep brisket.
Coat	Topcoat has corkscrew curls; undercoat is thick and soft.
Tail	Curved loosely over the back.

Cavalier King Charles Spaniel

- The ideal urban dog
- Friendly, sporting, and adaptable
- Prone to medical problems

The affable and energetic Cavalier is justifiably popular, partly because it is so accommodating to our moods. A Cavalier is willing to curl up on a sofa in bad weather, but equally eager to walk and run for miles when the occasion arises. However, increasing demand for the dog has led to intensive in-breeding, which has caused substantial increases in lethal heart conditions. The life expectancy of affected dogs is reduced from 14 to just 9 years.

History In the 1920s, an American, Roswell Eldridge, offered a prize to anyone exhibiting King Charles Spaniels with long muzzles, as they appeared in Van Dyck's painting of King Charles II and his spaniels. By the 1940s, these dogs were classified as a unique breed and were given the prefix Cavalier, to differentiate them from their forebears.

Key facts

Country of origin
Great Britain

Date of origin
1900s

Life expectancy
9–14 yrs

Temperament
Warm, gentle, affectionate, and graceful.

Maintenance
High incidence of inherited disease demands a thorough check of family history.

Coat may be black and tan, ruby, tricolour, or Blenheim

Compact, feathered feet

31–33 cm
(12–13 in)

Weight 5–8 kg (11–18 lb)

Physical characteristics

Head	Nearly flat between the ears. Well-developed lips.
Eyes	Large, round eyes contribute to the dog's sweet, endearing expression.
Ears	Long, with plenty of feathering.
Body	Small and well-balanced with a regal appearance; moves with an elegant gait.
Coat	Long and silky, with a slight wave.
Tail	Well-feathered.

Pekingese

- Calm and affectionate with its human family
- Regal appearance
- Can be self-important, wilful, and aloof

According to the rules set by the Chinese Empress Tzi Hsi, the Pekingese should have short, bowed legs so that it cannot wander far, a ruff of fur around its neck to give it an aura of dignity, and selective taste buds so that it appears dainty. She omitted to mention its other striking qualities – the stubbornness of a mule, the speed of a snail, and the condescension of the haughty. The Pekingese is a pleasure for those who enjoy the companionship of an amusing, independent dog. Chinese legend says that it is the result of a union between a lion and a monkey, combining the nobility of the former with the grace of the latter – this is an apt description.

History At one time the exclusive property of the ancient Chinese Royal Courts, and strongly associated with Buddhism, the first four Pekes arrived in the West in 1860.

Key facts

Country of origin
China

Date of origin
Antiquity

Life expectancy
12–13 yrs

Temperament
Good natured with those who have earned its respect.

Maintenance
Thick coat needs weekly brushing for at least one hour to prevent knotting and matting.

Other names
Peking Palasthund

Long, heavy mane makes a cape around the neck

Feathering on the backs of the thighs

Thick undercoat beneath coarse, straight topcoat

15–23 cm
(6–9 in)

Weight   3–6 kg (6–13 lb)

Physical characteristics

Head	Large and wide, with a long wrinkle in the shape of an inverted V separating the upper and lower parts of the face. Black on the lips, nose, and around the eyes.
Eyes	Round, dark, and shiny.
Ears	Heart-shaped, set at the front of the skull.
Body	Compact body is heavier at the front.
Coat	Full and long, in a variety of colours.
Tail	Carried curved over back.

Papillon

- Extravagant, flamboyant appearance
- A loyal and active companion
- Fine-boned, elegant, and graceful in motion

With ears reminiscent of butterfly wings (papillon means butterfly in French), small size, and a fine, silky, and abundant coat, this breed looks like a classic lapdog, content to spend its life watching the world go by. Not so. If handled correctly the Papillon excels at obedience training and is a well-constructed, physically fit breed, suitable for town or countryside. As with most toy breeds, it may suffer from slipping kneecaps and there is a psychological tendency for this breed to be possessive of its owner.

History The Papillon is believed by some to be descended from the 16th-century Spanish Dwarf Spaniel. Its shape and long coat, however, suggest northern spitz blood in its origins.

Key facts

Country of origin
Continental Europe

Date of origin
1600s

Life expectancy
13–15 yrs

Temperament
Alert, intelligent, and friendly, showing little aggression.

Maintenance
Coat requires less grooming than expected.

Other names
Continental Toy Spaniel

White, narrow, clearly defined blaze

Profuse frill on chest

Fine feet, like those of a hare

20–28 cm
(8–11 in)

Weight 4–5 kg (8–11 lb)

Physical characteristics

Head   **Dainty, pointed muzzle, abruptly thinner than the head, is tipped with black nose.**

Eyes   **Round and rather low on skull.**

Ears   **Drop or erect. Always heavily fringed, and set well back on the head.**

Body   **Longer than the height at the withers.**

Coat   **Thick silky topcoat with no undercoat. Multi-coloured, always including white.**

Tail   **Fringed and forward-arching.**

Dachshund

- Spirited, clever, and bold
- Ideal show dog
- A distinctive and recognizable breed

Today, most dachshunds are kept as household companions, but for hundreds of years they were bred as "earth dogs" – for their ability to follow badgers, foxes, and rabbits to earth. This accounts for their small stature, pronounced hunting spirit, and acute senses, especially scent. There are three coat varieties – smooth, longhaired, and wirehaired – and two sizes – standard and miniature.

History Ancient Egyptian sculptures show a pharaoh seated with three short-legged dogs – these may be ancestors of the dachshund. The smooth standard is perhaps the oldest dachshund and was once used as a tracker. The name dachshund, German for "badger dog", reflects the breed's original purpose.

Key facts

Country of origin
Germany

Date of origin
1900s

Life expectancy
14–17 yrs

Temperament
Loyal and highly courageous, even rash.

Maintenance
Longhaired varieties need constant grooming. All types are low in "doggy" smell.

SMOOTH STANDARD

LONGHAIRED MINIATURE

Short, dense, and lustrous coat

WIREHAIRED MINIATURE

Miniature and Standard:
13–25 cm (5–10 in)

Miniature Weight   4–5 kg (8–11 lb)
Standard Weight   7–11½ kg (15–25 lb)

Physical characteristics

Head	Sharply defined and narrow, tapering symmetrically to tip of the nose.
Eyes	Dark and oval in shape.
Ears	Rounded, set near top of the head.
Body	Long and low to ground, with short legs.
Coat	Variable; common colours include red, or patterns of black, chocolate, wild boar, grey, and fawn.
Tail	Depends on coat type.

Shetland Sheepdog

- An affectionate and responsive companion
- Devoted to its human family
- Easy to train

The Sheltie is consistently one of the most popular breeds in Japan, and is also popular in Great Britain and North America. Although it is rarely used as a working dog, it retains many of its guarding and herding instincts, and will efficiently protect its owner's home. Although once called the Dwarf Scotch Shepherd, the breed is a classic miniature, rather than a dwarf like a Dachshund. It is a smaller version of the large working sheepdogs of Scotland.

History The Sheltie has its origins in 18th-century Scotland, and may be the result of crossing local Shetland Island dogs with imported Rough Collies.

Key facts

Country of origin
Great Britain

Date of origin
1700s

Life expectancy
12–14 yrs

Temperament
Intelligent and biddable; an ideal family dog.

Maintenance
This dog's beautiful, long coat requires weekly brushing, and will shed twice a year.

Long, harsh topcoat

Profuse, long hair around neck and between forelegs forms the distinctive mane and frill

35–37 cm (14–15 in)

Weight 6–7 kg (13–15 lb)

Physical characteristics

Head	Tapers elegantly from ears to nose.
Eyes	Dark brown and almond-shaped.
Ears	Small, semi-erect ears are set close together on top of the skull.
Body	Well-proportioned; moves with a smooth and graceful gait.
Coat	Colour can be sable, blue merle, black and white, black and tan, or tricolour.
Tail	Low-set, and covered with abundant hair.

Poodle (Toy and Miniature)

- A proud and elegant companion
- Loyal, friendly, and alert
- Long coat can be cut in different styles

These Poodles are identical to the Standard Poodle *(see p.110)* but for their reduced size. The Miniature, extremely popular during the 1950s and 1960s, is slightly larger than the tiny Toy. Miniaturization can sometimes bring with it a heightened puppy-like dependence on people, but these poodles retain powerfully independent personalities, and at their best, they are responsive, trainable, and thoughtful.

History Herd-guarding and water-retrieving Standard Poodles were probably taken from Germany to France in the 1500s. By that time, the breed had been miniaturized.

Key facts

Country of origin
France

Date of origin
1500s

Life expectancy
14-16 yrs

Temperament
A faithful, sociable companion.

Maintenance
The Poodle's coat is not shed, so it requires regular clipping.

Other names
Caniche

MINIATURE POODLE

TOY POODLE

Woolly, springy hair

Hair on a puppy is shaved to a uniform length all over

Forearms are straight

Toy:
20–25 cm
(8–10 in)

Miniature:
28–38 cm
(11–15 in)

Toy weight: 6–8 kg (13–18 lb)
Miniature weight: 8–14 kg (18–30 lb)

Physical characteristics

Head	Long, narrow, and fine.
Eyes	Dark and almond-shaped eyes are slightly slanted and have a lively expression.
Ears	Long ears hang close to the face.
Body	Elegant and well-balanced; movement is free and light.
Coat	Profuse, dense hair is harsh in texture. Can be a variety of solid colours.
Tail	Was traditionally docked.

Shih Tzu

■ A happy and affectionate family friend
■ Outgoing, vibrant, and trusting
■ Distinctive long facial hair

Although it is very similar in looks to the Lhasa Apso *(see p.72)*, the Shih Tzu is different both in origin and temperament. A translation of the pre-revolutionary Peking Kennel Club's breed standard for the Shih Tzu says it should have, "a lion head, bear torso, camel hoof, feather-duster tail, palm-leaf ears, rice teeth, pearly petal tongue, and movement like a goldfish". The Shih Tzu is less aloof and more playful than its Tibetan lookalike, and this probably accounts for its greater worldwide popularity. The hair on the bridge of its nose tends to grow upwards, and is often tied up on the top of its head.

History Bred in the Chinese Royal Court over 400 years ago, the lively and outgoing Shih Tzu is without doubt a cross between Tibetan dogs and ancestors of today's Pekingese.

Key facts

Country of origin
China

Date of origin
1600s

Life expectancy
12–14 yrs

Temperament
A true companion dog; friendly even with strangers and other animals.

Maintenance
Long, thick coat requires daily grooming.

Other names
Chrysanthemum dog

Back is long and level

Hair forms a long moustache

Firm, well-padded feet

25–27 cm (10–11 in)

Weight 5–7 kg (11–15 lb)

Physical characteristics

Head	Round, broad head, with a short, square muzzle and a black nose.
Eyes	Very dark, large, round eyes.
Ears	Large, drooping, and hidden under a thick coating of long hair.
Body	Sturdy and compact.
Coat	Luxurious, long, straight coat; can be a variety of colours.
Tail	Heavily plumed tail is carried over back.

Lhasa Apso

- A dignified, friendly dog
- Protective of its human family
- An alert watchdog

The Tibetans bred dogs for temperament, not for looks. The Lhasa Apso was used as a sentinel: it would bark aggressively at unfamiliar sounds or sights – its bark is the basis for its Tibetan name, *Abso Seng Kye*, which means "bark lion sentinel dog". Dogs of this nature were most common in wealthy areas, especially in the palace of the Dalai Lama. There was some confusion when the Lhasa Apso was introduced into the West, and it was initially grouped into one category with the Tibetan Terrier and Shih Tzu. In 1934, all three were recognized as distinct breeds.

History For a long period of time, this ancient breed was exclusive to Tibet. The first Lhasa Apso arrived in the West only in 1921.

Key facts

Country of origin
Tibet

Date of origin
Antiquity

Life expectancy
12–14 yrs

Temperament
Playful and spirited; a loving companion.

Maintenance
Requires regular grooming, and plenty of attention.

Other names
Abso Seng Kye

Heavily feathered ears

Body is longer than it is tall

Round, cat-like feet have firm pads

25–28 cm
(10–11 in)

Weight   6–7 kg (13–15 lb)

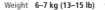

Physical characteristics

Head Covered with abundant hair that falls forward over the eyes.

Eyes Medium-sized, dark-brown eyes.

Ears Hang down against the head. Tips of ears may be dark-coloured.

Body Well-balanced and sturdy, with a level topline and muscular loins.

Coat Long, heavy, straight hair.

Tail Carried well over the back.

Miniature Schnauzer

- A devoted and playful companion
- Intelligent and eager to please
- Suitable for urban living

Named after its most prominent physical feature (in German, Schnauze means nose or snout) the Miniature Schnauzer, although once a formidable ratter, is now an almost perfect canine companion. Less noisy and feisty than its British terrier equivalents, this breed has become one of North America's favourite town companions. A classically calm dog, it is easy to obedience train and is not snappy. An enthusiastic barker, it also makes an excellent guard dog.

History Almost a perfect replica of the Giant and Standard Schnauzers, the Miniature descends from this root stock, with the addition of Affenpinscher and Miniature Pinscher bloodlines. Developed in Germany in the 1400s, it is unlikely, as some sources suggest, that Poodles played a role in the development of the breed.

Key facts

Country of origin
Germany

Date of origin
1400s

Life expectancy
14 yrs

Temperament
Good with children and other dogs. Can have medical problems if poorly bred.

Maintenance
Frequent grooming is required.

Other names
Zwergschnauzer

Topcoat is hard and coarse; undercoat is soft

Front legs are straight; elbows are close to chest

30–36 cm
(12–14 in)

Weight   6–7 kg (13–15 lb)

Physical characteristics

Head	Rectangular, with a bushy beard.
Eyes	Medium-sized, dark, oval eyes with arched, bristly eyebrows.
Ears	Small and set high on the head.
Body	Sturdy, short, and deep.
Coat	Colour can be pure black, black and silver, or "salt and pepper" (a mixture of light and dark grey).
Tail	High-set tail was traditionally docked.

Boston Terrier

- An affectionate and lively family pet
- Alert and sensitive
- An effective and alert watchdog

Well-mannered, thoughtful, and considerate, this true New Englander is a perennially popular dog in North America, making a sprightly, entertaining, active, and durable companion. Terrier in name only, it has lost any ruthless desire for mayhem, preferring the company of humans, although male Bostons will still challenge other dogs if they feel their territory has been invaded.

History This powerful-looking breed was developed in the 1800s by crossing the English Bulldog, Bull Terrier, Boxer, and extinct White Terrier. The Boston originally weighed over 20 kg (44 lb), but was bred down to its current smaller size.

Key facts

Country of origin
United States

Date of origin
1800s

Life expectancy
13 yrs

Temperament
Happy and friendly; loves children.

Maintenance
Requires a moderate amount of exercise. Short, smooth coat is easy to care for.

Other names
Boston Bull

Moderately long neck

Straight forelegs

38–43 cm
(15–17 in)

Weight 4¹/₂–11¹/₂ kg (10–25 lb)

Physical characteristics

Head	Square, flat skull, with a short muzzle.
Eyes	Large, round eyes are set well apart.
Ears	Small, thin ears are placed at the corners of the skull, and are carried erect.
Body	Short and well-balanced; moves with an easy and graceful gait.
Coat	Smooth, fine-textured coat can be brindle, seal or black, with white markings.
Tail	Short, tapering tail is set low on the back.

Jack Russell Terrier

- A playful and affectionate family friend
- A courageous hunter
- Energetic and excitable

Bred to be a working terrier, the Jack Russell conforms to its first breeder's requirement for long legs to enable the dog to keep up with horses on the hunt; it is also small enough to burrow and bolt foxes. The English vicar who developed the breed preferred wirehaired dogs, but today, both smooth and wire coats are equally popular. Sprightly and robust, this breed is a popular companion, especially in the United States. In its native Great Britain, however, a smaller version of Jack Russell is more common.

History The Jack Russell Terrier was developed in the 19th century by Reverend John Russell, a parson from the west of England, and a founding member of the Kennel Club of Great Britain.

Powerful jaws

Strong, straight legs

Compact feet with hair between the toes

Key facts

Country of origin
Great Britain

Date of origin
1800s

Life expectancy
13–14 yrs

Temperament
A fun, active dog.

Maintenance
Requires regular exercise and mental stimulation.

Other names
Parson Jack Russell Terrier

25–26 cm
(10–12 in)

Weight   4–7 kg (8–15 lb)

Physical characteristics

Head	Proportionate to the size of the body.
Eyes	Medium-sized, dark, almond-shaped eyes with a keen expression.
Ears	Small, V-shaped ears drop forward.
Body	Balanced and square, with a straight back and a narrow chest.
Coat	Dense, harsh, weather-resistant topcoat, and a short undercoat.
Tail	Traditionally docked in working dogs.

Border Terrier

- A good-natured, friendly companion
- Loyal and obedient
- A fearless hunter

The Border, an uncomplicated and genuine terrier, and little altered from its original form, is built to be small enough to follow a fox down the narrowest hole, but with enough leg to keep up with riders on horseback. It has never achieved the show-ring popularity of other terriers, and has therefore remained true to its original form and function with its durable, weather-resistant coat, its long legs, and its superb stamina. The Border is easy to train and has an amenable personality, making a superb family dog.

History The exact origins of this breed are unknown. There is evidence that it existed in the borders between England and Scotland, in close to its present form, in the late 18th century.

Key facts

Country of origin
Great Britain

Date of origin
1700s

Life expectancy
13–14 yrs

Temperament
Affectionate and sensitive; loves children, and is happy with other pets and horses.

Maintenance
An active dog, so needs plenty of energetic exercise.

Coat can be red, grizzle and tan, blue and tan, or wheaten

Hind legs have sturdy loins

Straight front legs

25–28 cm (10–11 in)

Weight 5–7 kg (11–15 lb)

Physical characteristics

Head	Skull is broad, with a short muzzle and powerful jaws.
Eyes	Dark, medium-sized eyes have a keen and alert expression.
Ears	Small and V-shaped.
Body	Fairly long, deep body, and a sound gait.
Coat	Harsh, dense, wiry topcoat, with a short undercoat and thick skin.
Tail	Fairly short and tapering.

Cairn Terrier

- A robust and plucky working terrier
- Lively and independent
- Can be quite affectionate

Until recently, when the West Highland White and Yorkshire Terriers superseded it, this was the most popular terrier in Great Britain. Breeders early last century were careful to retain the Cairn's natural shaggy coat, sturdy body, and terrier abilities. Equally at home in the town or the country, the Cairn makes a good watchdog, and is easier to obedience train than many other terriers. However, the terrier temperament is always there and males, in particular, can be bossy, and should be monitored when meeting children for the first time. The Cairn's small size, good health, and lack of stubbornness make it a delightful companion.

History The Cairn may have originated on the Scottish Isle of Skye where, since at least the time of Mary Queen of Scots, it worked the cairns, searching for hiding foxes.

Key facts

Country of origin
Great Britain

Date of origin
Middle Ages

Life expectancy
14 yrs

Temperament
Active and bold, this breed is assertive but not aggressive.

Maintenance
Requires regular exercise.

Profuse topcoat covers furry undercoat

Front feet are larger than back feet

25–30 cm
(10–12 in)

Weight   6–7 kg (13–15 lb)

Physical characteristics

Head	Broad, with strong jaws and a black nose.
Eyes	Dark hazel eyes, set wide apart, and topped with shaggy eyebrows.
Ears	Small and pointed; carried erect.
Body	Strong and well-proportioned. Back is level and of a medium length.
Coat	Colour can be grey, red, cream, wheaten, or nearly black.
Tail	Short tail is well covered with hair.

Scottish Terrier

- A dependable and loyal pet
- Assertive and courageous
- Can have a hot temper

This solid, muscular, quiet, and even dour dog has always been more popular in North America than in its native Great Britain. The American president Franklin Delano Roosevelt often travelled with his Scottie, Fala, and Walt Disney perpetuated the gentlemanly image of this breed in his film, *Lady and the Tramp*. Although built for penetrating underground passageways in the pursuit of small mammals, the Scottish Terrier is primarily a companion. Reserved and independent, this bold dog can seem aloof, but makes an excellent guardian.

History The Scottie of today is probably a descendant of dogs from the Scottish Western Isles, which were selectively bred in Aberdeen in the mid-1800s.

Key facts

Country of origin
Great Britain

Date of origin
1800s

Life expectancy
13–14 yrs

Temperament
A sensitive, independent dog with a feisty nature.

Maintenance
Requires a moderate amount of exercise, so is suitable for urban living.

Other names
Aberdeen Terrier

Hindquarters are extraordinarily powerful

Harsh, dense topcoat with a soft undercoat

25–28 cm
(10–11 in)

Weight 9–10 kg (20–22 lb)

Physical characteristics

Head	Long, flat skull, and a large nose.
Eyes	Small, almond-shaped eyes are set under distinctive long eyebrows.
Ears	Neat, pointed ears have a fine texture.
Body	Compact and sturdily built, with a firm, level back and a very deep chest.
Coat	Colour can be black, wheaten, or brindle.
Tail	Moderately long tail is thick at the root, but tapers to the tip.

West Highland White Terrier

- A devoted, understanding companion
- Self-confident and lively
- A popular show-dog

Although the West Highland White and Cairn Terriers share a common ancestry, selective breeding has produced breeds with quite different personalities. The Westie (along with the Scottish Terrier) is recognized worldwide because of the part it plays in advertising a Scotch whisky. White is also a fashionable colour for dogs, signifying good luck, or simply cleanliness. The consequence is that the Westie is very popular in North America, Great Britain, Europe, and Japan. The breed has a very high incidence of allergic skin conditions, and may have an excitable temperament.

History The Cairn Terrier occasionally used to produce white puppies. In the 19th century, the Malcolm family of Scotland selectively bred these, producing a breed easily visible on the Scottish moors.

Key facts

Country of origin
Great Britain

Date of origin
1800s

Life expectancy
14 yrs

Temperament
Feisty and proud, the affectionate Westie loves people and makes a good watchdog.

Maintenance
Requires regular grooming to maintain its appearance.

Head has profuse hair

Coarse topcoat covers soft undercoat

Feet have thick, black pads and black nails

25–28 cm
(10–11 in)

Weight   7–10 kg (15–22 lb)

Physical characteristics

Head	Broad skull gradually tapers to the eyes.
Eyes	Medium-sized and slightly sunken. Set wide apart, with a sharp, intelligent look.
Ears	Small and erect, with pointed tips.
Body	Compact and strong, with a level back and powerful loins.
Coat	Long, harsh topcoat is always white.
Tail	Relatively short and covered with hard hair, with no feathering.

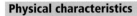

Fox Terrier

- A friendly, confident dog
- Lively, alert, and full of fun
- Always ready for action

The Smooth Fox Terrier was once a classic working dog, but today it is foremost an attractive, although frequently obstinate and strong-willed, companion. With persistence, this athletic dog can be obedience trained. The breed's agility and joy in exercising off the lead make it a good dog for the countryside. Its more popular cousin, the Wire Fox Terrier, is not demonstrative with people; it can be wilful, and perhaps snappy. One of the breed's instinctive traits that has not diminished over the years is its joy in digging. Its enjoyment in challenging other dogs to fights is almost as great.

History At one time, all dogs that went to earth in the pursuit of a fox were called fox terriers. It was not until the 19th century, however, that controlled breeding began, resulting in the breeds of today.

Key facts

Country of origin
Great Britain

Date of origin
1800s (wire)
1700s (smooth)

Life expectancy
13–14 yrs

Temperament
An active, happy dog with boundless energy.

Maintenance
Requires early obedience training and a firm owner to minimize its natural hunting instincts.

Wire Fox Terrier has a dense, strong coat

Straight, lean forelegs

36–39 cm
(14–15 in)

Weight   7–8 kg (15–18 lb)

Physical characteristics

Head	Flat, narrow skull, with strong jaws and a black nose.
Eyes	Dark, round eyes with a bright expression.
Ears	Small and V-shaped.
Body	Short, strong, and level back; chest is deep and loins are powerful and slightly arched.
Coat	Predominantly white, with markings in a darker colour (Wire and Smooth).
Tail	Was traditionally docked.

Norfolk Terrier

- Outgoing and inquisitive
- A lively and charming pet
- Hardy, fearless, and energetic

The Norfolk is a delightful little dog, although it has an instinctive terrier-like desire to attack and throttle any rodent it sees. Like virtually all terriers, it must be introduced to cats carefully, so that its natural instincts can be harnessed. Good natured and robust, the breed makes an excellent companion. This breed is identical in appearance, origin, personality, and function to the Norwich Terrier, except for its drop ears.

History The Norfolk was developed from the Norwich Terrier. From the 1800s, when the Norwich was first bred, puppies were produced with both erect and drop ears. The arguments this created resulted in the drop-eared Norfolk Terrier being recognized as a separate breed in 1965.

Slightly rounded skull

Coat can be wheaten, red, black and tan, or grizzle

Small, round feet have firm pads

Key facts

Country of origin
Great Britain

Date of origin
1800s

Life expectancy
14 yrs

Temperament
A good guard dog, as it has acute hearing and will bark at strange noises. Loves attention and does not like being left alone.

Maintenance
Requires regular lively exercise and a weekly brushing.

23–25 cm
(9–10 in)

Weight   5–6 kg (11–12 lb)

Physical characteristics

Head	Broad skull, with a strong, wedge-shaped muzzle and a clean jaw.
Eyes	Dark, oval eyes give a keen expression.
Ears	Slightly round-tipped, V-shaped ears hang close to the cheeks.
Body	Compact and strong, with a level back and short, powerful legs.
Coat	Straight, hard, and wiry.
Tail	Tapering tail; was traditionally docked.

Staffordshire Bull Terrier

■ An affectionate and loving companion
■ Hardy, brave, and tenacious
■ Requires an experienced owner

Here is a true split-personality dog, a genuine, canine Jekyll-and-Hyde character. There is probably no breed that is more loving with its family, and often with strangers and even veterinarians, than this kinetic mass of solid bone and thick muscle. It thrives on affection and devotes itself to being accepted as part of its human family. However, when it sees another dog – or any other animal – it can quite suddenly reveal a different side of its character. Sweetness and light become a force of darkness, as it becomes overwhelmed by a desire to destroy. Selective breeding has successfully reduced, but not eliminated, this tendency.

History Originating in Staffordshire, Great Britain, in the 1800s, this powerful, loyal breed traces its ancestry to crosses between ferocious, well-muscled bull baiters and agile, feisty local terriers.

Well-muscled hind legs are parallel

Key facts

Country of origin
Great Britain

Date of origin
1800s

Life expectancy
11-12 yrs

Temperament
Trustworthy, sweet-tempered and gentle; good with children.

Maintenance
A strong and determined dog, so needs firm obedience training. Regular exercise is required to avoid excessive weight gain.

Chest is wide and deep

Medium-sized, strong, well-padded feet

36–41 cm
(14–16 in)

Weight 11–17 kg (24–38 lb)

Physical characteristics

Head	Short, deep head, with a very broad skull, strong jaws, and large teeth.
Eyes	Round, medium-sized, and set well apart.
Ears	Small, wide-set, half-prick ears fall away from the cheeks.
Body	Muscular, short body has a clean outline.
Coat	Smooth, short, close-fitting coat.
Tail	Medium length; set low on the back and carried straight.

Bull Terrier

- Devoted and affectionate with its human family
- Fun-loving and playful
- Can be aggressive with other dogs

The Bull Terrier was created to be the ultimate fighting dog by breeder James Hinks of Birmingham, Great Britain. He favoured white Bull Terriers, and these became, and still are, fashionable companions. However, in selecting for this colour, Hinks had also unwittingly selected for a range of inherited medical problems that, in the coloured Bull Terriers, occur at a much lower incidence. The Bull Terrier is an even-tempered breed that is good with people. It also has lower-than-average tendency to snap and bite, although when it does, the damage can be considerable because it does not let go easily.

History This breed was developed in the 1800s by crossing the Bulldog with the now-extinct White English Terrier to produce a dog that dazzled observers in both the dog-fighting pit and the show ring.

Key facts

Country of origin
Great Britain

Date of origin
1800s

Life expectancy
11–13 yrs

Temperament
Despite its tough look, this breed makes a friendly and sensitive companion.

Maintenance
Requires frequent exercise to maintain its muscular appearance.

Other names
English Bull Terrier

Forelegs are straight and parallel

Round, compact feet have neat toes

53–56 cm
(21–22 in)

Weight   24–28 kg (53–62 lb)

Physical characteristics

Head	In profile, head curves downward from top of skull to tip of nose.
Eyes	Small, dark, triangular eyes are set obliquely and close together.
Ears	Small and thin.
Body	Well-rounded, with a short, strong back.
Coat	Short and flat, with a glossy appearance. In winter, may have a soft undercoat.
Tail	Short, tapering tail is carried horizontally.

Airedale Terrier

- An affectionate family companion and guard
- Outgoing and confident
- An aggressive hunter

Although it is far too large to live up to the definition of the word "terrier", which in French means an ability to go to ground, in all other ways the Airedale is the essence of this group of dogs. A born watchdog, it has a delinquent tendency to get into street brawls with other dogs. The tough, hardy Airedale has been used as a police dog, a sentry dog, and a messenger. Were it not for its inherently strong, stubborn streak, this alert and fearless breed would be a popular and successful working dog.

History The Airedale Terrier originated in Yorkshire, England, in the 19th century, when working men in Leeds crossed the Old English Broken-haired Terrier with the Otterhound, so producing this extremely versatile "King of Terriers".

Ears, head and beard are always tan

Long, powerful thighs

Forelegs are perfectly straight and thickly boned

Key facts

Country of origin
Great Britain

Date of origin
1800s

Life expectancy
12 yrs

Temperament
Friendly and intelligent; good with children, but should be supervized.

Maintenance
Coat is shed twice a year and may occasionally require professional grooming.

Other names
Waterside Terrier, Bingley Terrier

56–61 cm
(22–24 in)

Weight   20–23 kg (44–50 lb)

Physical characteristics

Head	Well-balanced, with a long, flat skull and powerful jaws covered with a beard.
Eyes	Dark and small, with an alert expression.
Ears	Small and V-shaped.
Body	Short, strong back and muscular loins; chest is deep but not broad.
Coat	Hard, dense, wiry coat; requires expert grooming for the show ring.
Tail	Set high on the back; not curled over.

American Cocker Spaniel

- Devoted, affectionate, and sensitive
- A wonderful companion
- Can adapt to city or country life

This affectionate and most popular of all American-born breeds descends from the working English Cocker Spaniel *(see p.86)*. However, although attempts have been made to work the American, and it still retains hunting instincts, its popularity lies primarily in the gentle companionship it offers. Its beauty and charm are appreciated throughout North, Central, and South America, and also in Japan. The American Cocker Spaniel does, however, suffer from a wide variety of health problems, including skin disease, but its generous and affable nature makes up for any physical shortcomings.

History Legend has it that the first spaniel arrived in the United States in 1620, with the Pilgrims on the *Mayflower*. Originally, all spaniels were classified together, but eventually the American Cocker was bred for desired traits, and was recognized as a separate breed in 1946.

Coat is silky with dense feathering on the legs

Excessively long hair on ears is almost impossible to keep neat

Key facts

Country of origin
United States

Date of origin
1800s

Life expectancy
13–14 yrs

Temperament
Playful and friendly; ideal for the elderly and good with children.

Maintenance
Long, soft coat requires regular grooming to maintain its silky appearance.

Other names
Cocker Spaniel

34–39 cm
(13–15 in)

Weight   12–15 kg (26–34 lb)

Physical characteristics

Head	Rounded skull, with a deep, square muzzle.
Eyes	Round, with a soft and alert look.
Ears	Long and well-feathered; set in line with the lower part of the eye.
Body	Sturdy and compact, with a strong back sloping from the shoulders to the tail.
Coat	Flat or slightly wavy; profuse feathering on ears, chest, abdomen, and legs.
Tail	Was traditionally docked.

English Cocker Spaniel

■ An exuberant and joyful family friend
■ Responsive and gentle
■ Well-bred background essential

An adept working dog, the English Cocker is also an extremely popular household companion throughout both Eastern and Western Europe, and in British Commonwealth countries. Unfortunately, it has a worrying variety of inherited disorders, including a plethora of eye conditions, numerous skin complaints, and kidney problems. Behavioural problems are also not uncommon, such as rage syndrome in solid-coloured dogs. It is always best to obtain details of family history before acquiring a Cocker Spaniel.

History By 1800, the small land spaniels were divided into two groups, "starters", whose function was to spring game, and "cockers", which were used to flush and retrieve woodcock from dense undergrowth. The English Cocker descends from dogs developed in Wales and south-western England.

Key facts

Country of origin
Great Britain

Date of origin
1800s

Life expectancy
13–14 yrs

Temperament
Gentle, engaging, and willing to learn.

Maintenance
This faithful dog needs plenty of attention, exercise, and grooming.

Other names
Cocker Spaniel

Pendulous, long, silky hair on ears dips in food when dog eats

Firm, round, cat-like feet

38–43 cm
(15–17 in)

Weight   12–15 kg (26–34 lb)

Physical characteristics

Head	Well-developed, slightly arched skull, with a square muzzle.
Eyes	Bright, alert, brown eyes.
Ears	Set low, and lie close to the head.
Body	Compact and strong, with a deep chest. Back slopes gently downward to tail.
Coat	Flat or slightly wavy coat is well feathered, with a dense undercoat.
Tail	Was traditionally docked.

English Springer Spaniel

- A willing and affectionate companion
- Fun-loving and eager to please
- An active dog that thrives on exercise

A gundog with unlimited stamina, the English Springer thrives on physical activity, be it flushing game in marshes, or retrieving tennis balls in city parks. This leggy and powerful dog needs constant mental and physical stimulation; when these are denied, it can be quite destructive. Today, it is Great Britain's most popular working spaniel. It is an excellent companion and even the most urban individual probably retains sound working abilities.

History Perhaps the rootstock of all working spaniels, identifiable members of this breed are portrayed in paintings from the mid-1600s. It was not until the late 1800s that springers and cockers were separated into distinct breeds.

Key facts

Country of origin
Great Britain

Date of origin
1600s

Life expectancy
12–14 yrs

Temperament
Good-natured and quick to learn. Can adapt to city or country life.

Maintenance
Requires frequent exercise and regular grooming.

Thick, straight, silky topcoat covers a short, soft, dense undercoat

48–51 cm
(19–20 in)

Weight   18–23 kg (40–50 lb)

Physical characteristics

Head	Fairly broad skull, with a straight, square muzzle and strong jaws.
Eyes	Dark and medium-sized.
Ears	Lobe-shaped, close-set ears have excellent hair cover, and are set in line with eyes.
Body	Compact and well-proportioned.
Coat	Can be liver and white or black and white, and may have tan markings.
Tail	Was traditionally docked.

Brittany

- A popular and affectionate companion
- Happy, alert, and active
- An excellent hunter with a rugged look

The most popular native breed in France, and the stalwart companion of hunters in Canada and the United States, the Brittany is a superb medium-sized dog. An excellent setting and flushing gundog, the breed is often assumed to be a spaniel, much to the chagrin of its admirers, and in many countries it still carries that appellation. It may be spaniel in size, but in function it is a classic pointer, probably the world's only pointer with a stumpy tail. Rough-and-ready in appearance, the Brittany makes a trustworthy, reliable, and obedient companion.

History The original Brittany of 18th-century France, as represented in old accounts and illustrations, had almost died out by the early 1900s, when a local breeder, Arthur Enaud, rejuvenated the breed.

Key facts

Country of origin
France

Date of origin
1700s

Life expectancy
12–14 yrs

Temperament
A friendly and loyal dog which loves to work and is eager to please.

Maintenance
Requires frequent, long walks, but only minimal grooming.

Other names
Épagneul Breton, Brittany Spaniel

Lightly fringed ears

Straight, well-muscled forelegs

44–52 cm
(17–20 in)

Weight   14–18 kg (30–40 lb)

Physical characteristics

Head	Round and slightly wedge-shaped.
Eyes	Amber or brown, with an alert expression.
Ears	High-set, short, and fairly rounded. Set above the level of the eyes.
Body	Compact and strong; moves with a smooth, brisk, and efficient gait.
Coat	Colour can be orange, liver, or black combined with white; can be tricolour.
Tail	Naturally short.

Beagle

- A gentle, loving family pet
- Cheerful, friendly, and even-tempered
- A natural pack dog

Although the Beagle is an independent dog with a strong tendency to wander off when distracted, it is a popular companion because of its affectionate nature and low degree of aggression. An endearing trait of this tranquil breed is its rather elegant and harmonious voice. Its actual size and look vary quite significantly from country to country, and some kennel clubs recognize different varieties of Beagle dependent on size.

History This breed may be descended from the Harrier and ancient English hounds. Small hounds, capable of accompanying rabbit hunters on foot, have existed since the 14th century.

Erect tail

Muscular thighs have excellent propulsive power

Well-defined lips

Feet are round and firm with strong pads

30–38 cm (12–15 in)

Weight 8–14 kg (18–30 lb)

Key facts

Country of origin
Great Britain

Date of origin
1300s

Life expectancy
13 yrs

Temperament
Alert and robust; enjoys the company of people and other animals.

Maintenance
Requires obedience training and plenty of active exercise.

Other names
English Beagle

Physical characteristics

Head — Slightly domed skull; nose is broad with wide nostrils.

Eyes — Large and brown or hazel in colour.

Ears — Long, with a fine texture, and hanging in a graceful fold.

Body — Sturdy and compact, with a muscular, level back and a deep, broad chest.

Coat — Short, dense, and weather-resistant.

Tail — Moderately long and set high on the back.

Whippet

- An ideal companion
- Quiet, reserved, and obedient
- Robust and powerful, despite its appearance

The Whippet's aerodynamic body design is ideal for racing. Over short distances it is capable of achieving speeds of up to 40 mph (65 km/h). It may look and behave like a delicate breed, and it certainly enjoys the pleasures of curling up on sofas and beds, but in the field its personality changes to that of a fearless and successful hunter. This gentle and affectionate breed is friendly with both children and adults. Its coat requires little grooming, although its thin skin is prone to laceration.

History In the 1800s, rabbit coursing was a popular sport in the north of England. To improve the acceleration of the terriers used in this sport, good coursing terriers were bred with small greyhounds, producing today's graceful Whippet.

Key facts

Country of origin
Great Britain

Date of origin
1800s

Life expectancy
14–15 yrs

Temperament
Gentle, confident, and even-tempered.

Maintenance
Quiet in the house and easy to keep. Requires regular, short runs.

Finely textured ears are very mobile

Legs are well-muscled and strongly boned, and covered with very thin skin

45–56 cm
(18–22 in)

Weight   12–14 kg (26–30 lb)

Physical characteristics

Head	Long, lean, and tapering to nose.
Eyes	Bright, alert, brown eyes, with a quiet and retiring look.
Ears	Small and rose-shaped.
Body	Deep chest and strong back. Neck is long and well-arched.
Coat	Short, close, and firm in texture. Can be any colour or mix of colours.
Tail	Long and tapering.

Border Collie

- Highly responsive, and a willing worker
- Keen, alert, and eager to learn
- An outstanding sheepdog

Still the most popular working sheepdog in Great Britain and Ireland, the Border can make an affectionate but difficult pet, especially in cities. Border Collies from working lines have a strong predatory instinct, which is channelled through breeding and training into a superb herding ability. Without constant stimulation, this need to work will vent itself in destructive behaviour, such as herding other dogs or people, or snappiness.

History Although shepherds in the hilly Scottish Borders have used collies for over 300 years, this breed was not given its present name until 1915.

Key facts

Country of origin
Great Britain

Date of origin
1700s

Life expectancy
12–14 yrs

Temperament
Obedient and faithful, with a strong desire to please its owner. Can be over-excitable.

Maintenance
Frequent exercise and directed activities are essential.

Moderately blunt, tapering muzzle

Weather-resistant coat

Well-boned, straight forelimbs

46–56 cm (18–22 in)

Weight   14–22 kg (30–49 lb)

Physical characteristics

Head	Fairly broad skull; strong jaws and teeth.
Eyes	Large and wide-set, with an alert and intelligent expression.
Ears	Medium-sized; carried erect or semi-erect.
Body	Well-proportioned with an athletic appearance. Neck is strong and muscular.
Coat	Topcoat is dense with a medium texture; undercoat is short and soft.
Tail	Carried low, but with an up-swirl at tip.

Pembroke Welsh Corgi

- An excellent family companion
- Outgoing and friendly
- Happy to live in the city or country

The robust Pembroke Welsh Corgi is an instinctive "heeler", used extensively throughout Great Britain up to the 19th century to drive cattle to markets. Built low enough to the ground to avoid flailing hooves, the bold Pembroke drove livestock by nipping at its heels. The stamina and efficiency of this breed's ancestors made it a popular working dog. Today, although it is still worked, this alert, kindly dog is mostly kept as a family pet. The Pembroke Corgi is more popular than its cousin the Cardigan Welsh Corgi, which is distinguishable by its long, bushy tail and larger ears.

History Ancient records indicate that the Pembroke Welsh Corgi has existed in Great Britain since at least 920. One story tells that the breed accompanied Flemish weavers brought to Great Britain by King Henry I of England.

Key facts

Country of origin
Great Britain

Date of origin
900s

Life expectancy
12–14 yrs

Temperament
A lively and confident but obedient family pet. May have the occasional inclination to nip.

Maintenance
Frequent grooming is advisable. Requires regular exercise as can become overweight.

A shorter body than the Cardigan

PEMBROKE CORGI

Long, fox-like brush tail

CARDIGAN CORGI

25–31 cm
(10–12 in)

Weight   11–14 kg (24–30 lb)

Physical characteristics

Head	Fox-like in appearance, with an intelligent and alert expression.
Eyes	Medium-sized, oval, brown eyes.
Ears	Erect and slightly rounded; smaller than those of the Cardigan.
Body	Low-set and sturdily built.
Coat	Medium-length and straight. Undercoat is short, dense, and weather-resistant.
Tail	Often naturally bobbed.

Golden Retriever

- A happy and trustworthy family pet
- Reliable and friendly
- Obedient and easy to train

Originally bred to retrieve waterfowl, the attractive, affection-demanding Golden has a gentle mouth and will rarely snap or bite. Several breed lines have been developed: one variety works as a gundog, another is used in field trials, while the largest line is devoted to the show ring and family life. A fourth breeding line has produced dogs that are trained exclusively as assistants for blind or disabled people. Popularity has unfortunately produced inherited defects in some lines, such as allergic skin conditions, eye problems, and even irritable snappiness.

History This kindly breed was developed in the late 1800s, by crossing a light-coloured Flat-coated Retriever with the now-extinct Tweed Water Spaniel. The first Goldens were exhibited in 1908.

Key facts

Country of origin
Great Britain

Date of origin
1800s

Life expectancy
12–15 yrs

Temperament
Relaxed but responsive and reliable; especially patient with children.

Maintenance
Requires daily exercise and regular grooming.

Other names
Yellow Retriever, Russian Retriever

Neck is clean and muscular with loose-fitting skin

Coat colour varies from cream to gold, and lightens with age

51–61 cm
(20–24 in)

Weight   27–36 kg (60–80 lb)

Physical characteristics

Head	Balanced, with a broad skull.
Eyes	Dark brown eyes, surrounded by dark rims, with a kind and friendly expression.
Ears	Set at eye-level; hang with a slight fold.
Body	Well-balanced; moves with a smooth and powerful gait when trotting.
Coat	Firm topcoat can be flat or wavy, with a dense, waterproof undercoat.
Tail	Carried level or with a slight curve.

Labrador Retriever

- An ideal family friend
- Good-tempered and eager to please
- An energetic and playful water-lover

Water-loving, affable, gregarious, and family-oriented – a delicious range of adjectives describe one of the world's most popular family companions. Unfortunately, some individuals suffer hereditary physical problems including cataracts, hip and elbow arthritis, and occasional wayward temperaments. Despite this, the Labrador Retriever is one of the most loyal and dependable breeds in the world.

History The Labrador Retriever traces its origins back to the St. John's region of Newfoundland in the 1800s. There, it was known as the "Small Water Dog", to differentiate it from the larger Newfoundland. Trade in salted cod brought the breed to the port of Poole in Dorset, England, where local landowners refined its breeding for use as a gundog.

Key facts

Country of origin
Canada

Date of origin
1800s

Life expectancy
12–14 yrs

Temperament
A kindly, fun, and devoted companion. Gentle with children and other family pets.

Maintenance
Needs a fair amount of exercise, and will enjoy the occasional swim.

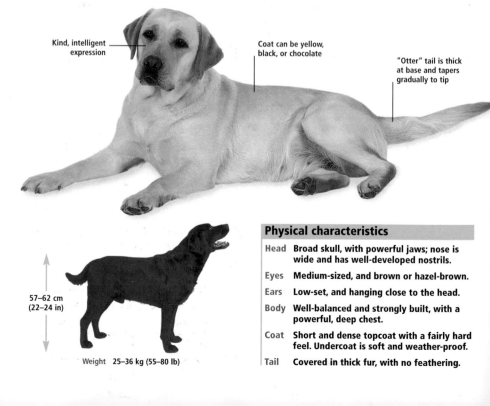

Kind, intelligent expression

Coat can be yellow, black, or chocolate

"Otter" tail is thick at base and tapers gradually to tip

57–62 cm (22–24 in)

Weight 25–36 kg (55–80 lb)

Physical characteristics

Head	Broad skull, with powerful jaws; nose is wide and has well-developed nostrils.
Eyes	Medium-sized, and brown or hazel-brown.
Ears	Low-set, and hanging close to the head.
Body	Well-balanced and strongly built, with a powerful, deep chest.
Coat	Short and dense topcoat with a fairly hard feel. Undercoat is soft and weather-proof.
Tail	Covered in thick fur, with no feathering.

German Pointer

- A faithful companion
- Athletic, active, and a keen worker
- Can be Wirehaired, Longhaired, or Shorthaired

Three breeds of German Pointer have been developed, each with its own distinctive characteristics. The Wirehaired Pointer is a marvellous family dog, as well as a hardy worker. Hip and elbow arthritis are known inherited conditions in this breed, so careful selection is important. The Longhaired Pointer (not recognized by the American Kennel Club) remains primarily a working dog, although it is calm and loyal, and makes a surprisingly good guard dog. The Shorthaired Pointer can be timid, but is an amenable companion.

History Although today's diverse group of German Pointers have a variety of origins, they are all a result of the intense activity that took place in dog breeding in Germany in the late 1800s, when German breeders introduced French and British breeding lines into national bloodstock.

Long forelegs have solid bone and close-fitting skin

A graceful outline

Good angulation to legs, with almost straight metatarsal bones below hocks

Key facts

Country of origin
Germany

Date of origin
1800s

Life expectancy
12–14 yrs

Temperament
Even-tempered and alert.

Maintenance
These energetic dogs require plenty of exercise.

Other names
Deutscher Drahthaariger Vorstehhund

60–65 cm
(24–26 in)

Weight   27–32 kg (60–70 lb)

Physical characteristics

Head	Proportionate to body; jaws are powerful.
Eyes	Oval (Longhaired and Wirehaired) or almond-shaped (Shorthaired).
Ears	Set high and hanging close to the head.
Body	Powerfully built; moves with a free gait.
Coat	Shorthaired: thick, flat; coarse to touch. Wirehaired: thick and harsh; a full beard. Longhaired: long and close-fitting.
Tail	Was traditionally docked (not Longhaired).

Irish Setter

- Lively and affectionate
- A loyal and protective family pet
- High-spirited and full of energy

Once known in Gaelic simply as the *Modder rhu* or "red dog", the Irish Setter was also called a red spaniel. This racy, active dog thrives on physical activity. Faster than most other companion dogs, it actively seeks out other dogs to play with, perhaps because it enjoys running rings around them. The Irish Setter is an exuberant extrovert. Its late maturation and joy of life give it an undeserved reputation for being flighty and overly excitable.

History As its name suggests, this breed has its origins in Ireland in the 18th century, with setting spaniels, early Scottish setters, and The Old Spanish Pointer playing a part in its development.

Key facts

Country of origin
Ireland

Date of origin
1700s

Life expectancy
13 yrs

Temperament
Friendly, mischievous, and full of fun.

Maintenance
Needs plenty of exercise and weekly grooming. A late developer, it may require more training than other breeds.

Other names
Irish Red Setter, Red Setter

Powerful hindquarters with well-developed thighs

Ears hang in loose folds close to the head

Long, silky, rich-chestnut coat

Small feet with firm, close toes

64–69 cm (25–27 in)

Weight 27–32 kg (60–70 lb)

Physical characteristics

Head	Long and lean, with an oval skull.
Eyes	Medium to dark-brown eyes have a gentle and intelligent expression.
Ears	Set low on the head, with a fine texture.
Body	Well-proportioned, with a deep chest; back is firm and slopes downward to the tail.
Coat	Long and straight; profuse feathering on belly forms a fringe.
Tail	Feathered tail, set low, and carried level.

Pointer

- A wonderful family dog
- Handsome, dignified, and sensible
- A strong hunting instinct

Gentle, obedient, and with a tendency to take life rather seriously, the Pointer's original purpose contradicted natural dog behaviour. Upon sighting a hare it would stand and point, permitting accompanying greyhounds to chase and seize the animal. Selective breeding has created an intensely biddable, noble, and giving individual, but one that is overly sensitive. Its kindly and gentle disposition makes it an ideal family companion.

History Although its exact origins are unclear, the Pointer was developed wholly in Great Britain and has been a hunting dog since the 1600s. At some stage in its development, Old Spanish Setter lines were probably used.

Firm, straight forelegs

Fine, smooth, hard coat with a good sheen

Thighs are lean and well-muscled

Key facts

Country of origin
Great Britain

Date of origin
1600s

Life expectancy
13–14 yrs

Temperament
Even-tempered and gentle with children. An effective and courageous worker.

Maintenance
Not ideal for urban living, as this active dog thrives on plenty of exercise.

Other names
English Pointer

58–71 cm
(23–28 in)

Weight   20–34 kg (44–75 lb)

Physical characteristics

Head	Fairly broad skull; deep muzzle has a slight arch, elevating the nose for scenting.
Eyes	Round, and hazel or brown depending on the coat colour.
Ears	High-set ears hang loose, even when alert.
Body	Sleek, muscular, and well-built.
Coat	Lemon, orange, liver, or black, either as a solid colour, or combined with white.
Tail	Straight, and held horizontally.

Weimaraner

- Friendly, alert, and responsive
- A bold, determined working dog
- Striking, steel-coloured coat

Rippling with muscles, this uniquely coloured gundog is popular both as a worker and, increasingly, as a companion. The Weimaraner usually has an obedient and fearless personality, and its natural disposition and strength make it a reliable watchdog. There are two coat varieties – the popular shorthaired version, and the less common longhaired variety. Both are reliable workers, proficient in field trials and obedience work, as well as in hunting. The breed has grace, speed, stamina, endurance, but perhaps most important of all, "star quality".

History The Weimaraner's exact origins are unknown, although grey-coloured hunting dogs were known in 17th-century Germany. Named after the court of Charles August, Grand Duke of Weimar, selective breeding in the 1800s created today's standards.

Shorthaired variety: coat is sleek and smooth

Strong, straight forelegs

Key facts

Country of origin
Germany

Date of origin
1600s

Life expectancy
12–13 yrs

Temperament
This confident, strong dog loves children and is a good guardian.

Maintenance
Can be dominant, so a firm hand is essential. Requires regular exercise.

Other names
Weimaraner
Vorstehhund

56–69 cm
(22–27 in)

Weight 32–39 kg (70–86 lb)

Physical characteristics

Head	Long, with an aristocratic look.
Eyes	Distinctive, light eyes are amber or grey.
Ears	High-set, and slightly folded.
Body	Medium-sized, with a straight, level back, and a deep, well-developed chest.
Coat	Coat colour shades from silver-grey to mouse-grey.
Tail	Was traditionally docked on working dogs, but is otherwise left natural.

English Setter

■ A devoted and affectionate family member
■ Mild-mannered and extremely friendly
■ A strong and effective working dog

A graceful, quiet, and considerate breed, the English Setter is marvellous with children and easy to train. This elegant breed is also a good, responsive worker in the field, capable of prolonged physical activity. In a small number of setters, there is an inherited tendency to blindness caused by a deterioration of the retinas. The predominantly white variety also has a higher-than-average incidence of allergic skin conditions.

History Setters are descended from spaniels with a hunting ability. British breeder Edward Laverack developed today's English Setter in the early 1800s.

Key facts

Country of origin
Great Britain

Date of origin
1800s

Life expectancy
14 yrs

Temperament
Very gentle, good-natured and happy.

Maintenance
Extremely active, so requires a great deal of exercise.

Oval skull with plenty of brain room

Topcoat is slightly wavy, long, and silky; undercoat is fleecy

Ears hang in neat folds, close to face

Parallel, straight forelegs

61–64 cm (24–25 in)

Weight   25–30 kg (55–66 lb)

Physical characteristics

Head	Long and lean, with a square muzzle.
Eyes	Colour ranges from hazel to dark brown. Oval in shape, with a bright expression.
Ears	Moderately long, with a velvety tip.
Body	Medium-length; elegant in appearance, with a free and graceful gait.
Coat	White, with flecking ("belton") in lemon, orange, liver, or black; can be tricolour.
Tail	Straight, feathered tail tapers to a point.

Chesapeake Bay Retriever

- Bright and happy
- Eager, brave, and willing to work
- An energetic and active water-lover

Along the duck-hunting shores of Chesapeake Bay, and throughout the United States, Canada, Scandinavia, and Great Britain, this tireless worker excels at retrieving game. It is a tougher breed than the Labrador Retriever, with a sharper personality. Like other retrievers, it is gentle with children and cordial to strangers. A loyal and affectionate companion, it is happiest in a country environment.

History Stories suggest that this breed descends from two Lesser Newfoundland puppies given to American George Law in 1807, by a British army captain. These dogs were bred with local hounds to produce the Chesapeake Bay Retriever. However, in form and function this breed is remarkably similar to the Curly-coated Retriever, which means that this industrious breed may also have English or Irish Water Spaniel, or English Otterhound blood in its history.

Key facts

Country of origin
United States

Date of origin
1800s

Life expectancy
12–13 yrs

Temperament
Alert and robust; a good guard dog.

Maintenance
Thick coat needs regular brushing and will shed profusely once a year. Requires plenty of daily exercise.

Ears hang loosely

Hare-like webbed feet with rounded toes

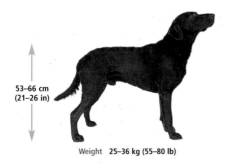

53–66 cm
(21–26 in)

Weight   25–36 kg (55–80 lb)

Physical characteristics

Head	Broad, round skull, with strong jaws. Pointed muzzle is of medium length.
Eyes	Wide-set, clear, and light in colour.
Ears	Small, and set fairly high on the head.
Body	Strong and well-balanced, with powerful hindquarters and a broad, deep chest.
Coat	Water-resistant; topcoat is harsh, thick, and oily; undercoat is dense and woolly.
Tail	Medium-length, with slight feathering.

Hungarian Vizsla

- Gentle and affectionate
- A powerful dog with a distinguished look
- Full of energy

The elegant Vizsla was originally developed in Hungary for pointing and retrieving, but its use has been extended to a third purpose in the last 20 years – that of a widely admired family companion. However, its original purpose has not been forgotten; in Canada, the wirehaired variety is commonly seen with weekend hunters. The Vizsla has a good nose, follows trails diligently, and retrieves either game or thrown tennis balls with enthusiasm.

History The name was first used in 1510 to describe the result of crossing the now-extinct indigenous Pannonian Hound with the Yellow Turkish Dog. By the 1850s, today's shorthaired gundog was established.

Key facts

Country of origin
Hungary

Date of origin
Middle Ages

Life expectancy
13–14 yrs

Temperament
Obedient, reliable, and healthy. Easily trained.

Maintenance
Requires daily exercise.

Other names
Vizsla, Magyar Vizsla, Drotszoru Magyar Vizsla

Smooth, shiny hair

Straight, strong, muscular forelimbs

Long thighs and legs, with low hocks

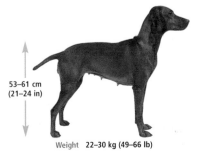

53–61 cm
(21–24 in)

Weight   22–30 kg (49–66 lb)

Physical characteristics

Head	Lean and muscular; long muzzle tapers slightly to square end.
Eyes	Medium-sized eyes are lively and alert.
Ears	Thin and silky with round tips, and hanging close to the cheeks.
Body	Strong and well-proportioned.
Coat	Dense, straight, and short; lies close to the body, and has no undercoat.
Tail	Was traditionally docked on working dogs.

Basset Hound

- A loving family companion
- Laid-back and sociable
- A natural and effective scenthound

Often stubborn, but usually benign and easygoing, the Basset was once a superb hunting dog. These dogs are excellent at trailing, very wise, and gentle in disposition. Today's typical pet Basset is heavier, longer, and a bit lower than its hunting counterpart and is the cartoonist's and advertiser's delight. In the United States, the cartoon character, Fred Basset, personifies droll good humour, while worldwide the Basset has been used to symbolize the comfort of well-fitting shoes.

History The Basset Hound may descend from "dwarfed" bloodhounds. It originated in France in the late 16th century, and is now popular in Great Britain and the United States.

Key facts

Country of origin
France

Date of origin
1500s

Life expectancy
12 yrs

Temperament
Affectionate and happy. Good with children.

Maintenance
Exercise is important to prevent excessive weight gain.

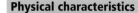

Ears are long and low-set

Full, deep chest

Weight is borne evenly on the centre of the paws without splaying the toes

33–38 cm (13–15 in)

Weight   18–27 kg (40–60 lb)

Physical characteristics

Head	Domed skull, covered in loose skin that wrinkles noticeably when head is lowered.
Eyes	Slightly sunken eyes with a sad look.
Ears	Fine, velvety ears hang in loose folds.
Body	Long and deep, with a level back and short, powerful forelegs.
Coat	Hard, smooth, and short hair; skin is loose and elastic.
Tail	Thick; carried with a slight curve.

Rhodesian Ridgeback

- An alert and willing watchdog
- Loyal and affectionate
- A handsome, strong, and athletic hunter

Contrary to myth and to its nickname (the African Lion Hound), this muscular dog was never used to attack lions, but acted as a true hound, trailing big game and then barking to attract the hunter's attention. Its sheer size and brute strength offered protection if it were itself attacked. Loyal and affectionate, few Ridgebacks are worked today; instead they serve as guards and companions.

History In the 1800s, European settlers in southern Africa bred their Dutch and German mastiffs and scent hounds with the indigenous ridgebacks to produce today's breed.

Short, dense, glossy coat with distinctive ridge along back

Well-arched toes have tough, round, elastic pads

Muzzle is long and powerful

Key facts

Country of origin
South Africa

Date of origin
1800s

Life expectancy
12 yrs

Temperament
Proud and dignified; can be aloof with strangers.

Maintenance
Clean and easy to keep, but requires regular exercise.

Other names
African Lion Hound

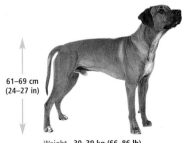

61–69 cm
(24–27 in)

Weight 30–39 kg (66–86 lb)

Physical characteristics

Head Broad, flat skull free from wrinkles.

Eyes Round, bright, and sparkling.

Ears Wide at the base, tapering to a rounded point and carried close to the head.

Body Strong and well-balanced.

Coat A characteristic ridge of hair grows along the back in the opposite direction to the rest of the coat.

Tail Tapering, with a slight upward curve.

Greyhound

- Lively, athletic, and even-tempered
- A dignified and loving companion
- The fastest of all dogs

Capable of reaching more than 40 mph (64 km/h), the elegant Greyhound is the dog world's most impressive speed merchant. It uses speed and sight to overtake prey, be it a living animal in the field or desert, or a mechanical rabbit on a dog track. The pet Greyhound is a delightful and relaxed companion, although retired racing dogs have a tendency to chase anything that moves.

History A 4,900-year-old carving on an Egyptian tomb confirms the antiquity of this breed. Exported to Spain, China, Persia, and elsewhere, the Greyhound was developed to its present form in Great Britain.

Key facts

Country of origin
Egypt/Great Britain

Date of origin
Antiquity

Life expectancy
10–12 yrs

Temperament
Alert and well-behaved; good with children. Muzzle may be required when off the lead as it can chase other animals.

Maintenance
Needs regular exercise and plenty of food.

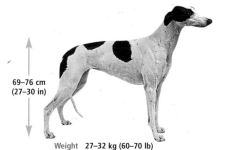

Powerful, arched loins

Fine, close hair on long, muscular neck

Long, straight forelegs are well-boned

69–76 cm (27–30 in)

Weight   27–32 kg (60–70 lb)

Physical characteristics

Head	Long and narrow head, with powerful jaws and strong teeth; flat skull.
Eyes	Bright, oval eyes are obliquely set.
Ears	Small and rose-shaped with a fine texture.
Body	Long, broad, square back and powerful, muscular hindquarters.
Coat	Short and smooth with a firm texture. Colour is highly variable.
Tail	Long, low-set and slightly curved.

Bearded Collie

- A family dog that adores children
- Friendly and self-confident
- One of Britain's oldest breeds

Exuberance is the cardinal personality trait of this vivacious and high-spirited breed. The Beardie needs constant mental and physical stimulation, and is ideal for people who have both time and energy. Having virtually disappeared as a working dog by the 1930s, this hardy breed always had a few staunch devotees among the shepherds and drovers of Peebleshire in Scotland. After World War II, Mrs G. O. Williamson revived the breed, starting with just two dogs.

History Like most shaggy herding dogs, the Beardie probably descends from the Hungarian Komondor. Mythically, these dogs were brought to Scotland by Polish traders in the Middle Ages.

Key facts

Country of origin
Scotland

Date of origin
Middle Ages

Life expectancy
12–13 yrs

Temperament
Stable, energetic, and cheerful; very accepting of other people and animals.

Maintenance
The long coat needs regular grooming to prevent matting.

Other names
Beardie, Highland Collie, Mountain Collie

Harsh, shaggy topcoat covers a soft, furry undercoat

Oval feet with well-padded soles

51–56 cm
(20–22 in)

Weight 18–27 kg (40–60 lb)

Physical characteristics

Head	Broad, flat skull, with a strong, full muzzle and a large nose.
Eyes	Large and expressive; set wide apart.
Ears	Medium-sized, set high on the head, and with a good covering of hair.
Body	Long and lean, with a firm, level back.
Coat	Increases in length from the cheeks to under the chin, forming the beard.
Tail	Long, with abundant feathering.

Old English Sheepdog

- A big, lovable family friend
- Even-tempered and trustworthy
- Active, with great stamina

Early in the 18th century, the Old English was well established as a drover, driving cattle to market. To show its tax-exempt status as a working dog, the tail was docked. This led to its nickname "bobtail" and to a practice that has endured. Today, the Old English Sheepdog is a faithful family companion and guard. While early training is necessary, this is mainly to control this breed's intense demands for affection.

History The Old English probably traces its origins back to continental sheepdogs, such as the Briard. Selective breeding began in the 1880s.

Key facts

Country of origin
Great Britain

Date of origin
1800s

Life expectancy
12–13 yrs

Temperament
Adaptable, calm, and self-confident.

Maintenance
Plenty of exercise is essential. Coat must be brushed frequently, and may need occasional trim for cleanliness.

Other names
Bobtail

Hair covers the eyes

Hard, shaggy coat

Strong, square, truncated jaws

53–61 cm
(21–24 in)

Weight 29–30 kg (64–66 lb)

Physical characteristics

Head	Capacious skull, well-covered with hair; nose is large and black, with wide nostrils.
Eyes	Dark eyes, set well apart.
Ears	Small ears lie flat to the side of the head.
Body	Strong, compact, and square, with a characteristic rolling gait when walking.
Coat	Profuse, harshly textured topcoat, with a waterproof undercoat.
Tail	Was traditionally docked.

Rough Collie

- Loyal and reliable
- An alert watchdog
- High-maintenance good looks

The elegant Rough Collie first attracted the attention of breeders, and then the public after Queen Victoria acquired the dog as a companion. However, the breed's popularity reached unprecedented heights when the Hollywood film industry invented Lassie in the 1940s. This responsive, fun breed is easy to obedience train and makes an excellent companion. Development of the Rough Collie for the show ring has tended to override its original herding abilities.
History Although shepherds in the hilly Scottish Borders used Collies for many years, this breed was not given its present name until 1915.

Key facts

Country of origin
Great Britain

Date of origin
1900s

Life expectancy
12–14 yrs

Temperament
Dignified, friendly, and responsible with children.

Maintenance
Long coat mats easily, so requires daily grooming.

Other names
Scottish Collie

Head has a smooth wedge-shaped outline

Dense, straight topcoat

56–66 cm
(22–26 in)

Weight   23–34 kg (50–75 lb)

Physical characteristics

Head	Flat skull; smooth, well-rounded muzzle with a black nose and strong jaws.
Eyes	Almond-shaped and slightly oblique.
Ears	Small and set fairly high on the head.
Body	Long, with a deep chest and a firm back; muscular forelegs are well-feathered.
Coat	Topcoat is abundant except on the head and legs; undercoat is soft and furry.
Tail	Long, bushy tail is carried low.

Australian Shepherd

- A loyal companion and a serious worker
- Good-natured and responsive
- Strong herding and guarding instincts

Virtually unknown outside the United States, the Australian Shepherd is now increasing in popularity because of its obedient and willing nature, as well as its natural good looks. Originally bred as a working shepherd suitable for the varied climate of California, the Australian Shepherd has adapted superbly to both family life and work as a service dog, especially in search and rescue. The breed has a temperament similar to those of Golden and Labrador Retrievers. It is affectionate and playful, but maintains a basic working instinct.

History This breed originated in California in the 1800s, although its ancestors include sheepdogs from New Zealand and Australia.

Key facts

Country of origin
United States/Australia

Date of origin
1800s

Life expectancy
12–13 yrs

Temperament
An active and even-tempered dog, although can be shy with strangers.

Maintenance
Requires regular and frequent exercise.

Muzzle roughly the same length as the skull

Thick fur on neck and chest forms a ruff

Broad, solid feet provide firm footing

46–58 cm (18–23 in)

Weight 16–32 kg (35–70 lb)

Physical characteristics

Head	Strong and clean-cut; size is proportionate to the body.
Eyes	Can be blue, brown, or amber, and may be flecked or marbled.
Ears	Triangular, and set high on the head.
Body	Medium-sized, well-balanced and solid; moves with a smooth, agile gait.
Coat	Weather-resistant and of medium length.
Tail	Naturally bobbed; docked in America.

Samoyed

- A friend for life
- Active, alert, and full of fun
- A striking dog with a smiling expression

Originally a hunter and guardian of reindeer herds, today's snow-white breed retains many of its original traits. The Samoyed is an exceptionally good-natured dog. It particularly enjoys human companionship, is good with children, and is not aggressive, although it makes a fairly good watchdog. As with most spitz breeds, the Samoyed does not take readily to training, and early obedience classes are advisable.

History The hardy and adaptable Samoyed accompanied the nomadic tribe of that name for centuries, as they traversed the most northerly regions of Asia. The breed was not introduced into the West until 1889 and, since that time, breeders have perfected its luxurious coat.

Key facts

Country of origin
Russia

Date of origin
Antiquity

Life expectancy
12 yrs

Temperament
Dependable and friendly with all – family, strangers, and other animals.

Maintenance
Heavy coat needs regular grooming and sheds profusely.

Other names
Samoyedskaya

Thick, weather-resistant coat

Feet are large and rather flat

46–56 cm
(18–22 in)

Weight   23–30 kg (50–66 lb)

Physical characteristics

Head   Powerful, wedge-shaped head.

Eyes   Almond-shaped and set well apart.

Ears   Thick, with rounded tips and well-covered inside with hair.

Body   Broad, very muscular body; chest is deep giving plenty of room for heart and lungs.

Coat   Long, harsh topcoat forms a ruff around the head; undercoat is short and woolly.

Tail   Well-covered and carried over the back.

Poodle (Standard)

- Smart, loyal, and fun
- A friendly, reliable companion
- Can be wary of strangers

The Standard Poodle is not simply a fashion accessory – it is a responsive and active dog with a dignified air. The breed has a lower-than-average incidence of skin complaints and does not shed, making it an ideal dog for people who have allergies. Not given to the hysterics that sometimes afflict its smaller relatives, the Standard remains at heart a working dog. Its French name, *Caniche*, meaning "duck dog", is descriptive of its original purpose – a duck retriever.

History Drawings by artists such as Albrecht Dürer reveal that the Poodle, developed in Germany in the Middle Ages, was originally a water dog. Today's distinctive clipping is based on historic grooming to reduce water resistance while working.

Key facts

Country of origin
Germany

Date of origin
Middle Ages

Life expectancy
11–13 yrs

Temperament
Lively and good-tempered; enjoys obedience training

Maintenance
Long coat requires frequent clipping.

Other names
Caniche, Barbone

Solid, even coat colour

Well-developed, muscular thighs

Hair on lower legs increases swimming power

38 cm and over (15 in and over)

Weight 20.5–32 kg (45–70 lb)

Physical characteristics

Head	Well-proportioned and elegant, with a long, straight muzzle.
Eyes	Dark-brown and slightly slanted, giving an intelligent expression.
Ears	Long, wide ears hang close to the head.
Body	Strong, muscular shoulders, a deep chest, and a short back.
Coat	Long, coarse topcoat with a harsh texture.
Tail	Was traditionally docked.

Dalmatian

■ A devoted family friend
■ Energetic and outgoing
■ Needs companionship

Although today the Dalmatian breed is kept solely as a companion, for centuries it was a superb working dog. In its time it has been a pack hunter, a retriever, and a bird dog, and used to herd sheep and catch vermin. Until the advent of motorized transportation, the Dalmatian was used as a carriage-dog, walking alongside horse-drawn carriages and clearing the road ahead in populated areas. A confident and exuberant dog, the Dalmatian can, uniquely, suffer from urate stones in its urinary system.

History Greek friezes over 4,000 years old show hunting dogs that are similar to the Dalmatian. Although Dalmatia, on the coast of the Adriatic, is described as this distinctive breed's home, there is convincing evidence that it originated in India, and was transported to ancient Greece by Indian merchant traders.

Key facts

Country of origin
Balkans/India

Date of origin
Antiquity

Life expectancy
12 yrs

Temperament
Spirited and confident; males can show aggression to other male dogs.

Maintenance
Needs plenty of exercise. Shedding can be minimized by daily brushing.

Long, broad back is perfectly straight

Shoulders are moderately oblique, clean, and muscular, leading to straight forelimbs

48–61 cm (19–24 in)

Weight   23–25 kg (50–55 lb)

Physical characteristics

Head	Smooth, square skull and a long muzzle.
Eyes	Round, bright eyes are fairly wide set.
Ears	Tapering to rounded tips and carried close to the head.
Body	Sleek and muscular, with a deep chest; moves with a smooth, effortless gait.
Coat	Short, dense, and glossy.
Tail	Strong, tapering tail is carried with a slight upward curve.

Shar Pei

- Serious and dignified
- Extremely devoted to its human family
- Distinctive crumpled appearance

No other breed in the dog world looks quite like a Shar Pei. Its Chinese standards eloquently describe its conformation – clam-shell ears, butterfly nose, melon-shaped head, grandmotherly face, water-buffalo neck, horse's buttocks, and dragon's legs. The first Shar Peis exported from Hong Kong and bred in the United States had severe eye problems, necessitating repeated surgery. Successive breeding has diminished these conditions, but has not reduced the very high incidence of skin problems.

History A long-time resident of China's southern province of Guangdong, this ancient breed appears to be descended from mastiff and spitz-type dogs. It is a fairly close relative of the Chow Chow. Driven almost to extinction by China's prohibition of dogs on the mainland, the breed was rescued by Matgo Law, a Hong Kong breeder.

Key facts

Country of origin
China

Date of origin
Antiquity

Life expectancy
11–12 yrs

Temperament
Calm and affectionate with its family, but cautious with strangers and animals.

Maintenance
Requires frequent grooming.

Other names
Chinese Shar-Pei, Chinese Fighting Dog

Prickly coat is very wrinkled

Straight, flexible forelegs

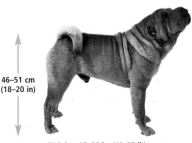

46–51 cm
(18–20 in)

Weight 18–25 kg (40–55 lb)

Physical characteristics

Head	Large relative to body; muzzle is broad and full.
Eyes	Dark, almond-shaped eyes, giving the appearance of frowning.
Ears	Small ears hang close to the cheeks.
Body	Compact, with a deep chest and muscular, sloping shoulders.
Coat	Harsh and straight; hair stands on end.
Tail	Thick, round tail is set high on the back.

Chow Chow

- A proud and loyal guard dog
- Powerful and independent
- Suitable for an experienced owner

The Chow Chow is probably entitled to be naturally aloof and stubborn. Throughout Mongolia and Manchuria its meat was once a delicacy, and its skin a popular fur for clothing. However, its name does not refer to the American cowboy's term for food, but originated in the 1800s, when English sailors named it after the term they used to describe miscellaneous ship cargo. Although it looks like an overstuffed teddy bear, the Chow Chow is not cuddly. It is a one-person dog, with a terrier-like tendency to snap or bite. **History** The ancient origins of the Chow Chow remain a mystery, although without doubt it is of spitz descent. In the early 1700s, historians described a black-tongued dog being used as food in the Orient. The Chow Chow first arrived in Great Britain in 1780.

Key facts

Country of origin
China

Date of origin
Antiquity

Life expectancy
11–12 yrs

Temperament
Quiet, dignified, and aloof. Can be possessive and wary of strangers.

Maintenance
Requires frequent and intense grooming.

Feet are small and cat-like

43–51 cm
(17–20 in)

Weight 20–32 kg (44–70 lb)

Physical characteristics

Head	Broad, flat skull and square muzzle; tongue is blue-black in colour.
Eyes	Small and dark; tight eyelids can cause medical problems.
Ears	Small, thick ears, slightly rounded at tips.
Body	Compact, powerful, and squarely built.
Coat	Rough or smooth types. Profuse hair around the head and neck forms a ruff.
Tail	Set high and carried over the back.

Boxer

- Loyal, courageous, and affectionate
- Expressive features
- Powerfully built and excitable

Boisterous, fun-loving, but gentle with children, the Boxer is in many ways an ideal family dog. However, its puppylike behaviour, fast reactions, and relatively large size mean that it can cause unintentional havoc in the home. A muscular and intimidating appearance make the Boxer an excellent guard dog.

History The Boxer is one of the great successes of the high-quality "designer" dog breeding that took place in Germany 100 years ago. Its primary ancestor, the old Bullenbeisser, was used for hunting boars and deer. Today's Boxer was developed by crossing Danziger and Brabanter Bullenbeissers with other Bavarian and foreign breeds.

Key facts

Country of origin
Germany

Date of origin
1800s

Life expectancy
12 yrs

Temperament
Playful and fun with friends and family, but wary of strangers.

Maintenance
Early obedience training essential to curb excitable nature.

Ribs well-arched, but not barrel-shaped

Front legs form a straight line from the shoulder

Well-muscled, powerful loins

53–63 cm
(21–25 in)

Weight   25–32 kg (55–70 lb)

Physical characteristics

Head	Top of skull slightly arched and lacking deep wrinkles; nose black and upturned.
Eyes	Dark brown in colour, not too deep set, giving an alert, intelligent expression.
Ears	Thin and wide-set.
Body	Sturdy, with balanced musculature.
Coat	Fawn or brindle in colour; short, shiny, and tight to the body.
Tail	Was traditionally docked.

Siberian Husky

- Willing, dignified, and tractable companion
- Great stamina and elegance
- Unusual colour and appearance

Smaller and lighter than most other breeds of sled dog, the agile, athletic Siberian Husky is designed for pulling moderate loads over great distances. In common with other ancient northern spitz types, it seldom barks, but engages in communal howling, much like wolves. The breed is dignified and gentle, lacking the possessive traits of a guard dog. The tireless Husky makes a very pleasant companion and has become especially popular in Canada, the United States, and Italy.

History Used as a draught animal by the nomadic Inuit, the Siberian Husky was chanced upon by 19th-century fur traders and brought to North America in 1909.

Key facts

Country of origin
Siberia

Date of origin
Antiquity

Life expectancy
11–13 yrs

Temperament
Gentle, eager, and robust, and friendly even with strangers.

Maintenance
Requires a fit, alert owner because it tends to wander and explore.

Other names
Arctic Husky

Tail held over the back in an arch when at attention

Alert, even mischievous expression

Compact, well-furred feet with cushioned pads

51–60 cm
(20–24 in)

Weight   16–27 kg (35–60 lb)

Physical characteristics

Head	Medium-sized, and in proportion to body.
Eyes	Almond-shaped; colour may be blue, brown, hazel, or non-solid.
Ears	Triangular, set high on head.
Body	Strongly boned, with a balanced shape.
Coat	Double coat is not so thick as to obscure the outline. Topcoat is smooth-lying, and may be black, white, or intermediate.
Tail	Well-furred and bushy.

Doberman

- A faithful guardian and companion
- Strong, intelligent, and obedient
- Can be nervous if poorly bred

The elegant Doberman is a classic example of the industriously successful dog-breeding programmes that took place in Germany just over 100 years ago. Today, this alert and resourceful breed is a companion and service dog all over the world. Due to unscrupulous breeding, shyness and fear biting can occur in some individuals.

History In the late 1800s, the German tax-collector Louis Dobermann used the Rottweiler, German Pinscher, Weimaraner, English Greyhound, and Manchester Terrier to develop this powerful breed.

Key facts

Country of origin
Germany

Date of origin
1800s

Life expectancy
12 yrs

Temperament
Bold, energetic, and loyal.

Maintenance
Early and careful obedience training is vital. Requires regular exercise.

Other names
Doberman Pinscher

Lean but well-muscled neck

Smooth, glossy coat

When standing, hock to foot area is perpendicular to the ground

Legs are perfectly straight and parallel

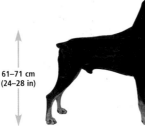

61–71 cm
(24–28 in)

Weight   30–40 kg (66–88 lb)

Physical characteristics

Head	Long head emerges distinctly from neck; skull is covered with tight-fitting skin.
Eyes	Dark, almond-shaped eyes are moderately deep set and have an alert expression.
Ears	Small and set high on the head.
Body	Muscular and powerful, with a square body shape. Back is short and firm.
Coat	Short, thick, and close-lying.
Tail	Was traditionally docked.

Irish Wolfhound

- Friendly, reliable, and sociable
- A powerful and effective presence
- The tallest of all breeds

Affectionate and loyal, the giant Irish Wolfhound loves to be with people, and makes an excellent companion. Despite its enormous size, it has a quiet nature and can be trusted with children. However, it needs a great deal of space and is therefore not ideally suited for city life.

History Present in Ireland almost 2,000 years ago, this noble breed had almost completely vanished by the mid-1800s, when it was revitalized by Captain G.A. Graham, a British army officer. Originally used by the Celts to hunt wolves, this majestic dog was probably first transported to Ireland by the Romans.

Muscular legs and forearms, with sturdy, straight bones

Wiry topcoat is long over eyes and under jaw

Key facts

Country of origin
Europe

Date of origin
Antiquity

Life expectancy
11 yrs

Temperament
Powerful yet kind, sensitive, and gentle.

Maintenance
Requires a considerable amount of exercise, and has a large appetite so food bills can be expensive.

71–90 cm
(28–35 in)

Weight   40–54 kg (88–120 lb)

Physical characteristics

Head	Long, with a slight indentation between the eyes. Muzzle is slightly pointed.
Eyes	Dark and oval.
Ears	Small, with a fine velvet texture.
Body	Gracefully built, with a long, well-arched neck and muscular shoulders.
Coat	Rough, hardy topcoat.
Tail	Long, slightly curved tail is well-covered with hair.

Bloodhound

- A gentle and affectionate dog
- Keen to please
- Not easy to obedience train

The Bloodhound thrives on the hunt rather than the kill – it revels in tracking and has been used to hunt animals, criminals, runaway slaves, and lost children. Today, this affable, plodding, sonorously voiced breed is both tracker and companion.

History For centuries, the monks of the St. Hubert monastery in Belgium bred superb scent-tracking hounds. At the same time, virtually identical hounds were bred in Great Britain. Both breeds had a common source – they accompanied crusaders who were returning to Europe from the Middle East.

Key facts

Country of origin
Belgium

Date of origin
Middle Ages

Life expectancy
10–12 yrs

Temperament
Kind and sensitive; friendly both with people and other dogs.

Maintenance
Strong and energetic, so requires considerable exercise and a fit owner.

Other names
St. Hubert Hound, Chien St. Hubert

Extremely long ears tend to curl inwards and backwards

Muscular thighs

58–69 cm
(23–27 in)

Weight 36–50 kg (80–110 lb)

Physical characteristics

Head	Long and narrow.
Eyes	Set deeply in their sockets; lower lids fall away revealing part of the inner surface.
Ears	Thin, soft ears are set low on the head.
Body	Strong back, powerful shoulders, and a well-muscled neck.
Coat	Short, fairly hard coat covers body; hair feels softer on skull and ears.
Tail	Long and thick; carried curved above back.

German Shepherd Dog

- Loyal and dependable
- A versatile and tireless working dog
- Well-bred background essential

When bred carefully, the German Shepherd Dog is an excellent breed – calm, reliable, and obedient. Indiscriminate breeding has, unfortunately, produced both physical and behavioural problems, the result being that the quality of individual dogs varies quite considerably. Poorly bred German Shepherd Dogs can suffer from medical complaints such as arthritis, eye disease, and gastrointestinal problems, and behavioural traits such as nervousness, fearfulness, timidity, and aggression to other dogs are not uncommon.

History The German Shepherd Dog has its recent origins in the extensive breeding programme initiated by Max von Stephanitz at the end of the last century. By the beginning of World War I, the breed was popular throughout Germany, and swiftly spread to other parts of the world.

Coat can be long or short and a variety of colours

Powerful, straight forelegs

Key facts

Country of origin
Germany

Date of origin
1800s

Life expectancy
12–13 yrs

Temperament
Faithful, steady, and responsive.

Maintenance
Frequent and regular exercise is important. Will respond well to training.

Other names
Alsatian, Deutscher Schäferhund

55–66 cm
(22–26 in)

Weight   34–43 kg (75–95 lb)

Physical characteristics

Head	Well proportioned to body, with a strong muzzle and firm lips.
Eyes	Slightly slanting, almond-shaped eyes do not bulge.
Ears	Erect and high-set.
Body	Powerful and well-muscled. Neck is of medium length.
Coat	Straight, hard topcoat; thick undercoat.
Tail	Bushy-haired; hanging at least to the hock.

Great Pyrenees

- Gentle, affectionate, and elegant companion
- Loyal and protective
- Can be reserved and aloof

The first Pyreneans to be kept as household pets had rather assertive, warrior-like personalities. In the last 30 years, breeders have succeeded in diminishing this characteristic, while retaining other attractive qualities such as patience, nobility, and courage. Originally bred for guarding sheep on the mountains of the Pyrenees, this elegant dog will still, however, go into a defence mode if its territory is invaded. Its great size makes it unsuitable for urban environments.

History One of the great, white guarding mastiffs that spread across Europe, this magnificent breed is probably related to the Italian Maremma, Hungarian Kuvasz, Slovakian Kuvac, and Turkish Karabash. It thrived principally in Andorra in ancient times, before it was "discovered" early in the 20th century.

Key facts

Country of origin
Europe

Date of origin
Antiquity

Life expectancy
9–11 yrs

Temperament
Tolerant and attentive, but can be strong-willed and territorial.

Maintenance
Abundant coat requires regular brushing.

Other names
Pyrenean Mountain Dog, Chien de Montagne des Pyrénées

Ruff of hair around neck and shoulders

Woolly feathering on forelimbs

65–81 cm
(26–32 in)

Weight 41–60 kg (90–132 lb)

Physical characteristics

Head	Medium-sized, with a slightly rounded crown; black nose and lips.
Eyes	Amber-coloured and set obliquely.
Ears	Small, hanging against head.
Body	Well-balanced shape, with broad, level back, and a slightly rounded ribcage.
Coat	Topcoat consisting of abundant long, white hair, with a woolly undercoat.
Tail	Well-plumed; carried low or over the back.

Akita

- Large, strong, and loyal
- An alert and effective watchdog
- Requires an experienced handler

Poised and regal, this impressive dog has a powerful presence. By nature the breed is undemonstrative and aloof, which can make obedience training and handling difficult. Males, in particular, have a greater tendency to be aggressive towards other dogs than many other breeds. Well-trained individuals make excellent companions, although they can be reserved with strangers. Alert and responsive, the Akita makes a fearless guard dog.

History The largest of all Japanese breeds, this powerfully built dog was originally developed around 400 years ago for large game hunting and dog fighting. By the 1930s, numbers had declined to near extinction, but formation of the Society for the Preservation of Japanese Breeds assured the survival of this dignified breed.

Key facts

Country of origin
Japan

Date of origin
1600s

Life expectancy
10–12 yrs

Temperament
Aloof and dignified. Can be difficult to handle.

Maintenance
Very active, so requires frequent exercise.

Other names
Japanese Akita, Akita Inu

Relatively small, deep-set eyes

Thick and muscular neck

60–71 cm
(24–28 in)

Weight   34–50 kg (75–110 lb)

Physical characteristics

Head	Large, but in proportion to body, with a strong, broad muzzle.
Eyes	Almond-shaped and dark-brown.
Ears	Small relative to the head; firmly erect.
Body	Wide, deep chest and a level back.
Coat	Straight, coarse topcoat covers a soft, dense undercoat.
Tail	Full, curled tail is set high and carried over the back.

Rottweiler

- A natural and fearless guard dog
- Good-natured with its human family
- Can be aggressive with other dogs

Powerful in body and jaws, the Rottweiler can offer formidable protection. Today, this impressively handsome dog, the descendant of ancient boar hunters, is popular throughout the world as both a family dog and a guard dog. The Rottweiler can have a tendency to show its temper, although breeders, notably in Scandinavia, have reduced this trait. However, it is willing to learn, and with an investment of time and training, this robust dog can make a calm, courageous, and loyal companion.

History The Rottweiler was originally bred in Rottweil, Germany, in the 1800s, as a droving and guard dog.

Slightly arched neck is round and muscular

Coarse, flat topcoat

Thick-boned legs

Key facts

Country of origin
Germany

Date of origin
1800s

Life expectancy
11–12 yrs

Temperament
Self-confident with a natural desire to protect home and family.

Maintenance
Obedience training and regular exercise are vital.

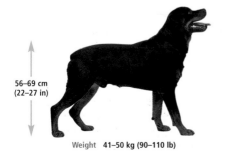

56–69 cm
(22–27 in)

Weight   41–50 kg (90–110 lb)

Physical characteristics

Head	Broad skull, with a moderately arched forehead; nose has large, open nostrils.
Eyes	Dark-brown in colour, and not too deep-set giving a self-assured expression.
Ears	High, wide-set ears.
Body	Robust, compact, and powerful.
Coat	Dense, medium-length topcoat is black with rich tan markings.
Tail	Was traditionally docked.

Bullmastiff

- A faithful and affectionate family companion
- High-spirited, agile, and strong
- Needs a firm, loving owner

In theory, the Bullmastiff should be one of the world's most popular guard dogs. Its speed, strength, and endurance were developed so that it could overtake and capture intruders without mauling or killing them. Handsome and powerful, it has spread throughout all the continents of the world, but it has never attained the popularity of its German equivalent, the Rottweiler. The reason for this is that the Bullmastiff can be a stubborn breed, resistant to obedience training, and overly protective of its human family.

History The foundation stock of the Bullmastiff is 60 per cent English Mastiff and 40 per cent Bulldog. It was produced in Britain in the 19th century to act as a gamekeeper's assistant, with the ability to chase and immobilize poachers on estates.

Key facts

Country of origin
Great Britain

Date of origin
1800s

Life expectancy
10–12 yrs

Temperament
Confident, loyal, and alert; can be wary of strangers.

Maintenance
A large appetite so can be expensive; needs regular and frequent exercise.

Arched, muscular loins

Broad, deep, and dark muzzle

Chest is wide and deep

Powerful forelegs are straight and well-boned

61–69 cm
(24–27 in)

Weight   45–59 kg (100–130 lb)

Physical characteristics

Head	Large, square head, with a short muzzle; fairly wrinkled when alert.
Eyes	Dark, medium-sized eyes are separated by a distinct furrow.
Ears	Small and V-shaped; set high and wide.
Body	Compact and well-balanced, with a short back and a slightly arched, muscular neck.
Coat	Short, dense, and weather-resistant.
Tail	Strong and tapering; set high on the back.

St. Bernard

- A gentle giant
- Courageous and trustworthy
- Unsuitable for urban living

Whether the St. Bernard ever actually rescued snowbound alpine travellers is debatable, but that image is irreversibly established. The Benardine Hospice has kept this kindly breed since the 1660s – Bernardine monks used it for draught work, and boasted to potential purchasers of its hauling abilities.

History Descended from alpine mastiffs first brought to Switzerland with the passing Roman Army, the St. Bernard was once an aggressive, short-coated breed. At one time it was virtually extinct, but it was revitalized, possibly with the use of both Newfoundland and Great Dane blood. This impressive breed's name came into general use in 1865.

Key facts

Country of origin
Switzerland

Date of origin
Middle Ages

Life expectancy
11 yrs

Temperament
Laid back and friendly.

Maintenance
Needs plenty of room and regular exercise.

Other names
Alpine Mastiff

Shorthaired variety; there is also a longhaired variety

Large, compact feet with well-arched toes

61–70 cm
(24–28 in)

Weight 50–91 kg (110–200 lb)

Physical characteristics

Head	Massive, with a short muzzle, a wrinkled forehead, and a broad nose.
Eyes	Dark-brown, friendly eyes are set to front.
Ears	Tender flap of ear is triangular in shape.
Body	Well-proportioned, with a broad, straight back and muscular, powerful shoulders.
Coat	Dense and smooth (shorthaired); thick and flat (longhaired).
Tail	Broad, powerful tail curls slightly at tip.

Alaskan Malamute

- A friendly and loyal pet
- Dignified but playful if invited
- A strong and active working dog

Although wolf-like in appearance, the Alaskan Malamute is an affectionate but powerful dog with outstanding stamina. When Jack London referred to the great strength of huskies in his novels of life in the frozen North, he was probably describing the Malamute. Popular in Canada and the United States as a family companion, this breed thrives on activity and excels in sled-racing competitions.

History Named after the Mahlemut Inuit living on the Arctic coast of western Alaska, this breed was used as a draught animal long before Europeans visited the Americas.

Key facts

Country of origin
United States

Date of origin
Antiquity

Life expectancy
12 yrs

Temperament
Affectionate even with strangers, but can show aggression towards other dogs.

Maintenance
A true pack animal, so early training is essential.

Dense coat makes the breed prone to heat stroke

Heavily muscled, strong-boned legs are ideal for traction and weight pulling

Densely furred tail carried over back in typical spitz fashion

Large, compact feet with thick pads

58–71 cm
(23–28 in)

Weight 34–43 kg (75–95 lb)

Physical characteristics

Head	Large, powerful head, broad between the ears but narrowing to the eyes.
Eyes	Brown and almond-shaped.
Ears	Triangular, erect, and small in proportion to the head.
Body	Well-muscled and strong, with a level back and a deep chest.
Coat	Thick and coarse, with a dense undercoat.
Tail	Plume-like tail is set fairly high on back.

Great Dane

- Reserved but dependable
- An excellent family pet, if you have room
- Needs attention and companionship

The dignified but affectionate Great Dane is the national dog of Germany. Its origins can almost certainly be traced to the dogs brought to Europe by the Alans, a Scythian tribe from what is now Asian Russia. These fighting mastiffs were probably crossed with Greyhounds, producing the elegant, distinctive, and giant breed of today. The sheer size of the Great Dane can cause medical problems, including a greater-than-average incidence of hip and elbow arthritis, and bone tumours.

History The Great Dane traces its origins back to the massive Alaunt of the 13th century.

Key facts

Country of origin
Germany

Date of origin
Middle Ages

Life expectancy
9–10 yrs

Temperament
Alert, loving, and outgoing.

Maintenance
Well-behaved and easy to groom, but sheer size means plenty of exercise and large food bills.

Other names
German Mastiff,
Deutsche Dogge

No loose skin
on elegant neck

Short, dense coat

Very deep V-shaped
chest with well-
sprung ribs

71–81 cm
(28–32 in)

Weight   45–54 kg (100–120 lb)

Physical characteristics

Head	Long, rectangular skull, a broad muzzle and thick, firm lips.
Eyes	Deep-set, medium-sized, and dark.
Ears	Triangular ears are set high on the head and folded forward.
Body	Powerful and smoothly muscled, with a strong back and a long, well-arched neck.
Coat	Thick, short, and sleek.
Tail	Long, tapering tail.

Newfoundland

- A brave, devoted companion
- Gentle and docile
- An energetic water-lover

One of the friendliest of all breeds, the Newfoundland was originally used in Canadian cod fisheries to haul nets ashore and to pull boats. Today, teams of Newfoundlands are used in France to assist the emergency services in sea rescue. If this benign, happy breed has a behavioural drawback, it is its inclination to rescue anyone from the water, regardless of their desire or need to be rescued.

History Descended from the now-extinct Greater St. John's Dog, this noble giant has been bred to its present standard for over 100 years. Native North American, Viking, and Iberian breeds may be included in its background.

Key facts

Country of origin
Canada

Date of origin
1700s

Life expectancy
9–11 yrs

Temperament
Extremely placid and even-tempered.

Maintenance
Full, thick coat requires weekly grooming. Loves the outdoors, so needs plenty of exercise.

Water-resistant coat

Feet are large and well-shaped with broadly webbed toes

Thick tail is well-covered in hair

66–71 cm
(26–28 in)

Weight 45–68 kg (100–150 lb)

Physical characteristics

Head	Broad and massive head, with a short, square, clean-cut muzzle.
Eyes	Small, dark, deep-set eyes.
Ears	Relatively small ears lie close to the head.
Body	Back is broad and level, with a deep chest and strong muscular loins.
Coat	Topcoat is flat, dense, somewhat coarse, and oily.
Tail	Fairly thick tail hangs downward at rest.

Mixed breed dogs

- Less susceptible to inherited diseases
- Regional variations
- Wonderful canine companions

Mongrels lack the cachet of pure-bred dogs, never having been bred for a specific purpose or look. But call them what you will – curs, mutts, or Heinz 57s – mixed breed dogs are just as loving and protective as the most expensive purebreds. Moreover, they are less likely to suffer from inherited medical problems, such as blindness, heart disease, and hip dysplasia.

Many people favour pure-bred dogs because they believe that selective breeding produces dogs with predictable characteristics. This is only partly true,

because a dog's temperament and personality are shaped by early environment and training as well as genetics. Mixed breed pups raised in a stable home environment and exposed to a variety of controlled situations grow into responsive and reliable adults, just like purebreds. Sadly, not all mutts are so lucky; many are the result of unplanned pregnancies and are unceremoniously discarded by their owners.

Give mutts a chance

Mongrels have a bad reputation. Many people think that because most strays are mixed breed individuals, mutts must have a natural wanderlust. Not so. The mutt's desire to wander is no stronger than that of a purebred. Lack of human responsibility is what produces this behaviour. Mutts are

Mongrels are certainly cheaper to run than some purebreds and make great companions.

Rescue dogs

Mixed breed dogs form the majority at dog shelters, and good homes for them are always needed. Mutts from shelters may have higher levels of anxiety-related behavioural problems, such as barking when left alone, destructiveness, and fear-biting. However, perseverance and consistency in training can turn even the hardest cases into affectionate and playful family pets.

cheaper to buy than purebreds, but this can be curiously detrimental to their well-being. When an investment is made in the purchase of a dog, owners wish to protect their assets. As a result, expensive dogs are far more likely than mongrels to receive good veterinary attention, such as preventative vaccination. The notion that mutts are sickly and dirty is again an idea that can be attributed to lack of care by their human owners.

Feral dogs are different

Feral dogs are not the same as mongrels. They eat, breed, give birth, and survive independently, depending upon the detritus of human habitation for survival.

Few ferals exist in North America or northern Europe, but they are common in Central and South America, in parts of the Balkans and Eastern Europe, in Turkey and the Middle East, in Africa, and in Asia. The behaviour and conformation of feral dogs varies from region to region, but often these dogs tend towards tan in colour. Their coats range from double and dense in regions such as the Balkans to smooth and short in the tropical regions of Asia and Africa. Although ferals breed randomly, they often breed true to type. When breeding is brought under human control, as it was with the Canaan Dog in Israel, they may be redesignated as pure-breds.

Selecting a mixed breed dog

It is best to acquire a mixed breed dog as a puppy from a known litter – the offspring of a friend's dog, for example. The behaviour of the mother is already known, and the father might be too. You'll have a good idea of your dog's temperament, as well as its adult size, coat type, and colour. And by selecting a puppy, you eliminate the unknown variables of early learning that so dramatically affect later temperament.

Reputable dog shelters charge reasonable fees for their mutts and always check out potential owners.

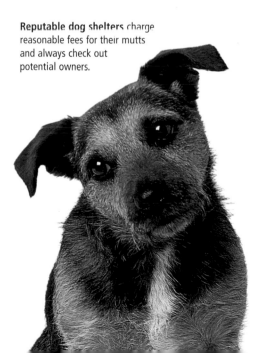

CHAPTER THREE

Behaviour

In curious ways, dogs and people share many
behavioural traits – indeed this is one of the reasons
that we live together so successfully. Like us, dogs are
socially outgoing animals that thrive on interaction
with their own kind, and they have a lifelong curiosity
about the world. However – and this is a big however
– dogs are not people in fur coats! They owe the sum
total of their inherited behavioural potential to their
wolf ancestors. The way a dog thinks, eats, hunts,
marks territory, grooms itself, mates, gives birth, and
cares for its young is rooted in the wolf pack. Through
contact with us early in life, the dog accepts us as
members of its pack, and forms a deep, lasting and
pure relationship with us. You could even call it love.

Natural variability

- Fundamental traits are wolf-like
- Selective breeding has altered behaviour
- Males and females behave differently

For thousands of years, our ancestors chose to breed selectively from dogs that showed a natural inclination to behave in ways that were useful to the human community. Animals that barked loudly at approaching strangers, for example, had clear value in raising alarm at the human camp; those which were swift of foot and had keen

Hairless dogs like this Toy Mexican Hairless puppy were bred selectively not just as curios, but for the great warmth their bodies provided.

eyesight were used as breeding stock for hunting companions; strength and protectiveness made for good guards; and those showing docility and rapid weight gain were good to eat. Selection for these natural abilities helped create the multiplicity of today's dog breeds.

Recent intervention

In the last millennium, and especially over the past few hundred years, we have intervened extensively in dog evolution. Our influence on size, shape, coat, and temperament has been overwhelming. But while we may have altered looks and increased or diminished certain behavioural traits, we have not changed the fact that the dog is a wolf, albeit in elegant, sometimes curious, disguise, and to understand dogs, we must look to the pack behaviour of the ancestral wolf.

Natural comforters

The exact origins of the first domestic dogs are unknown. Anthropologists observe that it is a universal human desire to comfort and feed young furry animals, and because the dog shares a number of social behaviours with humans, it gives us comfort and security in return.

Since it first lived with us, it is likely that the dog was selectively bred to give affection to its care-giver and provide

Beware of the dog

By Roman times, many varieties of dog had evolved. The Romans mainly used dogs to guard and protect their homes, and often decorated mosaics with images of dogs, sometimes inscribing the words *Cave canem* – "Beware of the dog".

warmth on cold nights. It is only this century, however, that affection and constancy have become amongst the most important behaviour traits that dog breeders select for.

Sex differences in behaviour

Human intervention has created differences in behaviour between breeds, but there are also natural differences between male and female dogs of the same breed. Male dogs are generally more active and more destructive than females. They make urine marks more frequently and fight more, often for territory or over potential mates. Neutering a male will reduce his general activity level, and his urine marking, roaming, and fighting. Neutered males are also more affectionate, and more likely to be friendly with other dogs.

Female dogs are generally more playful and friendly than males, and are naturally inclined to be affectionate. They learn obedience more easily and are easier to house train. Unlike males, neutering has little outward effect on a female's personality.

Colour differences and behaviour

Recent research has revealed a relationship between coat colour and temperament in the canine family. The results of a survey of thousands of professional breeders who breed dogs that can be a variety of solid colours, such as Labradors, Poodles, and Cocker Spaniels, suggest that chocolate or black dogs are easier to train, more reliable and better with children than blond, yellow, or apricot colours.

Scientific studies on another member of the canine family – the fox – back up this theory. In Russian foxes, certain coat colours are related to reduced fear and aggression, and a link was found between these colours and body hormone function – in particular, the hormones associated with the fight or flight response *(see p.31)*. A similar linkage might also explain coat-colour behavioural differences in dogs.

Male dogs not only behave differently to female dogs of the same breed, but are often bigger and more "masculine-looking".

MALE

FEMALE

Pack mentality

- Dogs fit in well to the human pack
- We assume pack leadership
- Dominant dogs may occasionally challenge their position

People and dogs share a surprising variety of basic social behaviours. Both of us are gregariously sociable. We are inquisitive, not only about others of our own kind, but also about other animals. We share common social signals with dogs, using similar body language to display our feelings. Because of these similarities, dogs will accept a human family as their pack.

Similar signals

Like dogs, we cower when confronted by superior force and show our teeth when we aggressively confront danger. We enjoy relaxing with our own kind, especially our

extended family, and we instinctively protect our family and our home. Dogs and people are both naturally territorial – we have resting places and hunting territories that we aggressively defend from others of our own kind. We are omnivores, willing to taste and eat almost anything. Equally important, although seldom mentioned, is that we are both naturally "neotenized" – we retain a life-long, child-like curiosity about the world around us. Even in adulthood, both humans and dogs enjoy play virtually as an end in itself.

Pack mentality

In the wolf pack, pack behaviour is well defined. A leader – nearly always a male – and his almost equally dominant consort, control most of

The top dog in the Husky pack jumps up to greet the real pack leader.

Pack security

All members of the pack are equally responsible for the security of their territory, and, for a companion dog, the pack means his human family. Most dogs will alert other members of the pack by barking, sometimes aggressively, but just as often simply to tell the rest of the pack that someone or something is approaching their communal space.

the pack activity. The rest of the pack willingly follow their leader, although dominant members occasionally challenge the leader's authority. The domestic dog's pack behaviour is less clearly defined but still present. We become the pack leader and our dogs willingly obey us. They will defend the pack's territory – our homes – as well as their own personal space.

Part of the human pack

The domestic dog experiences a few months of natural pack activity before it leaves its litter and joins a "human pack". In the litter, each pup learns how to behave with its litter-mates and with its mother. The mother is the leader because she controls food, warmth, and security. When a pup is taken from its litter – between 7 and 12 weeks of age – and is homed with people, it naturally transfers its innate pack mentality to our distinctly different species. People are acceptable to dogs as pack members and natural leaders because, like their mother, we too control food, warmth, and security.

Follow the leader

As a young dog matures into adulthood, his pack behaviour naturally evolves, influenced both by the cumulative experiences of his early life, and by the onset, at puberty, of sex hormone production. Within typical human households, the adult dog's pack instinct drives him to find a suitable niche in the family.

The dog's position in the pack is not always static, and, especially while young and robust, he may challenge in an attempt to move closer to pack leadership. Dominant dogs – males in particular – can challenge their designated position in the human pack at any time between sexual and emotional maturity, usually between 8 and 24 months of age. A dog may do so by refusing to follow instructions given by another pack member, or by intentionally challenging the pack member he considers to be the weakest. A dog might, for example, threaten or bite a child over possession of a toy, or he may refuse to obey a command given by the child's mother, but will still obey the same command given by the deeper-voiced, more assertive-sounding father.

Pack members willingly follow the "top dog"; this allows us to train our dogs.

Canine genetics

- Inheritance is controlled by genes
- Genes influence physical as well as behavioural traits
- Breeding matters

Chromosome

The four bases of DNA specify the genetic code

DNA is tightly coiled in chromosomes

Most cells contains a full set of chromosomes

A dog's physical characteristics, personality, and behaviour are shaped by a complex interplay of factors. Diet, environment, and social development all play a role, but your dog's basic "ground plan" is set out in its

Tissues and organs are made up of building blocks called cells

this molecule are chemical bases – the "letters" of the genetic code. There are just four letters in the genetic code – A, C, G, and T – but many permutations in their sequence mean that long strings of these letters can encode a vast library of information – enough to store this book and 100 more like it.

genes – strings of chemical code that tell cells what to do and how to develop. Physically, these strings of code are held within microscopic strands called chromosomes, contained in almost every cell in a dog's body. Each cell carries exactly the same set of chromosomes but different genes in different cells are selectively switched on or off. The activity (or inactivity) of specific genes determines the fate of a cell – whether it develops into a nerve cell or a skin cell, for example.

Physical characteristics, such as ear shape, are determined by genes. The Norwich Terrier has genes that specify erect ears, while the genes of the Norfolk Terrier code for lopped ears.

Canine code

Genes are made up of DNA (deoxyribonucleic acid), a long helical molecule. Strung along the length of

The dog's genetic code is a "blueprint" of the dog's design. The four-letter alphabet of the DNA code is organized into genes which specify the proteins that make up the dog's body. DNA is arranged in chromosomes – dogs have 78 in a cell. A dog's body is made up of millions of cells; almost all of these contain the complete set of genes that make up the genetic code.

Genes and proteins

One gene is a section of code carried by a DNA molecule. Its job is to instruct a cell to manufacture a particular protein – this could be a digestive enzyme, a neurotransmitter, or a structural protein that makes hair, for example – or to control the activity of other genes. Some genes control a single, simple characteristic, such as the rate at which hair grows, but the effects of others are felt widely throughout the body. Many complex characteristics, such as behaviour, are influenced by the interplay of many genes.

Behavioural influences

In the development of the domestic dog, we have used selective breeding to enhance and diminish a wide range of behavioural traits. For example, breeds developed for herding sheep, such as the Border Collie, are exquisitely sensitive to movement, and will silently approach sheep in a manner identical to that of a predatory wolf silently approaching a potential meal. The wolf, however, follows through with the chase and kills its prey. In the sheepdog, selective breeding has enhanced the genetic tendency to

The founder effect

Within a population of dogs, there typically exist many different versions of a particular gene – a gene that sets paw size, for example, may be present in small, medium, and large paw variants. In a large interbreeding population, these genes are constantly reshuffled, with the result that paw size remains "average". However, if just a few individuals from this large population split off and start their own small group, they are likely to take with them an unrepresentative sample of genes. When these individuals breed, the skewed sample of genes produces new or exaggerated characteristics not seen in the original population. This so-called "founder effect" has been recorded many times as human travellers have taken dogs to new parts of the world, such as Australia.

The Australian Shepherd perpetuates coat colours inherited from its collie ancestors

detect slight movements and stalk prey, but has diminished the instinct to kill.

Problems develop when this enhanced behaviour occurs completely out of the context for which it was developed. The genetic potential of the Border Collie to concentrate on the slightest movement may be triggered by the most insignificant event: an ant walking by or a blade of grass swaying.

This can lead to some domestic collies displaying "neurotic" or "obsessive-compulsive" behaviour that may even require veterinary treatment. We have manufactured these problems by selectively breeding dogs for enhanced behaviours, then taking them out of the environment we bred them for, and raising them in our homes.

Courtship and mating

- Familiarity between male and female is important
- Courtship is perfunctory
- The pair become "tied" after mating

Courtship is brief, and involves a range of stereotypic behaviour. The female often demands "play" before accepting mating.

Although the modern dog is well removed from its wolf origins, its mating rituals are still rooted in the behaviour of a pack animal. While the wolf comes into season only once each year – in the spring – most dog breeds have twice-yearly seasons when females are receptive to mating. In the pack, who mates with whom is dictated by social structure, and the dominant male rarely permits other males to mate with receptive females. Females rarely mate with unknown males, but with a ready supply of available and familiar males, females ovulate and mate with their partners several times. The likelihood of successful pregnancy is very high.

In the rather unnatural circumstances of modern mating

During mating the female remains passive while the male clasps her waist and starts making pelvic thrusts.

rituals, the dog owner often takes her female to an unfamiliar male and expects her to mate willingly – something she is often reluctant to do.

Ever-ready males

The male dog is an opportunist. He is sexually active year-round and attracted to the scent of any female in season.

The female is more particular. For most of the year she is hormonally inactive, but under the influence of her twice-yearly production of the hormone oestrogen, she becomes attracted to the scent of the male dog and is pyschologically ready to mate. Oestrogen also stimulates the release of eggs from the female dog's ovaries; these descend down her fallopian tubes to her uterus, where they await fertilization by sperm.

Mating

When the male has selected his mate, courtship does not last long. The female often demands play, and may drop to the "play bow" position or play mount the male. She scents his penis and permits the male to scent or lick her vulva. If she is unready for mating, she rolls over. After these rituals have been completed,

Avoid unwanted offspring

1 Do not even think about breeding from your dog unless you know you can find homes for every one of the resulting litter.

2 Do not breed from your dog, male or female, because it is "natural". It is far less natural to let your dog mate once, and then expect it never to want to breed again.

3 Always exercise your female dog on a lead when she is in season.

4 Only breed from females who are emotionally mature and do not carry known inherited diseases.

5 Do not expect the mother to do all the upbringing if you do decide to let her breed. It is your responsibility to ensure that pups are well socialized before they leave your home.

mating will then proceed. The mating process is swift; while the female stands firmly, the male mounts her back, clasping her body with his forepaws and thrusting with his pelvis. Pelvic thrusts often last for less than a minute after which the male ejaculates. During mating, a balloon-like region at the base of the male dog's penis swells. This prevents the couple from separating, and so after mating, the dogs are "tied" together for a short period. To protect themselves during this compromised time, the male swings his hind leg over the female so they remain rump to rump, and able to defend themselves if necessary.

After mating the male and female remain "tied" to each other for about half an hour.

Expecting puppies

- Few outward signs of pregnancy in the early stages
- False pregnancy is normal
- Emotional development begins before birth

Pregnancy in dogs lasts for approximately two months. One of the first signs that a female dog is pregnant, at about four weeks after conception, is that her nipples become slightly more prominent and pinker. By four to five weeks' gestation, your vet will be able to feel golf ball-sized swellings in her abdomen, and determine how many foetuses there are. Shortly after, her belly becomes visibly enlarged.

False or true pregnancy

After eggs are released from the ovaries, the vacated sites produce progesterone, the hormone of pregnancy. This hormone is responsible for initiating a variety of behaviours, including instinctive nurturing and milk production. Uniquely amongst all domesticated animals, the dog will naturally enter a two-month hormonal pregnancy stage whether she is pregnant or not. The consequence is that a dog may act and look pregnant after an oestrous cycle, but may only have a hormonal or "false pregnancy". During her false pregnancy, a female can experience a dramatic variety of mood and sensory changes. Affected females often collect soft toys or articles of clothing, which they carry to their nests and vigorously protect.

Diagnosing pregnancy

In other species, the presence of progesterone in the urine is a sign of true pregnancy, but because it is always present in the urine or blood of the female dog after she has ovulated, it cannot be used as a test for pregnancy in dogs. Although more sophisticated blood tests have been developed, the

A heavily pregnant female dog often finds that lying on her side is a comfortable way to distribute the weight of the litter of developing puppies in her swollen abdomen.

Pregnancy behaviour

Impelled by her need to nurture, this bitch has adopted an orphaned litter of kittens, which she grooms as she would her own puppies. Her behaviour derives from her past experience as a mother, and from progesterone, the hormone of pregnancy.

most practical way to differentiate between true and false pregnancy is either by a veterinary surgeon's physical examination for the presence of developing foetuses, or by ultrasound examination.

Risks during pregnancy

The greatest risk to unborn pups occurs during the first three weeks of development in the womb. Both drugs and infections can seriously impair healthy development. At birth, a pup inherits protection against diseases its mother has been exposed to. For example, if its mother has been vaccinated against distemper, maternal antibodies against this disease are passed on to the pup in the first mother's milk – the colostrum. Dogs should be vaccinated before they are pregnant, to increase the amount of passive protection they pass on.

Influences in the womb

Emotional as well as physical development of pups begins in the womb. Through his research, Dr. T. Berry Brazelton at Harvard University has shown how human infants are influenced in the womb by their mother's lifestyle, and the same applies to pups: whatever the mother dog eats, and whatever emotions she experiences while pregnant, affect the development of her pups.

Unlike humans, however, there is an additional influence from the position in the womb in which a pup develops. The dog's uterus has two distinct "horns", and foetuses develop in rows along each of these; pups in the middle of each horn of the uterus are more likely to receive better nutrition than those at either end.

A pup's "neighbours" in the womb may also influence its development. As a male pup's testes develop, they secrete bursts of the hormone testosterone. This travels to the foetus's developing brain, where it helps to forge connections that mould future male sexual characteristics, such as inherent dominance. Female foetuses that develop between two males may be exposed to small amounts of testosterone, predisposing them to develop a slightly masculinized brain, and, consequently, a more dominant and aggressive personality.

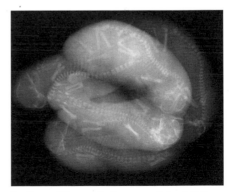

An X-ray of the womb of a pregnant dog, late in her two-month pregnancy, reveals the multiple skeletons of the developing puppy foetuses.

Giving birth

- Problems are rare
- Don't fuss with your dog
- Monitor her activities

Puppies are delivered at intervals ranging from a few minutes to a couple of hours in length.

About 24 hours before labour begins, a pregnant dog stops eating. She spends more time in her chosen nest site – typically a covered, isolated spot. Some dogs given access to the outdoors will dig a den in the earth to nest in, while indoor dogs often choose open cupboards or the space under beds. Many become more irritable and snappy, and, as labour approaches, become restless. Once minor contractions begin, the first water bag is squeezed into the birth canal and breaks, leaving a puddle of fluid similar in size to a typical emptying of the bladder. Contractions then become firmer and more rhythmic.

Delivery

The first pup is delivered within the next two hours. Most pups are delivered head first, although it is not unusual for some to be delivered tail first. Most females lie on their side and deliver their pups on to the ground, but some prefer to stand, allowing the pups to drop a short distance.

The firmest contractions are necessary to get the pup's head and shoulders through the birth canal. Once these are visible, the rest of the pup follows easily. Each pup is born

The mother licks the birth sac from the puppy's face and chews through the umbilical cord.

enveloped in a membrane, which the mother licks from its face and body. The massaging of her tongue is sufficient to stimulate the pup to take its first breath. Licking also dries the pup, reducing the risk of hypothermia. After the delivery of each pup, the mother expels an afterbirth or placenta. In the womb this was the pup's nutritional lifeline, feeding into its umbilicus. The mother usually eats the afterbirth, chewing off the umbilical cord about 3 cm ($1^1/_4$ in) from the pup's body. Within 30 minutes she is in labour again, expelling the next pup and its afterbirth.

With each subsequent birth, the mother licks the pup dry and eats its afterbirth, but otherwise concentrates on subsequent contractions rather than feeding. Healthy pups, attracted by the heat from her body, stay close. As a general rule, larger dog breeds have large litters, while smaller breeds have smaller litters. Only after the last pup has been delivered does the typical mother relax on her side and provide milk for her newborn litter. She does so by exposing her nipples, which she has groomed and cleaned throughout the final stages of her pregnancy.

Immediately after birth

For the next 24 hours the mother does not leave her pups. Their crying concerns her; crying usually means hunger, and she quickly positions herself to feed them. She

Rooting for milk

New-born pups stay close to mother, using heat sensors on their noses to locate the warmest spot on her abdomen. When a pup's head touches the mother (or another puppy) a rooting reflex is triggered; the nipple is located through a combination of touch and taste sensitivity to the sugar in the mother's milk.

licks their anogenital regions to stimulate them to urinate and defecate, consuming their body waste products to hide evidence of their vulnerable presence. If a pup wanders away but does not cry, she ignores it. Typically, in a litter of seven, one pup is born with a visible or invisible handicap and dies within a day or two of birth. The mother concentrates on her healthy pups, offering warmth, nourishment, and protection.

Complications

Our intervention in breeding has complicated birth for some. Certain breeds, exemplified by the Bulldog, give birth to pups with heads often too large to pass through the birth canal. Other breeds, such as the Yorkshire Terrier, give birth to litters of pups so large they often must be delivered by Caesarean section. Dalmatians can give birth to such large litters the mother simply cannot produce enough milk for all of her young to survive. Others may experience difficulty letting down milk. Prompt veterinary advice is usually sufficient to overcome most potential problems.

The mother licks her puppies dry, and they immediately seek milk and warmth.

Dependent on mother

- Mother provides security and discipline
- Pups learn by copying mother
- Independence comes early

For two weeks after birth, the pup is wholly dependent on its mother, but by three weeks of age it is tentatively standing, scenting, hearing, seeing, and responding. In the next two weeks, the pup enters a transitional period during which it begins to move away from total maternal dependence. The world opens up: the pup growls, barks, wags its tail for the first time, and notices us. Its temperature control mechanism improves sufficiently to allow it to leave the warmth of its mother. By seven weeks of age, a puppy is walking, running, and jumping.

Dependent for nourishment

The pups feed only on milk for the first three weeks. In the next three weeks, the mother may supplement their milk diet with regurgitated food or even

A mother dog instinctively disciplines her puppies, reprimanding them with a growl or even a controlled bite if they get too boisterous.

some of her own solid food. During the following weeks, she will allow the pups to suckle – not so much for nourishment but rather for comfort and security; a worried or frightened pup may run back to its mother and suckle to settle its agitation. If a pup acts too gregariously, she will discipline it.

Pack behaviour

Puppies are born with the instincts of a pack animal, and learn pack behaviour through watching their mother and copying her behaviour. They learn cooperative behaviour through relationships with their littermates. Early learning also ensures that pups have the ability as adults to hunt collectively or to communally protect territory. These abilities are at the core of the dog's success in integrating itself into the lifestyle of a different species – humans.

Early influences

The dog's brain develops at an astonishing rate from birth to three months of age, and a pup's brain and hormone development can be significantly influenced during this early development. Early mental stimulation accelerates body growth, reduces emotionality, and may even increase resistance to certain diseases.

What is "intelligence"?

A dog's mind is most adaptable and open while it is young, and many dogs display remarkable abilities to learn and be trained. We often talk of a dog's "intelligence", usually without fully understanding what we mean by the

Early exploration reveals an exciting world of new experiences for a young puppy.

word. For example, it is often said that early learning improves a dog's intelligence, but does this refer to its problem-solving capacity, its willingness to listen, or its performance in the field? Is success at guarding or retrieving a sign of intelligence? In fact, the dog lacks certain aspects of what we consider to be intelligence in humans. Compared to primates, it has limited puzzle- or problem-solving abilities: if a dog learns to open a door by the handle, it first does so by accident rather than premeditation. Dogs vary in their inherited abilities, and also in their ability to listen and learn. When talking about dogs, we often confuse instinctive abilities or trainability and obedience with intelligence.

Father's role

The father has a limited role in the pup's early life. Some males will occasionally lick and groom pups, but they rarely regurgitate food for them as mothers sometimes do. Fathers are more likely to teach discipline by nipping pups when they become too exuberant.

Early socialization

- A dog's brain matures quickly
- Frequent handling is essential
- Personality develops rapidly

A dog's social life commences at about three weeks of age when it starts to communicate with other dogs and with its human family. It is a puppy's open willingness to learn from us that makes it such a great companion. Daily exposure to people when under six weeks of age ensures a lack of fear of humans. For the next six weeks, the pup's mind remains fully open to a vast range of experiences; the more it smells, sees, tastes, hears, and touches, and the more it has to deal with different situations, the more adaptable it will be later in life.

Better than humans

Compared to us, the dog's ability to learn is phenomenal. What can take us years, a pup can learn in a matter of weeks: physical dexterity, the importance of relationships, the difference between right and wrong. In the wild, early learning is vital for survival as a member of the pack. What differentiates the dog from most other animals is that it exists primarily to live in harmony with us. Its success depends on its ability to live in and contribute to human society.

First impressions are vital if your dog is to enjoy future trips to the vet.

Good learning

1️⃣ Do not allow female dogs to breed if they are not "emotionally competent" to raise their pups, as the early lessons a pup learns from its mother are vital for its normal development.

2️⃣ Offer balanced nourishment to the mother while she feeds her litter to ensure that she is healthy and producing sufficient milk.

3️⃣ Do not isolate young pups – handle them frequently, and carefully expose them to as wide a variety of situations as is practical.

4️⃣ Think of how the pup will live as an adult; introduce other animals early in life.

Early learning

A puppy learns by watching its mother and littermates, by trial and error, and – most important for a good relationship with us – through training.

By lucky chance, the dog inherited from its wolf ancestors a prolonged socialization period lasting for roughly the first 12 weeks of life. If, during this time, a pup is exposed to other individuals or other species, it can "bond" with them, and will look upon them as members of its own group rather than as predators or prey. It is during this socialization period that a puppy readily and effortlessly bonds with us. The period of socialization ends because, later in life, other animals, including us, other dogs, and larger animals, are potential threats. If a dog does not have any contact with humans during the first three months of life, it is likely to fear people in its adult years.

During this sensitive stage of a puppy's early learning, she will make her first visit to the vet. If this visit goes badly, the result could be a lifelong fear of the veterinary clinic. If, on the other hand, the dog is allowed to sniff new, exciting odours, to meet a healthy, relaxed "clinic dog", and if the vet offers it a food treat while carrying out the examination, the puppy is more likely to learn that the clinic is at worst benign, or better, downright fun. In this way the puppy can be "conditioned", early in life, to accept visits to the vet.

Potent rewards

Learning is enhanced when a pup receives a reward for its behaviour. Food is a potent reward, and for a young pup, so too is touch. In the wild, the mother dog will find a meal, consume it, and return to her den where her pups beg by licking her mouth. In response to their begging she rewards them by regurgitating a meal. Our dogs do the same with us, trying to lick our faces when they greet us in the hope of receiving a reward.

Pups get rewards more subtly too. Physical play, chewing, or simply attention from mother or other littermates are rich rewards, and drive early learning. Fortunately for us, so too do sounds. Pups learn that soft sounds are positive and harsh growls are negative; this enables us to communicate with our dogs using different tones of voice.

Early encounters shape future relationships with other pets.

Joining the human pack

- Dogs are dogs, not furry people
- Your dog will treat you like a dog
- Be realistic about your dog's potential

When a dog enters your home, joins your family, and becomes part of your life, it doesn't expect you to treat it like a human – it expects you to act like a dog. Failing to understand how your dog thinks, as it moves from its mother and littermates to you and your family, is at the core of future training, behaviour, and social problems.

The dog is a gregariously sociable species. That's what this chapter is about – its interactions with its mother, its littermates, and then you, your family, and your other pets.

Superb observers

The most important – in fact, the essential – feature of a pup's new environment is us. A pup possesses superb natural observation skills, and it uses these skills on its new human pack, just as it would if it remained in a dog pack. Vocal communication is important; a gruff tone from a human is akin to a growl from another dog, but it is our body language that is most keenly observed and studied by dogs.

As a species, we use words to communicate our thoughts and feelings, and its easy to forget that we also unwittingly send out powerful signals through primate body language. Our shoulders slump and our heads droop when we are unhappy. We walk with a spring in our step when we feel

Dog behaviours may be superficially similar to our own, but sometimes they have very different meanings.

fresh and elated. If provoked enough we bare our teeth in anger. Interestingly, canines and primates have a shared vocabulary of body language, so almost every move you make is subject to interpretation and helps to shape the developing canine mind.

Clever dogs

If there is one statement I hear from nearly all dog owners, it is how clever their dog is. And it is true – your dog is clever. It anticipates your actions because it reads your body language so well. It reminds you if you forget to feed it because it has a wonderfully accurate biological clock. (I know of one Cocker Spaniel who brings her food bowl to her owners at 6 pm every day, only getting it wrong when the clocks change to Summer Time.)

Subliminal detection

Dogs also respond to the subtlest changes in household routine. That's why your dog seems to know that something is about to happen – for example, if you are about to take a family holiday – even before the suitcases appear. We are not aware of these subtle changes in routine, but they rarely escape a dog's attention.

Unwarranted expectations

Dogs are clever, but their cleverness should not be confused with human cerebral intelligence. The canine thinking process, or cognition, is not the same as ours – it has evolved along a very different course.

Even compared to monkeys, for example, dogs are surprisingly bad at so-called detour tests in which they have to navigate around obstacles to reach food. This is because dogs can't think symbolically; to them, fear is pleasure is pleasure, and that is that. So next time you threaten your dog with a conditional clause – "if you jump up on the kitchen counter one more time Logie, there will be big trouble" – you should not be surprised if your words are ignored. If we treat dogs like humans, we send them signals that are confusing or simply incomprehensible, and we end up disappointed when our dogs fail to behave according to our unrealistic expectations.

Dog thinking is the key to training

The way to communicate successfully with a dog is to think like a dog. Your dog expects you to be the leader of the new pack it has joined. It expects you to show leadership by providing security, food, and protection. It will respond to your leadership role by working with you, not against you, and by listening to what you say. Your dog's training and its eventual disposition – how it eats, sleeps, plays, and cooperates – depend on how well you can get your messages across at the canine level.

Food is perhaps the most powerful reward for your dog and should be used carefully during training.

Table manners

- Dogs are competitive eaters
- Scavenging is natural, but should be discouraged
- Vomiting is part of a dog's life

Pack behaviour explains why dogs eat like, well... dogs. In the competitive world of the litter, and then the pack itself, whoever eats first and fastest gets the most and the best food.

Gorge – never share

While we evolved as food grazers, nibbling through the day, the dog is a wolf at heart, with a digestive system equipped to cope with plenty of food when the pack makes a kill, and little food in between. In the wild, dominant members of the pack feed first, gorging until they are satisfied, then letting the "subdominant" pack members eat. Only after all of these dogs have

eaten can the submissive dogs eat what remains. The companion dog inherits this instinctive pack behaviour – confident dogs boldly eat their food, while ill-at-ease individuals eat quietly and silently when no one, including their owner, is watching.

Scavenging

Selective dog breeding has enhanced the scavenging behaviour inherited from the wolf, broadening the variety of the dog's diet. Like the wolf, dogs scavenge carrion but they will also search out anything else that potentially has nutrient value. That can include roots, berries, long grass, and even animal droppings,

Dogs are scavengers by nature – if they find food, they will quickly eat as much as they can.

Competition starts early in life, and a puppy that is successful at winning the best food at this stage is likely to grow into a dominant and confident dog.

especially herbivore droppings such as rabbit, sheep, deer, and horse manure. Though disgusting to us, droppings have genuine nutritional value for a dog. Some dogs also scavenge omnivore droppings, such as pig manure, while a select band willingly eat cat droppings, or their own or other dogs' droppings. These activities are normal in a biological sense but can dramatically increase the risk of bacterial gut infection, so dogs should be trained not to scavenge these dubious delicacies.

Bones and sticks

Bone burying is a behavioural vestige of the dog's genetic past. Many wild carnivores, including wolves and foxes, routinely bury food when there is a food surplus, then return to the food store in time of famine. Most dogs bury symbolically rather than practically, forgetting about their buried treasures. Some, however, do go back, often around one to two weeks later, to recover the buried bone and eat it. Dogs that do not have access to a garden may take a bone or a small, hard dog treat, and try to bury it in the carpet, often in the corner of a room.

Chewing on sticks is a dog's simple alternative to chewing on bones, because it satisfies the same biological need to crush hard objects. Dogs carry sticks around as they would bones, position them with their forepaws and chew with their large carnassial teeth. Chewing and eating sticks and bones can be dangerous, however, resulting in mouth and throat injuires that may require an emergency visit to the vet.

Regurgitating

Dogs experiment by tasting. Spring grass looks succulent and is eaten; the plastic wrapping on cheese smells good and is swallowed; the bits of chicken carcass in the rubbish are enchanting and rapidly consumed. All of these are potentially troublesome meals, but fortunately the dog has an extremely sensitive vomiting reflex that evolved because mother dogs naturally regurgitate meals for their pups when they are moving from milk to solid food. Vomiting is certainly unpleasant to us, but it is a normal part of canine table manners: eat anything; if it was a mistake, chuck it back out again.

Many dogs love to chew on sticks, and may be protective of a stick as if it were a bone.

Marking territory

- Dogs deposit scent marks to transmit data
- Body odours also carry information
- Some dogs accentuate scent marks with visible signs

A dog leaves scent markings, mixed in its urine and faeces, throughout its territory. These deposits contain chemical substances called pheromones that primarily display whether the dog is male or female, but probably also transmit an array of further information to other dogs in a way that evades human comprehension.

Important business

After a dog empties its bowels, a muscular anal contraction squeezes out two drops of pheromone-laden substance from its twin anal sacs – small grape-shaped reservoirs on either side of the anus – and deposits this offensive-smelling cornucopia of scents on the faeces. Analysis of anal gland secretion shows that it contains at least twelve distinct substances, allowing for a large "vocabulary" of scent.

Pheromones in urine transmit information about the reproductive condition of the female and the authority of the male. Males try to leave as much information about themselves as possible, although the "cleaner" the environment, the less need a dog has to mark it. Urban dogs that share territories, such as parks, with many other animals, urine mark more frequently than those that live in the countryside. Often a male dog will deposit urine to cover the smells of previous visitors. Female dogs

Two dogs sniff each other to acquire information about sexual status, dominance, and pack position.

The dorsal tail gland

Canines such as wolves and coyotes have active dorsal tail glands, which they use to deposit scent on bushes as their tail brushes against them. In domestic dogs, however, these elliptically shaped glands are considered to be evolutionary relics, developing only in some individuals. They are sometimes visible as oily or crusty hairless regions on the dorsal surface of the tail.

Touching taboos

Most dogs enjoy being touched by humans, especially around the chest and face. However, many are reluctant to be touched around the tail and anus, and dominant animals may even show aggression when touched in this area.

only scent mark often when in season, but will sniff to pick up other dogs' scents. Occasionally, some females will leave elevated markers by lifting one leg slightly when urinating.

Visual markers

Both males and females occasionally supplement their scent markings with additional visual markers, by scratching at the earth or kicking up dirt around their urine or faeces. These physical signs not only act like arrows, pointing towards the scent mark, but are also scent marks themselves, impregnated with sweat gland secretions from the dog's feet.

Body odour

Dogs produce odours in all body discharges and secretions, and these also transmit a variety of information. Dogs sniff each other to detect the wealth of different data presented in saliva, ear, and anal sac secretions, and in discharges from the vagina or penis and from glands around the anus and on the top of the tail. Ear odours and

discharges from the vagina or penis, in particular, may contain substances that indicate the sexual status of a dog. In addition to the substances discharged by the anal sacs to mark faeces, there are perianal glands surrounding the anus that produce sex-related pheromones.

Touch is meaningful

Dogs communicate eloquently by leaving scent markers on objects, but they also use touch to communicate needs or demands in a sophisticated manner. Of course, many dogs feel secure when they are in physical contact with their human pack leader, but many dog owners are familiar with how dexterous the touch of their dog's paw can be. While poorly socialized dogs fear physical contact, dogs raised from puppyhood in the presence of humans derive a life-long satisfaction in seeking physical comfort from their human family.

Scent markings left previously tell this Cocker Spaniel whether the depositor was a male or a female.

The importance of play

- Play enhances the social order
- Vital in developing hunting skills
- Play behaviour varies with sex and status

A willingness and desire to play are among a dog's most endearing qualities. By playing with its mother and littermates during its first formative weeks, a pup learns about social relationships, develops communication skills, creates life-long bonds, and practices all the physical and mental activities needed by a predator that once had to capture its own meals. Play begins in the litter when pups are about three weeks old.

A puppy "play bow" invites its littermates, its mother, or even us to play.

Learning physical control

Through play, puppies develop a variety of physical abilities, such as manual dexterity, improved coordination, how to grasp with their forepaws, the effectiveness of shoulder slams, and the advantage of momentum. Play allows pups to experiment and practice movements and actions in safe situations. Pups also learn about the authority of the "top dog" through play, and how to inhibit their biting: if a pup "jaws" its mother too hard, she reprimands it by nipping back. If the pup bites another pup too severely and hurts it, the hurt pup squeals in pain and stops playing.

Tug-of-war is a fun game, but is also a lesson in cooperative behaviour.

This is a potent lesson and is at the root of how we can control youthful exuberance when we train dogs.

Social relations
Play helps pups develop a social hierarchy in the litter. They test each other through play fighting, usually inhibiting their bites, but also using strength to test limits – to see how far they can go. Play also introduces cooperative behaviour: two puppies may join forces to stalk a third, or they both may chew on the same toy.

Play serves to reinforce inherent differences in the littermates' personalities. Pups learn about these differences, and incorporate this understanding into their play. For example, to perpetuate playful activity, a naturally dominant pup may learn how to "play submissive" – to "accidentally" fall down, permitting the lower-ranking dog to physically dominate it. Rather than developing a simple dominance–submission social hierarchy, through play, puppies learn that relationships are fluid.

Play is serious
A puppy learns, through play, how to show tolerance, friendliness, lack of aggression, and willingness to cooperate; all of these are aspects of a good future relationship with humans. It also learns the value of using threatening behaviour. Chases, ambushes, and pounces can all be mutually enjoyable fun, but watch a dominant pup's body language carefully and you will see that play can also be used to actively threaten other pups. During threatening play, the dominant pup places its paw on the other's back; it stares directly with dilated pupils, its hackles may be raised and it lifts its lip, snarls, and shows its teeth. There is an intensity to this pup's actions that is different from the similar, but more flamboyant, behaviours of relaxed play.

Early lessons for life
Through youthful play, pups develop a range of attitudes that last a lifetime. In normal play, sexual, predatory, or aggressive behaviour does occur, but it is out of context. Within the dog pack, these types of play lead to the development of confident dogs, on their way to leadership, and more dependent individuals, content for others to make important decisions. If a pup shows potentially dominant behaviour, avoid play fighting with it, as this could sow the seeds for later dominance aggression problems.

Supervised play
Poorly controlled playful activity can lead to social problems later in life. Intervene constructively; channel your pup's enjoyment of play into creative activities. With your vet's approval, arrange for your pup to meet other pups under controlled circumstances; puppies denied playful activity with other pups during the important months after leaving the litter can forget their social manners, and this may decrease their enjoyment of social encounters later in life, or result in behavioural problems (see pp.188–93). Organized puppy parties are ideal for training pups, through play, to enjoy exercise in public areas like parks, and to play happily with other dogs.

Controlled play teaches important social lessons

Regular groomers

- Grooming is a necessary daily ritual
- Dogs are highly adept at skin and coat care
- Perfume is important

After a good meal, a dog might wander over to the sofa and ritually rub one side of its face, then the other, against the absorbent fabric. Others spend their spare time chewing their nails, or inserting their claws into their ears, then licking them. These are intelligent, self-taught grooming techniques, but all are simply variations of natural grooming methods. All dogs use four standard actions to care for their skin: licking and nibbling, scratching and rubbing, rolling, and shaking.

Licking and nibbling

The teeth and tongue are a dog's natural grooming utensils. From early puppyhood, dogs intuitively tackle their basic grooming needs with licks and nibbles. Sometimes, when a dog licks itself, you can see it slipping into a gentle reverie. Licking becomes slow and rhythmic, and the dog may relax so much its tongue stops in mid-lick, glued to its leg. Nibbling is more active. The incisors are used to give a "needle massage" to the skin; like eating corn-on-the-cob, the nibbling action moves in lines back and forth along the legs or body. Nibbling has dual purposes: it stimulates the skin, while at the same time removing debris and surface parasites, such as fleas and ticks.

A wet dog vigorously shakes the water from its coat, flinging any drops of water out of its fur.

Strange perfume

Just like us, dogs love to cover themselves in attractive smells, but while we think that perfumed soap smells attractive, dogs are attracted to the more natural perfumes of dead fish, or the droppings of other animals. This is a remnant of wolf behaviour, perhaps serving to mask a wolf's own scent to improve hunting prospects.

Scratching and rubbing

Scratching is really only effective with the hind paws. Although some dogs become adept at using their forepaws to groom their heads, it's really more of a rub than a scratch. Some dogs use their claws to scratch inside their ear flaps, but classical scratching involves vigorously rubbing the shoulders, the top of the back, and the front legs with the hind paws' claws. During scratching activity, the dog extends its nails to get the maximum effect.

Rolling

Virtually all four-legged mammals body-roll to massage parts that their teeth and claws cannot reach. Rolling techniques vary from dog to dog. Some do virtual cartwheels, tucking their heads down, flipping over on to their backs, then arching left and right. Others drop to a crouch, then roll on to their backs, arching left and right to rub the skin; they then continue rolling over to complete a full 360 degree rotation. Yet others, while arching on their backs, extend their legs, exercising their muscles during their roll.

Some dogs like to give themselves dust baths by rolling on dry, sandy soil, while others prefer to roll after rain, or when dew is still heavy on the ground. Both methods help keep the hair

and skin healthy and surprisingly clean. Rolling to groom the skin is quite different from rolling to anoint the skin with canine perfume *(see left)*.

Shaking

Dogs shake for several reasons. Some shake upon awakening, to get their coats in order, improve circulation to resting muscles, and maybe even to flush the cobwebs from the mind. Most will shake after having a roll. The most glorious shakes occur after getting wet. A classic shake begins at the head and builds up in amplitude as it extends in a wave down the body, finishing at the tip of the tail. This grooming technique requires sophisticated, instinctive muscle coordination.

Scooting

Licking is an effective way to groom the anal region but so too is scooting – dragging the hind region along the ground. Dogs with tapeworms may scoot because of anal irritation, but the most common reason for employing this self-grooming technique is anal sac irritation *(see p.258)*.

A dog licks its fur to keep its coat clean, and uses its teeth to pull out entangled objects or external parasites.

Graceful aging

- Dogs are living longer
- Aging changes are inevitable
- Some age-related problems can be delayed

The rate at which a dog ages is under the control of a biological clock, which is set at conception in the animal's genes. The clock mechanism is located the hypothalamus – a part of the brain that controls the body's hormonal system (see p.30). As a dog ages, the brain produces ever-smaller quantities of a chemical called dopamine, which is somehow involved in the aging process; put simply, if dopamine production is maintained, a dog lives longer. For unknown reasons, small breeds tend to be better at producing dopamine in their later years than are large breeds, and as a consequence usually live longer.

Normal aging changes

The natural changes that dogs go through as they grow older are similar to those experienced by people. By 16 years of age, about 20 per cent of dogs pass urine or faeces in the house, with little or no warning, and for no medical or acquired behavioural reason. A quarter of all dogs of this age have altered sleep–wake cycles; they sleep more in the day but less at night, when they are more restless, but not because they need to eliminate.

A curious phenomenon of aging is that while females that have been neutered become more aggressive, neutered males get less aggressive as they grow older.

Ways to delay aging

A few simple changes can make your geriatric dog's life more comfortable. Provide short frequent walks rather than one long one. Groom your old dog often; it helps circulation. Feed it with smaller, more frequent meals. Take your dog out after each meal, just before bedtime, and first thing each morning. Change your dog's diet according to its medical needs, and keep its weight within a normal range. Provide warmth and comfort for sleeping and resting.

An older dog has thinner, more senstive skin, so requires gentle, careful grooming

By the age of 16, 60 per cent of dogs involve themselves less with their family; they greet less, follow their owners less, and solicit less attention. Interestingly, an earlier natural aging change involves following the owners more – not letting them out of sight.

A dog's mobility is usually reduced in old age, and as a result it may appear less responsive to commands and may become more aggressive, choosing to threaten and bite rather than retreat.

Over 70 per cent of 16-year-old dogs become naturally disorientated, going to the wrong side of the door when asking to go out, getting stuck in corners, or simply staring into space. Some dogs develop a disease similar to human Alzheimer's, a distictive form of dementia characterized by loss of short-term memory, behaviour changes, and general slowness of thought.

Mental stimulation

Routine mental exercise helps to postpone the natural decline in brain power that comes with age. Give your dog regular mental stimulation through creative activities, such as rolling a toy that releases food. Maintain the dog's physical dexterity by giving it work to do with its forepaws. Massages are also beneficial – they improve blood circulation to all parts of a dog's body, including the brain.

Aging and illness are different

With aging, dogs invariably slow down. In the absence of mental stimulation, the elderly dog becomes dull and lethargic, and its appetite may change. Similar changes also occur when a dog is unwell – lassitude or depression is often how a dog's body responds to the stress of disease or injury – so it is important to differentiate between natural aging changes and illness. Don't always assume that changes in your elderly dog's behaviour are just the changes of growing older. Elderly dogs benefit from twice-yearly veterinary examinations.

Natural aging changes include reduced appetite, but this is also a sign of illness; if your older dog's appetite changes, consult your vet.

Do dogs love us?

- Our relationship with dogs is unique
- People are good for dogs
- Dogs are good for people

Biologically speaking, living with humans has been a great success for the dog as a species. Without us, dogs would not have spread to all the continents and major islands in the world. Without us, they would not have become the world's most numerous large carnivore. We are also good for dogs as individuals, providing safe and secure homes, a constant supply of tasty food, and good health – sometimes through extraordinarily sophisticated medical treatments. We provide emotional support, too: a leg to lean against, someone to snuggle up to, and a hand to tickle a cheek or stroke a back.

Cupboard love

Most dog owners would profess to love their pets, but is the love dogs show for us in return no more than "cupboard love" – one dependent on our providing them with the basic needs of life? Having cared for over 10,000 dogs from puppyhood to the ends of their lives, I am convinced that it is far more, and would argue that the relationship a

Like people, dogs thrive on touch and enjoy social company and mental and physical activity. These shared traits make us believe that we can understand a dog's mind.

dog develops with its human family is virtually biological in its intensity.

Emotional attachments

There is no doubt that a dog's emotions are influenced by the people it lives with. In a study carried out at the University of Cambridge, England, it was found that Cocker Spaniel owners who were shy, undisciplined, and emotionally less stable than average, were more likely to have highly aggressive Cockers than people with average scores for these characteristics. And another piece of research showed that people who had high scores for neuroticism in personality tests had dogs that pestered for attention, were destructive when left alone at home, or sexually mounted people or cushions.

Dogs care for us

Outwardly, we appear to be the care-givers in the dog–human partnership. But the relationship is not one way – dogs offer us tangible physiological and emotional rewards. The American cultural anthropologist, Constance Perin, was the first to hypothesize about odd observations, such as the fact that our blood pressure drops when we stroke our dog. Perin theorized that the physiological rewards we get from stroking a dog evolved from the rewards we gained from physical contact with our mothers when we were infants. Stroking your own dog, Perin would argue, stimulates the same chemical pathways in our bodies as were activated when, as infants, we were in physical contact with our mothers.

Close contact with a dog is physiologically reassuring, and is proven to lower stress levels.

Is it love?

It is undeniably true that we have a deep-seated connection with our dogs, that they give us emotional sustenance, and that we share many of their character traits. But do they love us? Science cannot provide an answer and it is impossible to get inside a dog's mind to find out, so an objective response remains elusive. For me, however, there is only one satisfactory answer: of course they do!

Dogs are good for your health

Today, we choose to live with dogs primarily for social and psychological reasons. Dr. Warwick Anderson, at Monash University in Australia, discovered that dog owners have less risk of heart disease than non-pet owners. In another study, Dr. James Serpell, at the University of Pennsylvania, showed that dog owners tend to suffer from fewer minor health complaints, such as sore throats, lower back pain, and difficulty sleeping, than do non-pet owners, suggesting that dogs have an overall beneficial physiological effect on their owners. In the mid-1980s, the World Health Organization (WHO) reported that "Companion animals which are properly cared for bring immense benefits to their owners and to society and are a danger to no-one".

CHAPTER FOUR

Living with your dog

The first few days you spend with your dog sow the seeds for your future relationship. If you make mistakes at this stage, life can be frustrating for both of you. Choose your dog carefully, considering where you live and your family's lifestyle, then start as you mean to continue. Know what equipment you need, how your dog is to be housed, what toys you will provide, what you will feed and, most importantly, the essentials of basic training. Don't have unwarranted expectations, however: if there are training difficulties, in most circumstances the problem lies not with the dog, but with inconsistency on the part of the owner.

Choosing your dog

- Doing your homework is worth the effort
- Be sensible with your choice
- Choose for tomorrow not just today

Your cute puppy will become an adult very quickly and will need you throughout its life. You will be responsible not only for its physical health, but also for its emotional well-being. A mature dog needs lots of exercise and activity, and demands considerable mental stimulation.

Dogs cost money

Before you choose a dog, do some financial planning, especially if you are thinking of getting a big dog or one that needs extra attention, such as professional grooming. Make an estimate of monthly costs, factoring in regular expenses, such as food, dog equipment, grooming, and yearly preventative health care, such as vaccinations and parasite prevention. Do not forget to include the costs of kennelling your dog while you are away on holiday or business – they can soon mount up if you make a lot of trips. Allow for occasional medical bills or paying health insurance premiums (see p.209). Before buying, think carefully about the dent a dog will make in your household budget.

Dogs can cause problems

Before deciding whether to bring a dog into your home, consider some other potential problems. Allergic reactions to dogs are not uncommon, and it is heartbreaking to get a dog, only to have to part with it because someone in the

To raise a show champion look for a pedigree and award-winning parents. Even so, there are never any guarantees.

Dogs and the law

Different countries have different dog-related laws. These range from the pragmatic and regrettable to the downright unfair. In some places, the number of dogs you can own, or even their sex, is restricted. Specific breeds are illegal in some countries or states, and some breeds may need to be muzzled. Apartments usually have their own unique dog bylaws. In some there is a blanket ban on dogs, in others dogs must be carried on to and away from the property. Find out about local and national laws before you choose to buy.

family is sensitive. Dogs can also carry a wide variety of parasites and germs that can be dangerous to humans, especially to those with a compromised immune system – people receiving chemotherapy, for example, or who are HIV positive. Finally, dogs can bite your family or strangers; bites are not always covered by domestic or pet insurance policies.

Dogs need space

Generally speaking, big dogs need more space than little dogs, but the cliché that smaller dogs fit better into the urban landscape is not always true. Some small dogs have high energy levels and need spacious surroundings, while really giant breeds like the St Bernard may be content living in homes with small gardens. When choosing a breed, think smell too. A really big dog living in a little home can make your house smell like a kennel.

Dog or bitch?

There are no real rules for choosing between a male and female dog – it is a question of personal preference. There are differences in behaviour: females are generally easier to train and house-train, but may be more demanding of affection; male dogs are more likely to be aggressive with other dogs, and can be more dominant, more active, and more destructive. There are no differences between male and female dogs in terms of watchdog barking, playfulness, and excitability. Neutering almost always eliminates sexual drawbacks without inhibiting the attractions of that sex.

Choosing a purebred puppy allows you to have a good idea of the size, looks, and temperament your dog will have as an adult.

Puppy or adult dog?

The choice of whether to get a puppy or an older dog is a tough one. Puppies have some obvious advantages – they are putty in your hands, ready to be moulded to your family's lifestyle. Your dog will have fewer behaviour problems if you get it at about eight weeks of age and raise it in your own unique environment. However, adult dogs have their good points too: most are already housetrained, and many already have an understanding of obedience. Costs of purchase, training, and neutering may have been met. Virtually all adult dogs, given the need or chance, are emotionally capable of building a powerful new bond with you.

Purebred or mutt?

A pure-bred dog is one produced by mating two dogs of the same breed. The advantage of a purebred is that you know what the dog's eventual size and

Ask the breeder questions

If you are planning to get a dog from a breeder, ask these simple questions.

1 May I see the mother? (You should be able to.)

2 May I see the father? (Do not expect to. The best breeders go outside their kennels for fathers.)

3 Where do the pups live? (Pups raised indoors make better dogs than those raised in a kennel.)

4 Have they been seen by a vet? (Good breeders have parents examined before mating and pups examined before they are sold.)

5 When will they be ready? (Six weeks is too soon. Twelve weeks is too late. Eight weeks is usually just about right.)

temperament are likely to be. The disadvantage is an increased risk of certain medical inherited conditions, although this risk varies considerably between breeds. Mutts – crossbreds and random-bred dogs – benefit from hybrid vigour, which is the enhancement of good health that comes from mixing stock from different genetic backgrounds. Their disadvantage is that, as pups, it can be difficult to guess their eventual size and temperament. However, if you get a mutt pup and train it from early life to fit in with your lifestyle, there is every chance that it will turn out to be a great pet.

Where to find your dog

Pure-bred dogs should always be bought from reliable breeders. Some breeders are dedicated hobbyists, while others are more overtly commercial, but both types can

Pure-bred dogs are popular for their looks but mutts – crossbreds or random-bred dogs – suffer from fewer inherited illnesses.

be a good source of pups. Look out for dog-show rosettes on the walls and happy, relaxed dogs on the premises. Another sign of a good breeder is an inquisitive nature – if they are truly dedicated to the welfare of their dogs, they will want to know as much about you as you want to know about them.

It is not advisable to buy your pup from a pet shop. Some are excellent but many are not, and it is extremely rare for reliable breeders to sell their pups in this way.

Newspaper ads
Be very careful with the "dogs for sale" sections of the classifieds in your local newspaper. Some will be genuine ads from loving breeders, but many are private homes used as intermediaries by puppy farms – unscrupulous breeders who use bitches as puppy making machines and have little interest in anything other than a sale. However, if you exercise caution over your selection, it is possible to get a great dog through an ad.

Neighbours and vets
If possible, get your dog from a caring friend or neighbour. The pups will have been well socialized and raised in a known environment free of parasites and disease. Veterinary clinic noticeboards are similarly good, because the staff almost invariably know the parent dogs and their owners.

Adopting a rescue dog
Rescue dogs can make fantastic family pets, but before making a commitment, visit the dog at the rescue centre several times. Ask the staff plenty of questions, take the dog out for walks, and introduce it to your family. Signs of insecurity (cowering, barking, and unwillingness to leave the shelter) are to be expected, especially if the dog has been institutionalized for more than a few weeks. Some rescue dogs exhibit aggression, fear-biting, or an almost callous indifference to their adoptive family. In some individuals, these problems may take months of patient training to overcome.

Ask the rescue centre questions

If you are planning to get a dog from a rescue centre, ask these simple questions.

❶ Was the dog lost or handed in? (Vagrants often have a lifelong wanderlust.)

❷ If surrendered, why was it handed in? (Many dogs are discarded because they have behaviour problems that are not apparent until you live with the dog.)

❸ Has the rescue centre done any behaviour testing? (Progressive rescue centres analyse behaviour and give reports to potential adopters.)

❹ Can you help with any future problems? (The best rescue centres give continuing advice on behaviour problems.)

Thousands of wonderful dogs are always in need of loving homes. At rescue centres, young males typically outnumber other ages or females.

Dog equipment

- Get prepared for your dog's arrival
- Make practical choices
- Pups quickly outgrow equipment

All dogs need certain essential equipment: bedding, bowls for food and water, collars, identity tags, and leads. When buying these items, don't be led exclusively by cost or style. Think from the dog's perspective as well as your own – what will be comfortable, practical, and durable.

Food and water bowls

Choose robust and steady food bowls – ones that are unlikely to move across the kitchen floor as your dog eats. Heavy ceramic or metal bowls on non-slip rubber bases are excellent. If you feed canned food to your dog, use a separate can opener for the dog food and wash it often. Keep opened food cans, covered with plastic lids, in the refrigerator for no more than three days. Dogs are sloppy when eating and drinking; absorbent, washable mats under bowls help to catch the mess.

Collars and leads

Your dog should wear a collar and identification tag from day one. When you first put a collar on a young puppy, it may scratch at its neck and appear uncomfortable, but the sensation will become familiar within days. Make sure you buy a collar of the correct size – you should be able to slip two fingers between neck and collar.

Different collars suit different dogs. Meshed nylon with a simple buckle is comfortable and inexpensive. Wide, flat leather collars are excellent for long-necked breeds such as whippets, while rolled leather collars are good for

Built to last

Dogs invented the phrase "tested to destruction", so it is worth making the investment in good quality, hard-wearing equipment.

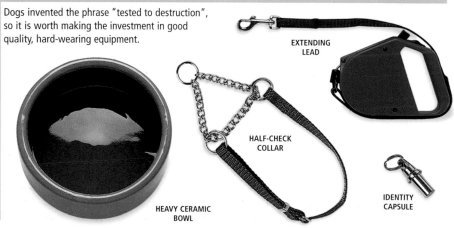

EXTENDING LEAD

HALF-CHECK COLLAR

HEAVY CERAMIC BOWL

IDENTITY CAPSULE

Canine clothing

Small dogs and delicate breeds with thin single coats may need additional protection from the winter rain and cold. A well designed coat has a waterproof exterior and a soft interior. If winter is particularly harsh where you live, you could consider insulated boots for your dog. In hot, sunny climates, a useful accessory for light-skinned dogs is sunscreen. Just like ours, dog skin burns when exposed to too much sunlight. Ask your vet about sunscreen products suitable for use on your dog.

As they grow older, some dogs may need a warm winter coat

Comfortable bedding

Your dog's bed should be hygienic, easily washable, protective, and comfortable.

1 Moulded plastic dog baskets are easier to clean and harder for your dog to damage than wicker models. The basket should be lined with a well-fitting washable mattress.

Chew-proof plastic is less attractive but more durable than wicker

2 Rectangular, round, or oval bean bags, filled with lightweight Styrofoam beads, make ideal beds. These usually come with zip covers that can be removed for washing. If the whole bag is soiled with urine or other liquids, it can be washed in the washing machine and dried on the clothes line.

Bean bags help retain the dog's body heat, making them ideal for small breeds

breeds with heavy coats. Half-check collars – a safe alternative to choke chains – are designed to control a dog without causing discomfort, and are excellent for big, lively dogs.

Leads should be thick enough to bear the strain of your dog pulling at full strength. Young dogs will often chew their leads when walking, so most are made of tough leather or nylon. Extending leads, which pull out to lengths of 10 m (30 ft), give your dog more exercise for less human legwork.

Baby gates

Within the home, baby gates can restrict a boisterous or unpredictable dog to parts of the building without interrupting your line of sight.

Body harnesses

Some dogs are not the right shape to wear a collar, and need a body harness instead. Bulldogs and Pugs have necks as wide as their heads, so collars slip

off. Small breeds like Yorkshire Terriers have soft windpipes; their collars can carry ID tags, but leads should be attached to a body harness for walking.

Canine identification

The most common form of ID is an engraved tag attached to the collar, carrying the dog's name and owner's telephone number. Collar capsules can carry more details, such as alternative contact numbers, but the most successful form of ID is the microchip – a tiny electronic transponder injected just under the skin in the neck. This emits a signal, which can be read by a handheld reader. The microchip has become the internationally accepted method of canine ID when it comes to travel between countries.

Crate training

- The crate is your dog's personal den
- Speeds up house training
- Crate should be large enough for adult years

A crate may look like a jail to us, but to a dog it is a natural den – a personal space where it feels secure and does not want to mess. It is worth training a puppy to eat, play, and sleep in a crate, because it will come to enjoy the reassurance of the crate when it is home alone, or when travelling in a car. In short, crate training provides the solution to a variety of behaviour problems before they happen.

Plan ahead

Get a crate before you bring your new puppy home. Choose one that will be large enough for your dog to stretch out in when it has grown to adult size. The crate should not be so large that your puppy can mess in one part and move away to sleep or play in another; when your pup is tiny, use a large

Some crates are designed to convert into puppy playpens, so that puppies can play alone or with their pals without causing havoc in your home.

cardboard carton to block off a section of the crate to make it smaller. Make the crate comfortable and put in some suitable toys, then introduce your puppy to the crate *(see opposite)*.

Training tips

Once your pup has become accustomed to walking into and playing in the crate, train it to use the crate by saying "Crate" while enticing it in with a treat. After a few repetitions, close the crate door for a few minutes while your pup plays happily within. Pups should never be left in a crate for more than two hours, and should always be exercised before confinement.

If your pup barks while in its crate or playpen, do not scold or admonish it, talk to it, or even look in its direction. If you pay any attention, you are telling your dog that noise gets results. After it is quiet for a few seconds, take it out and play with it. The only exception to this rule is if you think it has to relieve

Outdoor kennelling

Outdoor living is not advisable for most family dogs; it interferes with socialization, inhibits learning, and leads to problems associated with boredom. If there is no other option, plan for a combination of indoor and outdoor living. During the first months, restrict your dog to the kitchen and carry out crate training. At the same time, introduce the pup to its outdoor home. The dog house should be draft-free and dry, with hygienic, washable bedding, and should be large enough for your dog to stretch out. Make sure that you and your family spend quality time outdoors with the dog.

itself; if so, wait for it to stop barking for a moment, then take it outside. Never use a crate as punishment – it is meant to be enjoyed.

The crate becomes home

A dog instinctively feels comfortable in the security of its own den. Dogs like crates, in the same way that they like going under kitchen tables, behind sofas, or under beds. Crate training helps to speed up house training enormously, as dogs are not inclined to soil their own personal area. An additional benefit is that, once your dog is crate trained, travelling by car becomes far easier; the dog feels safe, secure, and relaxed in its crate, and the crate offers added protection in the event of an accident.

Introducing the crate

Have the crate ready when your dog comes home. Do not put it in an isolated part of the house: the best position is in a busy spot, such as the kitchen.

① Line the crate with newspaper, and equip it with soft bedding, a bowl of water, and an interesting toy. Leave the door open.

Use food and toys to encourage your puppy to enter the crate of its own accord

② Using a tasty snack, and the verbal command "Crate", entice the puppy into its new home. Your pup will willingly investigate, find the toy and treat, and consider the crate "a good thing". Keep the door open so that the puppy can leave the crate at any time.

③ Once the puppy has become accustomed to the crate, it will continue to use it without any further prompting from you.

The first 24 hours

- Start as you mean to continue
- Avoid excitement and create routines
- Supervise the first meeting with other pets

A dog needs time to explore and investigate its new home. Let it do so quietly and without fuss. Keep your family under control – and that includes grown-ups. There should be no screaming or jumping around the puppy, no feeding outside meal times, and no yanking, tugging, or pulling. Above all, the puppy should be treated consistently – your hard work and discipline is easily undermined.

Meeting other pet dogs

The first introduction of a resident dog to a newcomer should take place on neutral territory, after the resident has had plenty of exercise. Let them sniff one other and don't interfere unless either looks unhappy. Back at home, remove any bones, toys, and canine possessions from the garden to prevent jealousy. Older dogs do not much like exuberant puppy behaviour, and may snarl or snap. If you think your resident dog might attack, immediately put the pup in its playpen or crate.

Meeting your resident cat

Most pup–cat introductions go well. Typically, the pup retreats and learns to respect its feline housemate. If the dog starts to chase the cat, try distracting it. If it continues, place the pup in its crate; do not leave the dog and cat together unsupervised until the chasing problem has been resolved.

Who sleeps where?

Many dog owners feel it is best to make a new pup sleep in its permanent quarters – usually the kitchen or utility room – from day one. If this is what you want to do, you will need to be consistent and stoically ignore your

Contrary to cliché the relationship between cat and dog is usually friendly and playful.

Don't create problems

Put a pup on the sofa and it will think this is where it should stay. Allow a pup on your bed, and it assumes this is a good place to sleep. Give it food while you are eating, and it will expect this again. Do not create problems for the future by thinking you can get away with something just once. Dogs are smarter than you think.

A name is important

Dogs respond best to short, snappy, single syllable names like Rex, Bones, Ben, Meg. Choose a name that does not sound like another common word, and that you can shout without embarrassment!

pup's howling or crying. If you respond to the wailing, you'll simply teach it that making noise works.

I prefer pups to start in temporary sleeping arrangements – a high-sided cardboard box or crate in the bedroom, where the pup is comforted by the sight, sound, and smell of its family.

The first night

Make sure your puppy is tired and sleepy. Feed it a warm, milky meal, take it outside to relieve itself, then put the pup in its temporary sleeping box. Be quiet and calm, and disregard whimpers, howls, and cries.

When your pup wakes up in the night and tries to get out of the box, it probably means it needs to relieve itself. (Pups do not like to soil their own beds.) Take the pup to the toileting area and, when it relieves itself, give quiet praise and a treat. Then, without fuss, put it back in its box. Stick plugs in your ears for the next few minutes because it will want to play. Be resolute; it will learn that vocalizing does not work. Within a week, your pup will be ready to sleep on its own, in its designated "bedroom".

House rules

Consistency is vital. Create house rules and display them in a prominent place. They should include clear instructions on what your dog is and is not allowed to do and the responsibilities of each family member, for example:

• Macy is the primary responsibility of...
• Macy is restricted to...
• Macy sleeps only in....
• Do not give treats without Macy obeying a command;
• Always use Macy's name first when you want her attention;
• Consider Macy when making your plans or arrangements;
• Exterior doors are always kept closed;
• Everyone clears time to attend Macy's puppy classes.

The warmth of an insulated hot water bottle can comfort a puppy on the first night away from its mother.

House training

- Maintain a consistent approach
- Set realistic goals
- Reward appropriate behaviour

A dog is instinctively unwilling to soil its nest. In house training, you effectively take advantage of this instinct by teaching your dog that its nest actually extends to your entire home. House training is fairly straightforward, but it depends upon your vigilance.

Training in the great outdoors

It is easiest to house train a dog if you have immediate access to a park or a garden. A dog naturally wants to relieve itself after a meal, or following play, exercise, excitement, or waking up. Before squatting, it usually starts to run or circle, sniffing with its nose to the floor. When you spot these visual cues, immediately take your dog outside.

Be still and silent, and do not start playing games. As your dog begins to relieve itself, reassuringly speak a word or words that you have chosen to associate with toileting. Use the word cues consistently, and in time your dog will associate their sound with the need to go. After your dog has finished his business, give praise. Stay out a little longer if the weather permits – most dogs love the opportunity to be outdoors. Remember to take a scoop with you to clean up any mess.

If after five minutes nothing has happened, return indoors but keep an eye on activity so you are prepared for a quick return.

Indoor training

Using a crate *(see pp.170–71)* is a good way to house train your pup because it helps set up a simple routine. At any time your dog will either be in its crate, out of its crate toileting, or safely roaming about having "emptied its tanks".

Young pups empty their bladders about once an hour

1 Paper training is a practical way to train a puppy in a small apartment without fast access to the outdoors. However, if you use this method, you will prolong the training period because you will eventually need to retrain the puppy to mess outdoors. When the puppy starts to squat, quickly pick it up and take it to a selected toileting area. Place the puppy on the paper or litter tray.

Use word cues when your dog relieves itself in the right place

2 Praise the puppy after it has urinated on the paper. Keep a small piece of soiled newspaper along with the fresh supply; this provides the puppy with its own odour, encouraging it to use the paper again.

Training an adult dog

All the principles of toilet training apply equally to older dogs. The important difference is that older dogs may have to "unlearn" some toileting habits before learning new ones.

Apartment training

The same principles apply if you do not have easy access to the outdoors. Choose an area in your apartment where it is acceptable for your dog to toilet; it should be easy to clean and well away from distractions. Lay down a thick plastic sheet and cover it with newspaper, or put down a litter tray or commercially produced disposable pet pads. As before, when you think your dog wants to go, lead it to the designated toilet area. After it has relieved itself, give the pup (or adult dog) plenty of praise and reward it by letting it roam elsewhere in your home. Day by day, reduce the size of the paper-covered area; at the same time, take your dog out as frequently as possible so that it learns to use an outdoor "toilet" as well.

Accidents will happen

When you see your dog relieving itself in the house, get its attention by calling its name and attracting it to your back door (or the designated toilet area). You want to encourage it willingly to follow you. After the excitement is over, it will complete what it started earlier. When your dog has finished, keep it in another room while you clean up its mess. Don't punish your dog for what it did earlier. Delayed punishment is beyond its comprehension.

Smell and stain removers

Your veterinary surgeon can supply you with enzyme-containing odour eliminators to deal with stains on carpets and upholstery. Alternatively, make your own by mixing biological (enzyme-containing) washing powder with hot water and liberally soaking the area. Alcohol also breaks down odours, but avoid products containing ammonia, which is a natural body-product. It will attract rather than repel a dog from a site. If carpet is soiled, the underlay and even the floor beneath should be treated with odour-eliminating products. White vinegar and water is good for removing stains from carpets.

Submissive urinating

Dogs may urinate as a sign of submission. Do not mistake this for a lapse in house training. Submissive urination is a natural way for a low-ranking dog to appease a higher-ranking individual. If your pup piddles when it sees you, ignore it and walk away, either to an area where there is newspaper on plastic sheeting, or out of the back door. Encourage it to follow you and relieve itself.

Most pups outgrow submissive urinating as they mature and build confidence.

Practical toys

- Toys are educational
- Some "belong" to you, others to your dog
- Toys need not cost you a penny

Toys are fun, but they are also amongst the most important items you provide for your dog. Each toy has a purpose: to be chewed, to squeak, to be chased, or to play tug-of-war with. Use toys in the same way that you use food treats as rewards *(see pp.180–81).*

Chewable toys are your dog's own toys; ones you do not get involved with. Squeak and chase toys, on the other hand, belong to you, not your dog. Store these toys out of your dog's reach – it makes them more interesting when you bring them out, and also

powerfully communicates the message that you are in charge.

Don't overwhelm your dog with toys. If it feels like it lives in a toy shop, it will find it difficult to differentiate between what is a toy and what is not. As a result, it will play with and chew on virtually anything.

Chew toys

Dogs need and love to chew. Meat-flavoured nylon bones, rubber rings, a rubber ball on a nylon rope, and rawhide chews are all excellent chew toys. Avoid rawhide from countries where unknown preservatives might be used. Sterilized bones are also problematic: although dogs love them, teeth can be fractured by chewing hard bones *(see pp.252–3).*

If you need to leave your dog at home alone for a period of time, you should leave out toys that provide more

A dog provided with toys can exercise its mind and senses even when you are away from home.

Squeaky toys

Squeaky toys are great fun, but can lose their "squeak" if chewed too forcefully. They last a lot longer when rationed, especially when a pup is teething. They come in different guises: some are made of soft sheepskin-like material surrounding a squeaker, while others are thin-skinned rubber balls enclosing the squeaker. Dogs are less inclined to chew on squeak toys that collapse under the slightest pressure. Give a squeaky toy to your dog as a treat, for a short period, using a food reward as a distraction when taking it away.

Inappropriate toys

1 Do not leave electric cords dangling. Playful pups will tug on them, leading to damage to the appliance and potential danger for the pup.

2 Keep rubbish in a pedal bin: it is less attractive to your dog than a hanging plastic bag.

3 Do not give your dog an old shoe or slipper to chew on: a pup cannot differentiate your discards from your new dress shoes.

4 Teething puppies will chew almost anything – wooden kitchen table legs are ideal. Reprimand inappropriate behaviour and provide chew toys.

5 Temporarily remove throw rugs from a teething pup's territory – they are irresistable for chewing.

mental stimulation. Some chew toys, for example, are hollow inside and can be filled with something exciting, like peanut butter. Extracting the food gives your dog an engaging challenge. Other toys are designed to be nosed around the floor, dropping morsels of food out as they are rolled around; they can keep a dog occupied for hours.

Fetch and tug-of-war toys

A throwable toy, such as a ball, braided nylon rope, or a frisbee, is great for giving your dog exercise and improving its coordination. Training your dog to fetch and retrieve takes time and patience, plus plenty of food rewards and praise for correct behaviour. Arm yourself with lots of toys at first, or you will be the one getting the exercise!

Tug-of war is a good bonding game, and helps build strength, but be sensible. A strong-willed dog will genuinely want to win: occasionally you should concede defeat to maintain interest, but most of the time you

should come out on top. If you do not, your dog will think it is stronger than you; this can be the start of a loss of respect and consequential problems.

Instant toys

A small, empty plastic water bottle is a great activity toy. Even a small dog can grab it by the neck and drag it. A slight nudge with the nose gets it rolling. Add a little water, and it is more exciting as the water laps, glistens, and gurgles. This is a safe distraction, but do not leave it with your pup long enough for it to chew through the plastic.

Make sure your pup has toys to play with, or it will create its own chew toys from around your home.

Home and garden

- Be a considerate neighbour
- Dog-proof your garden
- Survey for possible dangers

Chances are your neighbours will welcome the new canine addition to your family, but do not leave it to chance; tell them what you are doing, make your garden secure, apologise for any initial barking and whining, clean up after your dog, and obey both local laws and common sense. Legally, you are responsible for your dog's actions. Check your home insurance policy for dog-damage cover; this should include direct damage, such as trashing your neighbours' flower beds or biting their cat, or indirect damage – for example, to a car that swerves to avoid your dog.

Home alone

Barking is part of standard canine communication, but is an activity that can really irritate your neighbours. It is up to you to control it. Dogs bark when they are left at home alone and are

Scoop poop

Train your family to clean up after your dog, in your own garden, on the road, and in the park. Poop scoopers come in a variety of materials and styles, most of which are designed to appeal to your aesthetic rather than practical needs. If you can get over your qualms, simply use impermeable, biodegradable plastic bags.

bored, or at strangers and other dogs if they are not well socialized. Prevent problems through proper training.

There will be times when your new dog will be home alone. You have a responsibility to your neighbours, and to your dog, to make the best possible attempt to ensure canine contentment in your absence. Consider installing a personal dog door so that your dog

A bored dog may bark, dig, or destroy while you are away from home.

Dog walkers, sitters, and day care

Professional dog walkers and sitters are available in most urban areas. In many cities, there are also doggie day care centres where busy couples can leave their dog while they are at work during the day. Investigate and interview any potential "dog help" thoroughly: find out if play is supervised, if there is a barking policy, and whether there are rest periods for your dog. Ask whether any training takes place, and if there are any health issues to consider.

can get into the garden when you are out: the most secure types are activated by a magnetic tag on the dog's collar. If it is unsafe to let your dog out, create a window seat indoors so it can see outdoor activity.

Dog-proof your garden

Make sure your garden is escape-proof and safe for your dog to explore alone:
• Remove potentially toxic or poisonous plants (see p. 229);
• Lock away garden, cleaning, and automobile chemicals (see p. 229);
• Clear the garage if your dog is allowed access to it;
• Take care when using any potentially dangerous garden equipment, especially the lawnmower;
• Keep garbage cans in a latched shed;
• If you have a swimming pool, ensure that the safety fence around the pool area, and the pool cover if you have one, are absolutely dog-proof;

• Check that the perimeter fence is high enough and cannot be dug under;
• Make sure that the gate is always closed securely – the safest gates spring shut automatically after opening.

Thick hedges are not sufficient for your garden perimeter – dogs are experts at finding even the smallest escape route. If you cannot fence your garden, "invisible" fencing is available. A cable is laid around the perimeter of your grounds; when your dog reaches the cable, it receives a mild electric buzz through an attachment on its collar.

Garden issues

Dogs are exuberant creatures. If you treasure your garden, restrict your dog to only those areas in which it cannot cause damage. Dogs love to dig; if you do not mind earthy paws and nose, consider installing a fresh earth-digging zone for your dog to enjoy.

Small dogs can use a cat-flap to go in and out of a secure garden.

Training essentials

- Consistency is vital
- Reward good behaviour
- Food, toys, and touch are effective rewards

Dog training is simple when you understand how your dog thinks – how it interprets your tone of voice, your body language, and your use of rewards and discipline. If you are inconsistent with your approach, you create problems that can be difficult to undo. Spend time now, learning how to manage your dog; any dog is trainable, but the younger it is, the easier it will be. Informal training should begin as soon as you bring a new puppy home.

Clicker training

Clickers are wonderful aids in dog training. Timing is exquisitely important: the clicker is clicked as the dog begins to respond correctly. Eventually it hears the clicker and does what you want it to. The best way to clicker-train your dog is to join a training class that uses clickers.

Be consistent

Dogs need to know the rules – what is allowed and what is not. Consistency is vital, especially when giving rewards or meting out verbal discipline, so make sure that all members of your family understand and stick to the rules.

When rewarding or disciplining your dog, good results depend on good timing. Give the reward as soon as your dog tries to do the right thing. Rewards given too late – even three seconds after the event – cause confusion, especially in young pups.

Rewards

Dogs need constant encouragement when they are being trained. Give your dog rewards to reinforce positive behaviour. A tasty treat is just about the most potent

Play with your dog after a training session, so it associates learning with fun.

Discover which is your dog's favourite toy – it can be a wonderful aid to training

Use touch

Physical rewards are important during training: praise your dog while stroking it along its body. Associate touch with food or toy rewards, and at the same time give a verbal reward. Your dog will soon learn that just the words "Good girl" or "Good boy" are satisfying on their own.

Combine touch with verbal praise

Physical contact is a potent reward

reward you can give most dogs; this works best when the dog is hungry. Just about anything is fine as long as it tastes good. Toys – especially chewable or squeaky toys – are almost as powerful. Use toys as rewards for dogs that are not greedy by nature.

Finish on a high note

Always finish training sessions with something that your dog enjoys. If your pup is struggling to get something right, for example, go back to a task it knows how to do well and end the session with that exercise.

Be careful, however, not to save the most powerful reward for the end of the session – if you do so, you are unwittingly training your dog to want the session to end so that it can receive its favourite reward.

Discipline

There are a variety of different forms of discipline that you can use to help your dog learn what is acceptable and what is not; these must never be used,

however, as a means to get revenge for bad behaviour.

"No!" is a powerful word, but use it wisely – save it for when you see your dog doing something wrong. Never shriek, mumble, or whine "No", or use it so frequently that your dog disregards it. Growl it, deeply and sharply, when you need to use it, and at the same time, give your dog a hard stare. Standing over your dog, saying "Bad dog!", then maintaining your stare is an extremely effective form of discipline. Use symbolic isolation as a potent form of discipline: if your dog misbehaves, take it to an empty room, shut the door, count to 30, then let it out, but ignore it for another minute.

There will be times when something more dramatic is needed. Water pistols, noise makers, even a rare, symbolic shake by the scruff of the neck are effective. When using discipline, never leave your dog on a negative note. After a reprimand, let yourself cool down, then do something positive.

Some dogs are extremely eager to learn, and can master even complex tasks with ease.

Basic training

- Train when you are alert
- Have realistic expectations
- Use daily rewarding situations

Most dogs willingly learn to come, sit, and stay because they want to please you, and because it is in their interest to do so. Train your dog when both its mind and yours are alert. Be prepared: know the words and gestures you plan to use and have your rewards available. Dogs thrive on instant gratification.

Puppy classes

Puppy classes are like playschool for young children – an ideal environment for early learning and moulding behaviour. Some puppy classes are better than others: ask your veterinary clinic to recommend good local classes – ones that restrict participation to puppies under 16 weeks old and encourage entire human families to attend.

How to begin

Start slowly: a one or two minute lesson is perfect for a pup. Five minutes is too long. Older dogs have greater powers of concentration, but dogs with even the best mental stamina cannot concentrate on training for more than about 15 minutes at a time. Pups are capable of concentrating on training several times during the day, although some may need to burn off a little excess energy before lessons.

All dogs are capable of learning basic obedience, but it requires patience, perseverance, and self-discipline from you and your family.

When to train your dog

An ideal time for training a puppy is just before mealtimes, giving you three or four ready-prepared training opportunities each day. As it gets older and you reduce the number of meals it has each day, train shortly after it awakens and after it empties its bladder and bowels. Choose the location for the initial training exercises carefully; a hallway, for example, is ideal – there is space to move about, but no distractions to interrupt proceedings. Once your dog reliably responds in that location, move on to a more distracting environment, like the garden; eventually move on to the most complicated surroundings, such as the street or a park. Train by increments: avoid leaps to a much higher level.

Don't get flustered

If your dog is not responding to training, avoid persistently repeating commands; it confuses your dog. If training is not going well, stop. Think about what you are doing. The problem is with you, not with your dog. Do not be shy about asking for help; front office staff at veterinary clinics can be a good source of sound advice.

Learning to come to you

This important lesson is one of the first that your puppy should be trained to understand (see right). Never use the word "Come" to call your dog from something exciting to something less interesting, or to call your dog to discipline. Never command your dog to "Come" unless you know it will obey.

Learning to wear a collar and lead

When introducing your pup to wearing a collar, put it on just before feeding, when its mind is distracted by the sight and smell of food. Take it off immediately after. Once it is used to wearing the collar, clip the lead on just before feeding and call it to dinner, applying very gentle tension to the leash. By associating these accessories with something as thrilling as food, your dog will not resent wearing either item.

Teaching your dog to come to you

This is the easiest command for a puppy to learn. Begin teaching this before mealtimes, when your puppy is alert and hungry.

1 Crouch down a short distance away from your puppy. Show it the food bowl, say its name, and, as it begins to move towards its meal, give the command "Come". As it approaches, say "Good dog" enthusiastically, and give it the meal. Between meals, carry out the same exercise a few times daily, using a food titbit.

Graduate to standing upright while getting its attention by calling its name, then saying "Come" as it starts to approach. Stroke it as your reward. Within only a few days, it will come to you willingly when it hears its name and the word "Come".

The puppy is rewarded for coming to you by receiving its meal

The lure of a tasty meal entices the puppy to approach

2 Older, strong-willed, or shy dogs may not come so willingly. If you are having difficulties, carry out the training with the puppy on a lead to ensure that it always complies with your instructions. This guarantees that you can always attract the puppy's attention, by giving a quick jerk on the lead. Do not use the lead to pull the dog towards you, but encourage it to come to you of its own accord, in return for a food or toy reward.

If you have a wilful dog, carry out all training exercises on a lead so it learns that you are in control

Teaching your dog to sit

Concentrate on your dog's head: control the head, and the body will do what you want it to do.

1 Stand facing your dog, and with food in your hand, command it to "Come". Depending on your dog, you may have to use a lead to ensure it responds.

Show your puppy the food as you command it to "Come"

2 When it reaches you, move your hand holding the food over the dog's head. As your dog's eyes follow the food above it, its rump will naturally go down. When you see your dog bending its hind legs, give the command "Sit".

Food is held directly over the puppy's head

3 As it assumes a sitting position, say "Good dog" and give the food immediately. Graduate to standing beside your dog while giving the command "Sit". Initially give food rewards, but after a while, start to give them intermittently. Finally, your words of praise alone will be sufficient reward for your dog.

A food reward is often the most effective for training, but if your dog is a picky eater, try using a favourite toy combined with verbal praise

Learning to sit

Puppies can be taught to "Sit" *(see left)* just as quickly as they learn to come to you. If you cannot entice your dog to sit for a food reward, hold its collar in one hand and use your other hand to tuck its hindquarters into a sitting position. Give the command "Sit" as you do this and instantly reward it with a food treat and a verbal "Good dog".

If food rewards are so exciting that your dog cannot concentrate on your commands, try other less stimulating but still interesting rewards, and train your dog on a fuller stomach.

Learning to stay

If your pup has mastered "Come" and "Sit", it has learned to follow a sequence of commands. The next stage is to add a third command: "Stay" or "Wait" *(see right)*. This will be vital for your dog's safety in future. "Stay" is simply a prolonged variation of "Sit".

If you are having trouble, try training to stay with your dog sitting at the base of a wall – this prevents it from sliding backwards. If your dog does not respond properly or does something wrong, avoid the word "No" – this should be saved for more serious misdemeanours. Instead, introduce a neutral word like "Wrong".

Learning to lie down

Teaching your dog to lie down *(see far right)* may take persistence and patience on your part, because you are asking it to do something that it already does instinctively: lying down is a submissive gesture between dogs. If your pup creeps forward on its haunches instead of lying down, kneel beside it and,

Teaching your dog to stay

After you have trained your dog to "Sit", graduate to "Stay", reinforcing the verbal command with a clear hand signal.

1 First command your dog to "Sit" – this will ensure that you have its full attention. Make sure that your dog's head is up, looking at your face, but do not stand too close; your dog should not be looking up vertically.

Dog sits patiently, waiting for your next command

2 After it sits, show your dog the palm of your hand while you command "Stay". Take a few steps away from your dog. If you are using a lead, walk back until the lead is extended. If your dog moves, start the exercise again from the beginning.

The dog concentrates on both voice and hand signals

3 Keep the duration of the "Sit-Stay" short, then conclude the "Stay" by introducing your release word – "Finished". Calmly give a small food reward and praise your dog. Gradually increase the duration of the "Stay", graduating to the command word alone without the food treat. Over a period of a week, repeat the exercise until you are giving the command at distance.

Save praise until after you have given your release word

Teaching your dog to lie down

"Lie Down" is a natural variation of "Sit" and "Stay", but requires a little more work by you and greater understanding by your dog.

1 With your pup in a "Sit" position, kneel to one side, tucking the lead under your knees and gently holding its collar.

2 Put the food treat in front of your pup's nose, and, using a sweeping action, move your treat-holding hand forward and downward in an arc. As your pup lies down to keep in contact with the now ground-level food treat, give the command "Down". Keep the treat clenched in your hand so the dog cannot grab it.

Control the movement of your dog by holding the collar

3 Continue moving the food along the floor until it is in a complete down position. Praise it with "Good dog" and reward it with the food treat.

Repeat the exercise frequently, until the puppy responds to words alone.

Teaching your dog to walk on a lead

Begin training in a place where there are no distractions. If you have not introduced the lead before, let your pup look at it and smell it.

1 Attach the lead to your puppy's well-fitted, comfortable collar. With your puppy to your side, hold the end of the lead and the food treat in one hand. Your other hand holds the slack in the lead. Avoid tension on the lead at this point. Command your pup to "Sit".

Lead is held in both hands

2 Start walking forward and as your puppy gets up to move, give the command "Heel". Let the dog feel only the slightest tension on the lead. If it surges forward, slide your hand down the lead, give a slight but firm pull on the lead, and command "Steady".

A light jerk on the lead brings the dog back into position

3 After only a few steps, command the dog to "Wait" and give the food reward. Verbally reward your dog, then try the procedure again covering the same sequence of events. Once it is walking to heel on its lead in a straight line, graduate to turns. When turning, either you walk around the dog, or, to turn the other way, your dog should walk around you.

while it is sitting, put the palms of your hands under its forelegs. Lift it gently into a begging position, and then lower into a lying position. Instantly reward it with praise and treats.

If your dog refuses to stay down, using both hands, apply gentle pressure on its back just behind the neck. Reward it for lying down, then give your release word – "Finished".

Walking the dog

Outdoor activities can be a delight when your dog walks obediently by your side. Before you start to train your dog to walk on the lead *(see left)*, make sure that it reliably understands basic obedience commands – "Sit", "Come", and "Stay" *(see pp.182–5)*. This is important because "Sit" is always the take-off point for walking to heel.

Always keep the first sessions short, beginning with only a few seconds and a few feet forward. Repeat this twice a day, increasing both time and distance. Be patient, consistent, and not too ambitious. It does not matter whether you start training your dog to heel on or off the lead; if, however, you start with walking off the lead, make sure that you train in a safe area – your dog may decide to chase after a cat rather than obeying you!

Solving problems

Walking on the lead is one of the most important lessons your dog will learn – a puppy that does not learn this lesson properly will be more difficult to control as an adult *(see pp.190–91)*.

It is important to "addict" your pup to the food treat you are using as a reward. Dried liver treats work well because they are smelly. If your pup

Head halters

Head halters are ideal for most dogs, but especially for rambunctious, bold, or independent individuals, as well as for those that chew excessively. The lead clips to a ring under the dog's jaw. If the dog pulls forwards, its own momentum pulls its jaws shut and its head down. If your dog has a small muzzle or a soft windpipe, a body harness that fits around the chest may be more appropriate.

Halter should not be too tightly fastened

Attach the lead to the halter ring under the dog's jaw

simply is not interested in food, a toy that triggers intense interest, such as a squeaky toy *(see p.177)*, is an ideal alternative. If your pup is a food-lover, try training after meals.

If your puppy jumps up to get at the treat, you are holding it too high. Move your hand lower, and at the same time use your free hand on your dog's collar to prevent jumping. If your pup loses concentration, you probably have chosen the wrong time or place for training. Try again when it is better prepared. Once you have trained your dog to walk to heel in the quiet of your home and garden, you are ready to graduate to walking in public areas.

Be patient

Training your dog involves teaching it a completely new language. Think about yourself being instructed in a foreign language. At first you will be frustrated because it sounds like gibberish. Be reasonable with your dog, and do not expect too much too quickly. Be patient, have fun, and remember: you are not a failure if you ask for help.

Common mistakes

When training your dog, avoid these common pitfalls:
• Never give excessive praise after releasing your dog from a command: it can overexcite your dog, and teaches it to jump around at the end of training;
• Never train when circumstances mean your dog finds it difficult to concentrate on what you are doing: if it is worried about the presence of other dogs, or more interested in investigating other activities, its mind will not be focused on you;
• Never give a command without ensuring that your dog complies: if you do so, you are actively training your dog to disregard that command;
• Do not try to train several dogs at the same time: it is virtually impossible to be successful.

With the basics of dog obedience mastered, you and your family will discover the joy of living with a happy, well-trained dog.

Behavioural problems

- All dogs develop behavioural problems
- Prevention is easier than cure
- Be sensible with retraining

Dogs do not behave badly because they are spiteful; they don't chew, bark, jump, dig, or destroy to get even. They do these things because they are excited or bored. We make the mistake, because we are an emotionally more complicated species, of assuming our dogs share our deviousness. A dog's life is really quite uncomplicated. Dogs needs physical, social, and mental stimulation; if these needs are not met, behavioural problems can develop.

Eliminate the cause

Many unwanted behaviours are minor and easy to live with, but some are sufficiently antisocial to need changing.

One simple way to do this is to minimize the chance that a problem will happen again. For example, if your dog has raided the rubbish, move the dustbin out of reach. If your dog is finding snacks in the cat litter tray, make the tray inaccessible, or if it is drinking from the toilet, close the lid. If your dog is destructive when left alone, keep it in its crate with a wonderful peanut-butter-filled chew toy.

Understand rewards

Try to understand the reason for your dog's bad behaviour. This is easy when the rewards for a certain behaviour are obvious: if your dog begs at the table, for example, and you notice a family member giving it a titbit. Sometimes, however, the reward is not as obvious. If your dog trembles when it sees another dog, and you pick it up, you are not reassuring your dog, you are rewarding it for trembling.

Destructive behaviour is often a sign of boredom – always provide natural outlets for your dog's physical and mental needs.

Retraining rules

Almost all bad habits can be diminished or corrected by following this basic program:

1️⃣ Go back to basic obedience. Make sure the dog understands the basic commands *(see pp.182–7)*.

2️⃣ Make sure your dog does something for you, such as sitting or lying down, before you give any kind of reward, even a verbal "hello".

3️⃣ Satisfy your dog's natural needs by creating acceptable outlets for natural behaviour.

4️⃣ Eliminate the satisfaction your dog gets from its unacceptable behaviour. Sometimes this will involve mild punishment.

5️⃣ Persevere. Do not expect overnight miracles. Typically, it takes about three weeks to overcome most common behaviour problems.

6️⃣ If you are unsure, or if aggression is involved, get professional help.

Where to get help

Help is available through puppy socialization classes, obedience classes, advanced training groups, residential kennel training, or personal trainers. Your veterinary staff will give advice on what may be appropriate for you and your dog.

If your dog likes to chew shoes, train your family not to leave shoes about, but provide it with a chew toy. If your dog jumps up to say hello, train it to sit when you come home and reward it for sitting rather than disciplining it for jumping. If your dog barks when it hears a noise, train it to fetch and carry: it is difficult to bark effectively when your mouth is filled with a soft toy.

Try automatic correction

Create circumstances where a dog teaches itself to stop doing something:
• Use bitter apple spray, Tabasco sauce, or other safe but disagreeable tastes to prevent it from chewing things you do not want to be chewed;
• Use inexpensive vibration-sensitive alarms for windows, or on beds or the sofa,

if you do not want your dog jumping on these in your absence;
• If you are at home and see your dog doing something you do not want it to do, a squirt from a handily placed water pistol, or a clunk on the floor from a soft-drink can filled with a few coins, can work wonders.

Boredom problems

Chewing, digging, howling and barking, fence jumping, or rhythmically pacing back and forth are all signs of boredom or separation anxiety. This is especially common in rescued dogs or those that have become overly dependent on their owners.

Prevention of boredom *(see over)* is always easier and better than trying to overcome any resulting problems. However, if your dog is displaying

A dog instinctively hunts for food at all times, and if it finds something tasty it will eat it. Train your dog to understand that stealing food from the table is unacceptable behaviour.

Howling and barking problems

The best way to turn off barking is to train your dog to "Speak" on command. This exercise takes time and patience on your part; if you can stick to it, you are a marvellous and dedicated dog owner.

1 Attach your dog's lead to a fence or a post. Stand a few feet away and tease your dog with a toy. When it barks in frustration, give a food treat. Give the command "Speak" the moment it barks, then give the reward. When it consistently barks to the word "Speak" in return for the toy or food, switch to a verbal reward like "Good girl".

Barking dog is rewarded with a toy

Watch body language to anticipate the bark

2 Once your dog understands "Speak", give the command "Quiet" when it is barking and reward it with the toy or treat as soon as it stops. Be patient; this takes time. Eventually switch to verbal rewards at a distance when it responds to your "Quiet" command. Now set up mock departures, giving the "Quiet" command before you leave. Stand outside: if it barks, make a noise, for example by dropping a metal dustbin lid. You want to startle your dog into stopping barking. Return and praise it for being quiet.

When your dog is barking, give the command "Quiet"

As soon as your dog stops barking, give a reward

Pulling on the lead

Pulling on the lead is one of the most common problems experienced by dog owners. Do not attempt to match your strength against your dog's by repeatedly pulling back on the lead. If your dog pulls persistently, retrain it in basic obedience commands (see pp.182–7), and use the following remedial techniques:

1 Retrain walking to heel, but now hold your dog's lead at your left, and slide your left hand down the lead to near its collar, to give you greater control.

Dog is sitting patiently and calmly

2 When the dog pulls, slide your left hand down the lead and pull back firmly. When the dog is in the correct heel position, command the dog to sit. Start to walk again, giving the command "Heel".

Keep the lead short to give greater control

3 If your dog pulls again, give another yank, command it to "Sit", and reward it with a food treat. Repeat the exercise, commanding your dog to "Sit" each time it pulls. Graduate to more distracting environments and circumstances.

Reward your dog with a food treat when it walks quietly without pulling

Preventing boredom

1 Make sure your dog has had physical, mental, and social activity before you leave it alone.

2 Feed your dog just before you go out.

3 Rub your hands on a favourite toy, to leave your scent, and give it to your dog.

4 Leave quietly. Draw the curtains if necessary and leave a radio or television on to mask distracting outdoor noises.

5 Never leave your dog at home alone all day.

6 If you must leave your dog at home alone, get a friend to visit, to play with and exercise your dog. Alternatively, use a dog walker *(see p.179)*.

behavioural problems due to boredom, try the following cures:

• **Destructive chewing:** apply taste deterrents to objects you do not want chewed, but at all times provide exciting chew toys.

• **Digging:** if your dog is a persistent digger, redirect its energy away from the flower beds or lawn, to an acceptable area, such as a sand pit. Chicken wire is also an excellent deterrent to digging.

• **Jumping fences:** for fence jumpers, create obstacles: tin cans strung on a rope about a foot from the fence and three feet off the ground make a nice, noisy, and natural deterrent. Chicken wire on the ground at take-off distance from the fence works well, but make sure the gauge of the wire is too small for your dog's foot to slip through.

Nipping

Overcome this unpleasant habit by training your dog to carry a toy in its mouth; if preoccupied with one job, it is difficult for it to carry out

another. Integrate toy carrying with basic "Sit–Stay" obedience *(see pp.184–5)*.

Excitement problems

Dogs show they are excited by barking and pulling on the lead *(see opposite)*, or jumping up. Try the following if your dog jumps at visitors or you:

• Plan ahead: make sure your dog is on a lead, or in another room, when visitors come into your home;

• Use a positive command, "Sit", rather than a negative one like "Off" or "No";

• Avoid eye contact, and go about your business until all four of its feet are back on the ground;

• Do not raise your voice, wave your arms, or increase its excitement in any other way.

Jumping up is a more serious problem if you have a large dog.

Dominance aggression

Dominance aggression is the most common reason why dogs growl at, or bite, their owners. Its onset may seem sudden, but it is not: your dog will have been assessing your position for some time and decided to challenge. If your dog is aggressive towards you or your family, follow these rules:

1 Avoid physical punishment: it is too provocative and may make matters worse.

2 Use body posture, facial expression, and the tone of your voice to leave your dog in no doubt that you are the leader of the pack.

3 Keep a lead or house line constantly on your dog's collar. Use this to move your dog to temporary (one minute) isolation from the family.

4 Review your relationship with your dog to determine why it thought it could challenge you. Remember, as pack leader, you eat first, and you go first through doorways. It is the little things in life that give signals to your dog.

Aggression problems

There is always a reason for aggression, obvious to the dog but not always as clear to us. Our problem is that we fail to see the warning signs, or if we do, we do nothing about them. Once it develops, aggressive behaviour never disappears on its own; we have to contain it, reduce it, then eliminate it.

If your dog behaves in any of the following ways, it has the potential to become aggressive:
• Growling at you, other people or other animals;
• Showing its teeth to you or your family;
• Snapping when you try to take a toy, bones, or food away;
• Cringing and hiding behind you when visitors approach;
• Barking and running to the door when delivery people arrive;
• Chasing after moving animals;

Possessive aggression

Possessiveness is a behavioural problem that is most often encountered in dominant dogs, but there are also breed predispositions: terriers, for example, are often possessive of food, toys, and rest areas.

1 Train your dog to release a toy on your command: with a tasty treat hidden in one hand, encourage the dog to take the toy.

2 Issue the command "Give", and when the dog releases the toy, reward it by saying "Good dog" and giving the food. Repeat the exercise immediately by giving the toy back to the dog, then commanding "Give" again.

• Nipping at your ankles when playing exuberantly;
• Giving you a glassy-eyed, hard stare that lasts for minutes.

Early learning is vital

While some dogs are born with a greater tendency to become aggressive, problems only occur in homes that wittingly or unwittingly encourage the development of a dog's aggressive potential. Early socializing with the human family, strangers, and other animals and exposure to a range of experiences dramatically reduce the likelihood that a dog will reach its "aggression potential" *(see pp.146–7)*.

Types of aggression

It is important to understand exactly what is going on when a dog shows aggression: biting you because you touched your dog where it hurts, for example, is perfectly justifiable aggression on your dog's part. On the other hand, biting you because you tried to push it off the sofa is a crime. If your dog shows any form of aggression, get immediate professional advice. There are several different forms of aggression, each with its own cause and treatment. These include:

• **Dominance aggression:** this kind of aggression can be towards people *(see opposite)* or other dogs. Aggression between two dogs is more likely to occur when both are relatively equal in age, sex, and size. Your instinct to comfort the underdog only increases the problem. To overcome this problem, determine which is the higher ranking dog, then treat it as such.

• **Territorial aggression:** some dogs are fiercely overprotective: prevent this problem by introducing your dog to regular household visitors when it is young. Talk to your postman and leave some food treats to be put through the letter box with the mail. If your dog is often in the garden, leave a favourite toy or food (in a

weatherproof box) at your gate, with instructions for it to be given to your dog when the gate is opened by a visitor. If you train your dog this way, it will still alert you when someone comes to your house, but will not be compulsively protective of its territory. Use the same principles in your car.

Other forms of aggression

Other common forms of aggression in dogs include:

• Chasing cats and livestock (predatory aggression);
• Biting in response to pain (pain-induced aggression);
• Biting through training (learned aggression);
• Biting when worried or afraid (fear-induced aggression);
• Fighting between males (sex-related aggression).

If your dog behaves aggressively with you, your family, or with other dogs, seek professional help.

Body maintenance

- Train pups to accept grooming
- Develop a grooming routine
- Report abnormalities to your vet

Your dog's coat and skin need regular bathing and brushing, and occasional cutting or clipping. Routine brushing keeps the skin and coat in excellent condition, and at the same time trains you to notice anything out of the ordinary that may indicate a medical problem. Smaller and older dogs need routine nail trimming, while dogs of any age benefit from your caring for their teeth, ears, and eyes.

Dog bathing

Dog hair is naturally self-cleaning, but most dogs benefit from bathing about once a month; longhaired breeds may need more frequent attention. Follow these guidelines for bathing your dog:
- Groom your dog before bathing to remove mats and tangles;
- Use a non-slip rubber mat in the bath to prevent slipping;

- Remove leather collars, but always have another collar on your dog so you can grab it if your dog decides to make a run for it while soaking wet;
- Ensure the water is not too hot: run it first to get the right temperature;
- Put balls of cotton wool in your dog's ears to prevent water from getting in;
- Use a "no-tears" shampoo, or if using any other type, take great care to avoid getting shampoo in the eyes;

Routine bathing keeps a dog's coat clean, but you will also need to wash your dog at other times – after it has rolled in manure, for example.

Clipping a dog

If you have a Poodle, or another breed with constantly growing hair, your dog's coat will need clipping. This is usually necessary every six to eight weeks, although a dog's coat can be clipped more often in summer, and less often in colder weather. If you want to clip your dog's coat yourself, it is best to get one-to-one instruction from an experienced "clipper". However, even if you do not want to try clipping, you should occasionally trim your dog's coat, to prevent tangles.

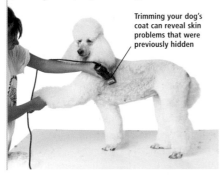

Trimming your dog's coat can reveal skin problems that were previously hidden

Professional groomers

Select a groomer as carefully as you select your vet. Word-of-mouth from other dog owners and veterinary staff is the best starting point. Most groomers can groom, wash, dry, and clip your dog in about four hours. Avoid groomers who want your dog tranquillized: they do not have the "golden touch" with dogs.

• Use a hand-held shower to wet and rinse your dog – if your bath is not equipped with one, get a rubber shower unit that fits on the bath tap;
• Have plenty of towels ready: your dog will want to shake;
• Regular bathing does not get rid of fleas, so if fleas are a problem, use a flea control product that is not washed off by routine bathing.

Coat brushing

A smooth coat like a Boxer's is the easiest to care for: use a rubber brush or a hound glove twice weekly, against the lie of the fur, to remove debris, dirt, and any loose hair. Afterwards, use a chamois cloth, stroking with the lie of the coat, to bring out the natural shine.

A short, thick coat like a Labrador Retriever's needs different tools. A slicker brush has soft, wire bristles and is ideal for removing tangles. Use it twice weekly, followed by a bristle brush to remove any remaining dirt.

If the coat is slightly longer, like that of a Golden Retriever, it needs to be slicker and bristle brushed more frequently; this should preferably be

Essential equipment

The items in your dog's basic grooming kit will vary according to its coat type: if the coat is smooth, for example, a rubber brush is essential to loosen dead skin and dirt; a short coat is easiest to clean with a bristle brush; tangles and mats in longer coats are removed with a metal pin brush and combs. In any coat type, a flea comb is used to remove fleas.

FLEA COMB   RUBBER BRUSH

TWO-SIDED BRUSH
(PIN AND BRISTLE)

WIDE-TOOTHED COMB

FINE-TOOTHED COMB

daily, for short periods, to get your dog used to this type of attention. Use a wide-toothed comb for combing through the feathery hair on the legs and tail. The long hair around the feet, chest, and hind legs needs occasional trimming with scissors.

Rough Collies and Shetland Sheepdogs have long coats combined with dense, thick, protective down. This type of deep coat mats easily without thorough grooming. Use a slicker brush to gently untangle matted hair and remove any knots or dirt.

Some breeds, such as the Yorkshire Terrier, have long, silky coats, but no protective undercoat. Take extra care when grooming these breeds – without insulating downy hair, it is very easy to scratch or irritate the skin. Yorkies should be brushed with a slicker brush, then combed daily, especially behind the ears, to prevent mats from forming.

Material in hair
All types of material can become stuck in a dog's hair. Never use paint or tar remover to remove substances. If your dog has chewing gum stuck in its coat, use scissors to cut out the gum and

stuck hair. Plant burrs are easiest to remove if you spray on a little cooking oil. Corn starch powder can help to untangle mats in your dog's coat, because it acts as a dry lubricant.

The rest of the body
Routine body maintenance keeps your dog in good physical condition, saves you avoidable veterinary expenses, and and strengthens the bond between your dog and you. Through routine examination, you will notice problems before they become serious. Dogs that are used to letting their owners carry out routine maintenance are far easier for a vet to examine and treat.

Nail cutters
While heavy dogs usually wear down their nails, lightweight dogs need theirs trimmed. The tip of the nail consists only of keratin, but the rest contains the "quick" – living, sensitive tissue. If you cut into the quick, this is very painful for your dog, and may cause bleeding. In translucent nails it is easy to see the quick, but most dogs have darker nails, making clipping more problematic. If in doubt, ask your groomer or veterinary staff to show you where to clip your dog's nails. Blood-stopping powder is available from pet shops in case of accidents, although using powdered corn starch works equally well.

Prevent bad breath
Bad breath usually means a tooth and gum problem – the most common reason that dogs are taken to the vet. From puppyhood, train your dog that tooth brushing is simply part of life's routine (*see opposite*). Check your dog's

Trim your dog's nails with a guillotine-type clipper – this gives a cleaner cut with less pressure.

Nails are softer when wet, so trim your dog's nails after a bath

Checking anal sacs

Anal sacs are scent sacs found on either side of the anus. When these are full, they feel like single, hard grapes under the skin, and your dog may lick or drag its rear along the ground. If your dog's anal sacs are full, they must be emptied. Wearing a disposable glove and holding a tissue, place your thumb and forefinger on either side of the anus and squeeze gently. If you are unsure about doing this or notice anything unusual, consult your vet.

Check your dog's anal sacs during routine grooming

Brushing your dog's teeth

With your dog in a comfortable position, let it smell a food treat, then raise its upper lip and brush the tooth–gum margin of the visible teeth using a small toothbrush and dog toothpaste. If the dog does not squirm, give it the reward. Repeat this exercise daily, each time increasing the time spent and the area of teeth covered until, after about two weeks of training, you are brushing all the teeth, top and bottom and from back to front.

Ask your vet for canine toothpaste

teeth and gums once a week: make sure there is no sign of gum infection or tartar build-up on the teeth, because this can lead to gingivitis, tenderness, and gum disease.

Ear inspections

Check your dog's ears routinely for odour, inflammation, or wax build-up. Floppy-eared dogs, such as Labrador Retrievers, Cocker Spaniels, and Basset Hounds, are more prone to ear problems because of the warm, damp climate in their ears. Do not worry about a little nondescript ear wax – this is a natural form of protection for the ears. If there is abundant wax, use a proprietary wax remover, available from your vet, or simply wipe the inside of the ear with a cotton ball moistened with mineral oil. If wax builds up again within a week, take· your dog to the vet for a checkup.

Ear hair

Hair growing down the ear canal can be a problem in wire-haired breeds, but also Poodles, Shih Tzus, Lhasa Apsos, and Yorkshire Terriers. This hair needs weekly or even daily removal. Grasp a few hairs at a time with your fingernails or with tweezers, and pull them out. Unless the hair is deeply rooted, this is quite easy and not upsetting to your dog, but always give a treat afterwards.

Eye checks

Some breeds develop "sleep" in the corners of their eyes; overnight, mucus forms a small, hard, crusty ball that catches in hair at the corners of the eyes. Often it is easy to pick this off with your fingernails, but if it is firmly adhered, soften it with a cotton ball dipped in luke-warm water. If the eyes and the skin around them do not look normal, consult your vet.

Good nutrition

- Feed a well-balanced diet
- Needs change with age
- Obesity is a common problem

A healthy dog has a nutritious, well-planned diet and produces well-formed, easy to clean-up droppings. There are many different ways to achieve a balanced diet: the easiest is to feed your dog one of the premium foods produced by high quality manufacturers. The alternative is to cook for your dog. Considering that few of us consistently cook a well-balanced meal for ourselves, however, acheiving this for our dogs can be a tall

Tailor your dog's diet to its specific energy needs, and discard any leftover food at the end of the day.

order. If you plan to cook for your dog, make sure you fully understand the basic principles of good nutrition.

A dog's dinner

Dogs are omnivores; they naturally have a mixed diet (see pp.38–9), but if given a choice, they prefer meat to all other types of food. A meat-only diet, however, will eventually lead to a life-threatening calcium deficiency, so commercial dog foods are produced to have a healthy balance of nutrients.

Over the last decade, canine nutritionists have realised that by carefully balancing the type of fibre in dog food, they can encourage healthy digestion. In your dog's intestines there is an elaborate ecosystem of bacteria, responsible for helping to digest food. In fact, these bacteria do even more: some boost your dog's immune system and provide protection from harmful bacteria. The best diets, with carefully balanced fibre content, nourish the good bacteria, and at the same time inhibit the development of the types of bacteria known to be associated with diarrhoea.

Commercial dog foods

Dog food manufacturers generally produce several ranges of food, each with different specifications. Premium products are made to fixed formulas, so the

Dietary needs for active dogs

If your dog works, or spends time outdoors in cold weather, it will have increased energy needs. Fat is the best form of energy in these circumstances. A variety of high calorie diets designed for active dogs are available from pet food manufacturers.

ingredients are always the same. At a lower price level, however, foods are manufactured to set nutritional and quality standards, but from a varying supply of ingredients. This difference is important to realise if you have a dog with fixed taste preferences or if certain foods give your dog an upset stomach.

Reading a food label

Dog food makers always list an analysis of the nutritional content of a food on the label: this usually includes protein, fat, fibre, and moisture levels. However, comparing the amounts of protein, fat, or fibre between prepared dog foods, is slightly more complicated than simply reading the label.

Dog foods vary in the amount of moisture they contain: a canned dog food, for example, may be 80 per cent moisture, and so only 20 per cent dry matter; a dry dog food may be only eight per cent moisture, and so 92 per cent dry matter. The only way to accurately compare basic protein and fat contents of one food with another is to first work out how much of each food is dry matter, and then calculate how much of the dry matter is made up of protein or fat. If you find this difficult, or want to save time, all pet food manufacturers can give you this information via their helplines.

Dry dog food

All-in-one dry food is a convenient way for you to feed your dog, although it

may not necessarily be the best tasting. These foods are cooked under pressure and then dried. Fat is sprayed on the particles for palatability, but because fat can go rancid, dry foods need an added preservative.

Substances called "antioxidants" are excellent preservatives, and these are also good for the dog because they destroy "free radicals" – reactive molecules in the dog's body that damage cell membranes. Vitamin C (ascorbic acid) and vitamin E (tocopherol) are antioxidants commonly used as preservatives.

Wet dog food

Canned food is highly palatable, but it provides no exercise for the teeth and

Speciality foods

Manufacturers such as Iams, Waltham, Hill's, and Purina produce ranges of foods, available through your vet, to nourish dogs with kidney, bladder, heart, liver, bowel, skin, or allergic conditions. These companies also provide veterinary surgeons with a variety of tasty, nourishing convalescing diets for debilitated dogs or for those who have had surgery. The choice is excellent and ever-increasing. As a home-cooked alternative, cooked chicken or fish and rice is excellent for a delicate stomach.

Ensure that even the smallest bones are removed from chicken before giving it to your dog

Your vet can recommend a dry or wet speciality dog food tailored to your dog's medical condition

Vegetarian diets

Dogs can survive on vegetarian diets because they can convert vegetable protein and fat into the ingredients necessary for all bodily functions. This is a path, however, that no dog willingly follows. Vegetarianism is a human ethical decision foisted, perhaps unfairly, on some dogs. If you think it is important that your dog shares your ethical principles about meat-eating, make sure you get professional advice from a canine nutritionist on how to create a balanced diet for your dog.

gums and is prone to contamination if it is not eaten immediately after opening. Heat sterilization and vacuum sealing prevent spoilage of wet dog food, so no preservative is needed. Most canned foods are nutritionally complete on their own.

Home cooking

Home cooking that is balanced for you is probably balanced for a young, healthy dog. Remember, however, that dogs do not chew food like a human, so nutrients that need chewing will pass through undigested. Avoid tofu and other bean products as food sources, especially if you have a deep-chested breed, like a Great Dane or any type of setter. These products stimulate mucus production and increase the risk of stomach bloat – a condition that can be life threatening *(see p.255)*. Be careful with dairy products – they can cause diarrhoea in some dogs *(see p.257)*.

Bones?

Dogs love bones, and like every vet in the country, I have had to open up dogs' bellies to repair the damage bones have caused. Bones are also perhaps the most common cause of fractured teeth. Gnawing on a bone does have some benefit, however, because it massages the gums and scrapes the teeth, but if you plan to give bones to your dog, introduce them as early as possible so that it develops "responsible bone eating" habits. Offer only the hardest bones, such as beef bones, and do not let your dog become possessive over them. As an alternative, try highly compacted biscuits that pups work on for days at a time.

Needs change with age

Your dog's energy needs change throughout its life, increasing the more active it

Chewing bones could damage your dog's teeth, so consider alternatives.

becomes, then decreasing as it reaches its senior years. Contrary to what many pet owners think, older dogs do not benefit from less protein in their diet, but gain from better quality, easier-to-digest protein. They also benefit from increased levels of many vitamins and minerals. Diets formulated for the older dog often have higher levels of antioxidants to boost the immune system and reduce tissue damage, more common in senior years. Dog food manufacturers produce a range of diets appropriate for the age and activity levels of your dog.

Sex and calories are connected

Male and female sex hormones affect metabolism. When these hormones are reduced, through neutering or advancing years, many dogs develop a tendency to become overweight. Weight gain after neutering is extremely simple to prevent: before your dog is neutered, make sure you know its exact weight. After the procedure, reduce your dog's food consumption by a certain amount – perhaps 20 per cent. This should mean that your dog will retain its pre-surgical weight, but if you do this and your dog is losing weight, return to the former meal size.

Eating during pregnancy

Pregnant dogs require very little increase in food until late in their pregnancy. Increase a mother-to-be's food intake by ten per cent during the last four weeks of her nine-week pregnancy. After she gives birth and is lactating, she will need up to three times her normal daily food intake.

Tackling fat

It is not easy to find out the calorie content of commercial dog foods; as a general rule, assume that any food labelled "low calorie" or "light" has 15 to 25 per cent fewer calories than that manufacturer's regular brand. The following guidelines may be helpful if you are trying to reduce the weight of an obese or overweight dog:
• Try to keep an accurate record of what your dog eats – you may be surprised to see how many snacks it is being given throughout the day;
• Feed low-fat, high fibre foods, to lowers calories while retaining bulk;
• If your dog is fit and healthy, increase the amount of exercise it is getting;
• Avoid crash diets: they may only drive your dog's metabolism to be more efficient and fat-storing in the future.

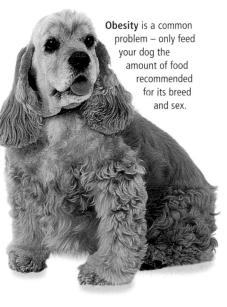

Obesity is a common problem – only feed your dog the amount of food recommended for its breed and sex.

Raw meat – a "natural" diet?

Raw meat is, generally speaking, more hazardous for your dog to eat than cooked meat – there is a risk of bacterial contamination and, in some regions of the world, the possibility of parasites.

New experiences

- Plan ahead for a baby's arrival
- Make travel plans for your dog
- Don't panic if your dog goes missing

During the lifetime of any dog, you may possibly move home, and will certainly take holidays and need to find someone to take care of your buddy. People and other pets will come and go, and nothing worries young dog owners more than the arrival of a new baby in the home. How will your dog react to these changes?

A new baby in the home

Plan ahead for the arrival: cool the intensity of your relationship with your dog, as this will inevitably change with a new baby in the house. Change any sleeping arrangements well before the baby arrives.

When your baby first comes home, let your dog smell the new smells, but try not to change any more of its routines. Set aside time to give your dog the attention it deserves. Never leave your baby and dog unattended. If your dog has even a remote tendency to snap, train it to wear a muzzle in the presence of your baby.

A new dog or cat

When bringing a new cat or dog into your home, restrict your new pet to one room while leaving the resident to go where it wishes. If the newcomer is a kitten or pup, let your resident sniff it while it is sleeping. If your new kitten awakens, hisses, and spits, perfect. You want your dog to respect your cat, and cats are outrageously good at teaching dogs to do this. If the newcomer is a puppy, as far as possible let your resident make all the first moves.

Holiday care

Friends and family are usually the best people to look after your dog while you are on holiday. Try to work out a reciprocal arrangement: you look after their pet when they are away. Professional pet sitters are an expensive alternative. If you plan to use a boarding kennel, always visit in advance. Inspect the facilities and

Your dog's travel crate should be twice as wide as your dog, slightly taller, and longer than the length from its nose to its tail.

What to do if your dog is missing

1 Stay calm. Think sensibly about what your dog may do if separated from you.

2 Carry out an immediate search of the local area, asking people if they have seen your dog.

3 Contact the police, local dog shelter, your vet, and all local veterinary surgeons, giving them a description of your dog and its ID number. Give these people at least two contact numbers for you, ideally your mobile and home phone, or email address. Keep a phone number list of everyone you contact.

4 Photocopy and post flyers to display around the local area, with the words "LOST" and "REWARD" in large letters. A reward is always an effective inducement. Include a picture of your dog on the flyers.

5 When your dog is safely returned, always contact your phone list to give the good news and to thank them for their help.

Car travel with your dog

Your dog should travel in its crate, behind a dog barrier fitted into your car, or on a back seat equipped with a harness attached to the seat belt anchor (below), allowing it to lie down. Stop every two hours for exercise. Carry a water bowl and bottle of water. If travel sickness is a problem, discuss the possibility of medication with your vet. Never, under any circumstances, leave your dog in your car in hot weather or direct sunshine: heatstroke in hot cars is one of the most common avoidable causes of death in dogs.

The best kennels provide a "home from home", with comfortable beds, tasty food, frequent contact with kennel staff, and activities with other dogs.

ask the kennel owner questions. Find out about the daily routines and care that your dog will receive so that you can have peace of mind while on holiday. You need to be organized, however: the best kennels can be booked up months in advance for the busiest seasons.

Travelling with your dog

Your holiday plans may sometimes involve travel by air, sea, or rail. Ensure that your dog's travelling crate is secure, the right size for your dog, and meets the carrier's regulations: your vet or the transportation company will be able to give you accurate guidelines. Make sure that your dog has visible ID, and, preferably, carries a microchip.

If you are flying, whenever possible book direct flights, and try to keep the length of time to be spent travelling to a minimum. Do not give your dog tranquillizers if possible; it may make you feel better, but can increase your dog's risk of accidents. Some airlines allow small dogs to accompany you in the passenger cabin.

Canine activities

- Dogs thrive on physical activity
- Events are sociable for us too
- Choose activity appropriate for both of you

Eating, sleeping, being petted, and having half an hour of outdoor activity each day can be a boring life for many dogs. There are a wide variety of canine activities where your dog can have fun, and you can meet other people with similar interests. Many dogs thrive on challenges, and enjoy obedience, work, or agility competitions; these are also demanding and rewarding for you, because they involve dedication and teamwork. A less physically demanding sociable pastime is showing your dog at dog shows.

Official dog show judges compare each dog in the competition against a set of standard characteristics defined for each breed.

Official and unofficial dog shows

An official show is an event sanctioned by the organization your dog is registered with. Showing usually involves joining a local dog club that is affiliated with the registration body, participating in local events, and working your way up to regional, then national, shows (see p.54–5).

Unofficial dog shows are those not recognized by a major registration organisation. These are more relaxed events that take place wherever there are dog owners. At these events, dogs may compete for the "waggiest tail" or the "sparkliest eyes".

Physical activities

If your dog could choose, these are the activities it probably would want to participate in. You could decide to compete in obedience or working trials, herding or sledding competitions, agility trials, or flyball. In these events, mental and physical abilities are rewarded. By joining an appropriate club, you give your dog the chance to think, and use its senses, reflexes, dexterity, and strength.

Obedience trials

In obedience trials, a dog and its handler work through a series of obedience exercises, such as sitting, heeling, and retrieving. While some

Agility training is an energetic and fun activity suitable for any well-trained dog and its enthusiastic owner.

Your dog leaps over the hurdles while you run along side

Herding and sledding

In sheepdog trials, working sheepdogs compete against each other to perform a set series of herding manoeuvres. The herding dog's ability to move groups of sheep or ducks is tested around a defined course.

Sled racing over a well-maintained snow course is popular in North America and Scandinavia. If snow is not available, dogs compete pulling a sled on wheels, called a gig.

Agility games

In agility trials, dogs compete with each other and against the clock to race through a course that involves weaving, jumping, balancing, and obedience. This is an extremely energetic activity that requires you as well as your dog to be in excellent health.

breeds, the Border Collie for example, excel at obedience, most trials are open to any dog, regardless of breed. All major kennel clubs sanction their own obedience trials.

Working trials

In working trials, dogs use the abilities they were originally bred for. In competition, they retrieve, point or set, herd, race, chase after lures, follow scent trials, or go to ground.

The most popular form of working trials is field work. Pointers, for example, will compete to search and find a bird, then hold a classic "point" while the handler fires a shotgun. Scent hounds and terriers competitively follow scent trails, while retrievers retrieve objects under a variety of circumstances.

Flymouse is a variation of flyball in which the dog catches a soft toy – the "mouse" – rather than a ball.

Flyball

In this fun sport, a dog races down a short course, leaping over a series of hurdles, then steps on a board that launches a tennis ball, which it catches in its mouth. It races back over the hurdles to the starting line. As it arrives, the next dog in the team flies down the course. A second team competes in an adjacent lane, and the fastest team to complete the relay wins.

The dog catches the "mouse" in its jaws as it flies through the air

Pressure on the lever on the box triggers the launch of the "mouse"

FLYMOUSE

CHAPTER FIVE

Health concerns

Everything in life carries an element of risk. Through simple and practical disease and accident prevention you can minimize these dangers and significantly cut your veterinary bills. Ensure that your dog is vaccinated against contagious diseases and protected from common parasites. Be responsible when your dog is near traffic or other dangers, and know what to do if an accident does happen. Make yourself familiar with the clinical signs of general illness and more serious conditions. If you think there is cause for concern, see your vet sooner rather than later; early diagnosis nearly always makes treatment easier and more successful.

Choosing a vet

- Location and convenience are vital
- Visit and ask questions
- You should feel comfortable with the personnel

Vets look after the medical well-being of all animals, from gerbils to giraffes. In urban and suburban areas, most vets restrict themselves to companion animals, and even in a rural agricultural practice there is often one vet who concentrates on pets. These are the people you are most likely to see with your dog. Amongst companion animal vets, some have chosen to focus on one species only – dogs, cats, or horses, for example. These vets are not necessarily "specialists" in the medical sense, but rather individuals who feel most comfortable with one animal.

Your choice of vet should reflect your dog's preferences as well as your own, although some dogs will be apprehensive with any vet.

Make an informed choice

Dog-owning friends and neighbours are the best source of information about local vets. Before committing yourself and your dog, arrange to visit the practice to see its medical facilities. Find out how many vets there are. How likely is it that you will see the same practitioner most of the time? What is their referral policy?

If you are interested in holistic care, ask whether complementary treatments are ever used. Ask to see behind the scenes – the operating area, dog accommodation, and diagnostic facilities. Although the clinic may appear a bit chaotic, it should be clean and well organized.

Facilities and costs

All veterinary practices should have a minimum of examination equipment, X-ray and emergency operating facilities, basic laboratory apparatus, and a post-anaesthesia recovery room. This minimum is necessary to cope with potential urgent cases. Many will also have more

Financial worries should not compromise the medical care that your pet receives. Taking out insurance with an experienced provider, recommended by your vet, will buy you considerable peace of mind. Pet health insurance has been available for more than 25 years. Premiums range from £80–£250 per year depending on the extent of cover you want, your breed of dog, and where you live.

Alternatively, you can act as your own insurer. For each of your dogs, invest a sum equal to an insurance premium in a secure investment. Insurance company figures show that claims are high in the first year, then drop until dogs are about eight years old when claims start to climb as the years advance. If your dog is typical, by the time it is a senior citizen you will have a nest egg tucked away for any unexpected veterinary bills.

Veterinary qualifications

To practise in the UK, a vet must be a member of the Royal College of Veterinary Surgeons, and will have the initials MRCVS or FRCVS after their name. Your vet may also be a "specialist" in a chosen field, having gained a Certificate (Cert.), a Diploma (Dip.), or a Specialist post-graduate qualification. It takes at least two years to gain a Cert., at least four years to gain a Dip., and five to become a Specialist. The more letters you see after a vet's name, the more qualified he or she is in a specific area. Ask your vet what these acronyms mean: Cert SAM, for example, stands for Certificate in Small Animal Medicine.

In the rest of Europe, "European Colleges" grant recognition in specialty areas. For example, the letters "ECVIM" means that a vet is a member of the European College of Veterinary Internal Medicine. You may see these letters in the UK, because when veterinary surgeons move from one country to another they take their advanced qualifications with them.

advanced diagnostic and treatment equipment, which may be reflected in the practice's charges. Every vet should also provide round-the-clock emergency cover. Find out how this is offered. Is there a special number to telephone, and who will answer your call? Does emergency cover rotate through different practices? Does your vet have a good arrangement with an emergency and critical care facility? If so, can they access your dog's medical records, or speak to your vet when they need to?

Ethical policies

Many vets, including myself, will not crop ears or dock tails – amputations that have no purpose or value for pet dogs. It is important to find out whether you and your vet share the same opinions because he or she could be faced with making agonizing, and possibly even life-and-death decisions on your dog's behalf. If you and your vet understand one another, those decisions are easier to make.

Specialist practices may have expensive state-of-the-art diagnostic and treatment technology; this is usually reflected in higher charges.

Examining your dog

■ Train your dog to be examined
■ Carry out routine examinations at home
■ Keep accurate records of your dog's weight

Routine home examination of your dog can reveal problems early, when they are easiest to treat. Regular, weekly sessions will also train your dog to submit to, and even enjoy, the process; it is far easier for a vet to make a diagnosis on a dog that willingly allows itself to be examined.

Do not attempt to take on too much in each session: examine just one area, then reward your dog with praise, petting, and treats.

Appearance and mobility

Your dog's general appearance is a good indicator of its health. The coat should retain its natural, rich appearance: increased dullness and lack of sheen can indicate a skin problem, such as parasites or infection, or may signal disease elsewhere in the body. Any of the following symptoms warrants seeing your vet the same day:
• Difficulty getting up, down, or getting comfortable;
• Staggering, falling over, walking in circles, or difficulty walking in a straight line;
• Overreacting to light, sound, or touch;
• Head tilted to one side;
• Unexpected restlessness;
• Bloated belly;
• Unusual chest movements;
• Muscle spasms;
• Any acute body swelling;
• Crying, yelping, or moaning.

What your dog's temperature means

°F	°C	CAUSE AND ACTION
over 106	over 41	Heatstroke: cool down immediately and get urgent veterinary attention.
105	40.6	Dangerous: seek same day veterinary attention.
104	40	High fever: seek same day veterinary advice.
103	39.4	Moderate fever: telephone your vet for advice.
102	38.9	Normal.
101	38.3	Normal.
100	37.8	Normal.
99	37.2	Sub-normal: seek same day veterinary advice.
under 98	under 36.7	Hypothermia: keep the dog warm and get urgent veterinary attention.

Taking your dog's temperature

A dog's normal body temperature ranges between 100.5°F (38.1°C) and 102.5°F (39.2°C), though it may rise with exercise or excitement. When taking a dog's temperature using a glass thermometer, first shake it down and lubricate with water-soluble jelly. Insert the thermometer about 2.5 cm (one inch) into your dog's rectum and hold in position for 90 seconds. Remove, wipe clean, and read. Digital rectal or ear thermometers are simpler to use. Never try to take a dog's temperature by mouth, or if the dog resents it.

Monitor your dog's weight

Weight changes are always significant. If you notice that your dog has suddenly gained or lost weight, consult your vet immediately. Changes are easy to spot if you record your dog's weight on a regular basis. To weigh a small or medium-sized breed, pick up your dog and weigh yourself on bathroom scales; subtract your own weight to calculate your dog's. If you own a larger individual, visit your veterinary clinic every few months to weigh your dog on their scales.

Examining the head

Changes in a dog's eyes and nose can signal more complex diseases elsewhere in the body. Routine checks can identify problems early.

① Check your dog's eyes for redness, discharge, cloudiness, or obvious injuries. Dilated pupils in bright light mean fear, pain, excitement, or shock.

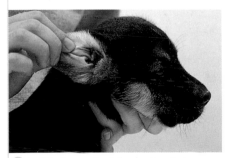

② Look in the ears for inflammation, discharge, excess wax, or physical damage. Check the skin on the ear flaps for abnormalities. The nose should be cool and wet with no sign of discharge from either nostril. Examine the lips, especially the lip folds. There should be no inflammation or unpleasant odour. Open your dog's mouth. The gums should be a healthy pink. Check the roof of the mouth: sticks may become lodged between the teeth.

Examining the body, skin, and coat

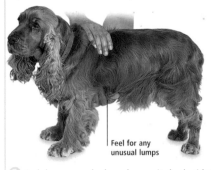

Swollen lymph nodes can signal infection in the head and neck

Look out for changes in the lustre of the coat

① Run your hands over the head, cheeks, jaws, and throat. Gently turn your dog's head left, right, up, and down. Resistance can mean pain.

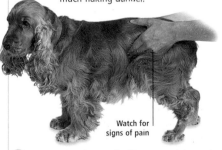

Feel for any unusual lumps

② Feel down your dog's neck, over its back, sides, and chest. Any stickiness might indicate a site of skin infection or a penetrating injury. Frequently part the hair to examine the skin which should look "quiet", without inflammation or too much flaking dander.

Watch for signs of pain

③ Run your hands over the hips, around the groin, and down each limb, feeling the joints for swelling or excess heat. Examine the feet, checking the pads for damage, and the length of the nails. Gently lift the tail and inspect the anus, which should be perfectly clean and odour free. Examine the genitals for any discharge or inflammation.

Practical prevention

■ Inoculate against infectious diseases
■ Some vaccines are better than others
■ Give boosters according to local risks

Preventing problems is better and cheaper than seeing your vet when your dog is in distress. By "problems", I mean infectious diseases, internal and external parasites, physical accidents, unwanted pregnancies, and diseases that might spread from your dog to you, or vice versa.

Vaccination is the most important measure you can take to ensure your dog's good health, but the subject has rightly become a topic of intense discussion. My advice is to read the following and then, with your vet, develop an appropriate inoculation schedule for your dog.

How vaccinations work

A vaccine contains disease-causing bacteria or viruses (or parts of them) that have been modified so that they no longer make your dog ill. Crucially, however, they retain the ability to "activate" the body's immune system, preparing it to fight off future infection. When a dog is vaccinated, against distemper, for example, some of its white blood cells "learn" to produce antibodies – complex chemicals that neutralize the distemper virus.

Vaccinations may be given as single inoculations, or as multivalent vaccines, where a single shot protects against a variety of diseases. The duration of the protection afforded by vaccines is largely unknown, with the exception of

Common infections and diseases	
DISEASE	CLINICAL SIGNS
Parvovirus	Severe vomiting and diarrhoea, possibly with blood; lethargy and listlessness; dehydration. Parvovirus can be fatal if untreated.
Distemper	Coughing; inflammation and discharge from the eyes; vomiting and diarrhoea; fever and dehydration; later neurological changes including seizures. Distemper can be fatal even if treated promptly.
Hepatitis	Vomiting and diarrhoea; dehydration; jaundice. Hepatitis can be fatal if not treated promptly.`
Leptospirosis	Lethargy; loss of appetite; kidney problems; liver problems. Leptospirosis is transmitted in rat urine and is often contracted from swimming in contaminated water. It can be transmitted to people.
Bordetella (canine cough)	Hacking, dry, non-productive cough; gagging; copious phlegm. This bacterial infection is particularly debilitating in breeds with delicate windpipes and in the elderly.
Parainfluenza	Coughing; retching; fever. This mildly debilitating infection increases a dog's risk of pneumonia.
Rabies	Increased salivating; increased aggression; increased docility; paralysis; lameness. The signs of rabies vary enormously. The disease is invariably fatal and highly contagious to people.

the rabies vaccine, which is known to be effective for a minimum of two or three years. Because no one knows how long protection lasts, many manufacturers and veterinary associations recommend annual boosters to keep immunity reliably high. However, some veterinary schools

Core vaccinations		
DISEASE	PUPPY SHOTS	ADULT BOOSTERS
Parvovirus	At 8 weeks, then 10 or 12 weeks, depending on manufacturer's advice.	Booster at 15 months then every two years.
Distemper	At 8 weeks, then 10 or 12 weeks.	Booster at 15 months then every three years.
Hepatitis/ Adenovirus	At 8 weeks, then 10 or 12 weeks.	Booster at 15 months then every three years.
Rabies	Only necessary if going abroad. At 12 weeks or over if mother inoculated; at 8 weeks or over if not.	Every two or three years.
Additional vaccinations		
Parainfluenza	At 8 weeks, then 10 or 12 weeks, depending on manufacturer's advice.	Booster at 15 months then every two years.
Leptospirosis	At 8 weeks, then 10 or 12 weeks, depending on manufacturer's advice.	Booster at 15 months then yearly.
Bordetella (canine cough)	At least one week before risk of exposure.	Booster at 9 months if risk continues.

and practitioners employ a three-year re-booster schedule. This schedule is based on the realization that immunization to viruses may persist for years or even throughout the life of the dog. They claim that reducing the frequency of vaccination may help reduce some immune system problems.

Protection plan

There is no general rule that dictates which vaccinations your dog will receive, but all puppies should begin a course of "core" vaccinations as soon as possible after eight weeks of age (see above). The youngsters should not be put at risk until fully protected. If your dog is over 12 weeks of age and has an uncertain vaccination history, it is best to vaccinate as you would do for a puppy, although, depending on the manufacturer, fewer injections may be needed.

Animals can occasionally react to vaccinations. These reactions are usually mild and short-lived, and may include muscular aches, mild fever, and drowsiness. Very rarely, there may be a more severe reaction, the most common side effects being vomiting, swelling of the face, and hives. In these cases, seek immediate advice from your veterinary surgeon.

Local knowledge

The risks to your dog will vary depending on where you live, so it is important that you discuss with your vet the core diseases against which your dog should be protected, and the frequency with which booster vaccinations need to be given.

Each patient is routinely given a clinical examination before vaccination.

Parasite control

- Get advice from your vet
- Regularly treat your dog and its environment
- Some alternative treatments work well

Dogs suffer from a variety of internal and external parasites. Regular grooming will help you spot early signs of infestation. Even some internal parasites leave telltale signs on the fur and skin. Particular vigilance is needed with puppies, which can inherit parasites from their mothers, and in warm weather when parasite populations explode, making all dogs more prone to attack.

Ask the vet

Q: How frequently should a dog be wormed?
A: Pups should be wormed for roundworms every three months until one year of age. Once yearly thereafter is fine in most areas except in specific circumstances. Your vet will advise you if there are additional risk factors for your area. Bitches should be wormed after each season, and during pregnancy, on the advice of your vet. You should also discuss extra worming with your vet if your dog has been on a course of corticosteroids, as this may have affected its immune system.

Internal parasites

TYPE	MEANS OF INFECTION	DIAGNOSIS AND TREATMENT
Roundworms (common)	Pups can pick up these worms from their mothers before birth, or from suckling on the mother's contaminated skin.	Severely affected pups are pot-bellied. Pups from 14 days of age and pregnant mothers are wormed routinely using products such as fenbendazole.
Tapeworms (common)	The most common tapeworm (Dipylidium caninum) is picked up by eating an infected flea. Other tapeworms can be contracted from uncooked offal from a variety of livestock, but especially sheep.	Tapeworms rarely cause signs of disease in dogs. The most common sign of infection is dried tapeworm segments that look like grains of rice in the hair around the anus. Worm with praziquantel. Avoid access to animal carcasses or feeding uncooked offal.
Hookworms (uncommon)	One species (Uncinaria) occurs in colder climates and is picked up when dogs lick material contaminated by worm eggs. Another species (Ancylostoma) occurs in warm climates and is also contracted through mother's milk or by larvae burrowing through the skin.	Weight loss, diarrhoea, blood in the droppings, or skin inflammation, especially around the paws or belly, can indicate infection. To treat, mother and pups are wormed, the environment is cleaned and clinical conditions, such as anaemia, are corrected. Worm with fenbendazole.
Whipworms (uncommon)	Worm eggs build up in the environment where they may survive for years in shaded areas. Eggs are accidentally eaten by dogs. They mature into tiny adult worms that cause severe damage to the intestines.	Signs of infection include diarrhoea, often very smelly and tarry with dark blood. In severe cases, the coat is dull and a dog loses weight and may have abdominal pain. To treat, the environment is cleaned and all dogs wormed. Get veterinary assistance.
Giardia (common)	A microscopic, single-celled parasite, picked up from contaminated water. This is an underdiagnosed cause of diarrhoea in dogs.	Diarrhoea, possibly with blood and abdominal pain is a sign of infection. Treat all water while hiking. Give fenbendazole or veterinary recommended treatment.
Heartworms (common in many parts of Europe, but not UK)	Eggs are passed on to a dog by mosquito bites. These mature into large worms that reside in the heart.	Coughing and debility do not occur until disease is well advanced. Dogs that live outdoors have a higher risk of infection. Prevent, using selamectin or ivermectin, or treat following your vet's advice.

Internal parasites

Dogs have internal parasites ranging in size from microscopic single-celled *Giardia* to grotesquely long tapeworms. Fortunately, there are effective, safe, and convenient worming medications available from your vet that prevent or eliminate virtually all dog worms.

Fleas in the home

Fleas are the most common external parasites. They leave their eggs and larvae in carpets, which must be treated to prevent reinfection of your dog. Professional sodium borate, tetraborate, or polyborate carpet treatments reliably destroy flea eggs. Do not use laundry grade borax as it may cause eye, respiratory, or kidney problems.

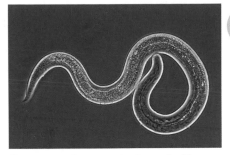

Toxocara **roundworms** pose a human health hazard. Their eggs can be passed to us through contaminated dog faeces.

Over-the-counter remedies

Some parasite control products are very effective while others – perhaps the majority – are older and less efficient. Always seek your vet's advice on the efficacy of over-the-counter products.

External parasites

TYPE	MEANS OF INFECTION	DIAGNOSIS AND TREATMENT
Fleas	Fleas are activated by body heat, vibration, and dog odours. Dormant larvae "come alive", mature into fleas, then hop on your dog for a blood meal. They spend the rest of the time making baby fleas. Fleas are picked up from the dog's environment as well as from other animals.	Fleas cause itchiness in most dogs *(see p.230)*. Look for fleas or flea dirt, shiny specks on the skin, especially over the rump. Prevent or treat with effective, safe medications. Always treat the environment as well as all dogs and cats. Use products that prevent the flea lifecycle completing or safe spray or "spot-on" substances that kill fleas.
Ticks	Ticks wait in long grass. A shadow, vibration, or even a change in temperature signals a meal has arrived. The tick attaches to the dog, burrows its mouth into the skin and sucks a meal until it bloats with blood and drops off. Ticks can carry a range of diseases including Lyme disease, *Babesia*, and *Ehrlichia*.	Ticks swell enormously and are easily seen when engorged. Apply alcohol to the tick to kill it. Then, using tweezers, twist it at its root in the skin to corkscrew it out. Just pulling may leave the mouthpiece and lead to infection. Prevent ticks by using a recommended product. Avoid squeezing ticks, as this releases more "poison" into the dog.
Mites	Ear mites are contracted from another dog, usually the mother, and are most active at night.	Dogs with ear mites produce wax and debris in their itchy ears. Treat with a veterinary ear drop or lotion.
	Demodex mites are inherited from mother. They cause problems in dogs with weak immunity.	Demodex often causes hair loss without itching. Your vet will dispense a prescription treatment.
	Sarcoptic mites are acquired from another dog, fox, coyote, or wolf. The mite tunnels into the skin, causing a skin disease called scabies.	Scabies is intensely itchy, often affecting the ear tips and elbows. It responds to selamectin and other veterinary treatments.
	Cheyletiella mites are most commonly a puppy problem, inherited from the mother.	These mites cause a thick dandruff over the back, often with no itchiness. They are easily killed with anti-flea treatments.
Lice	Dog lice are contracted in unhygienic environments such as puppy farms. The lice leave their eggs, called "nits", glued to the dog's hair.	Lice cause itchiness and, like fleas, if an infestation is intense they cause blood loss and anaemia. Lice are destroyed by many effective anti-flea treatments.

Responsible ownership
■ Prevent unwanted pregnancies
■ Prevent diseases transmissible to us
■ Prevent road traffic accidents

As dog owners, we not only have responsibilities to our dogs, but also to our families and the communities we live in. It is not difficult to behave in a sensible manner, keeping a dog on its lead to prevent road traffic accidents and neutering our pets to avoid unwanted pregnancies and the problems that accompany both male and female sex-hormone-induced behaviour. It is equally important to be aware of the limited range of diseases that dogs can transmit to us.

Dog bites

Dog bite injuries are, overwhelmingly, the most common condition that we suffer from as a result of contact with dogs. In the United States alone, between one and two million people are bitten by dogs each year. Most are children, with boys being more likely to be bitten than girls. Fortunately, most bites are not classified as serious, and fewer than five per cent become infected. In most dog bites that do become infected, the *Pasteurella* bacterium is involved.

Tetanus is rare in dogs, but can be transmitted to humans in deep bites.

Neutering and behaviour

Breeding – the natural consequence of sexual activity – is out of the question for most dogs, and lack of fulfilment can lead to social problems and destructive behaviour. Neutering can make life easier both for dogs and their owners. Neutered female dogs no longer experience twice-yearly heat cycles or unwanted pregnancies, and escape the mood swings associated with hormone production. Neutered male dogs wander less, are more responsive, and empty their bladders because they are full, rather than to leave scent messages for other males. And while they retain their territorial guarding behaviour, neutered males are less likely to indulge in aggressive behaviour with other male dogs.

Neutering has only a few potential drawbacks. The most common is weight gain – affecting one in three neutered dogs – but this can readily be controlled by changes to a dog's diet. Occasionally, a male dog's odour changes and other males try to sexually mount him. In even rarer circumstances, neutering can lead to hormone-related urinary incontinence. Neutering has little effect on the behaviour of female dogs, because they are only hormonally active during their twice-yearly heat cycles. However, in rare cases, neutering can trigger urinary incontinence in predisposed females.

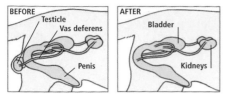

Male dogs can be neutered at any time. Under general anaesthetic, a small incision is made in the scrotum, through which the testicles are removed.

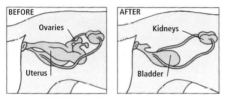

Female dogs should be neutered just before their first season, if physically mature. Both the ovaries and uterus are removed under general anaesthetic.

Transmissible dog diseases

A disease that can be passed to humans by dogs, or other animals, is called a zoonosis. Although these conditions are always of concern, almost all are rare. Dog owners are theoretically at risk of contracting the following:
• **Lyme disease:** ticks can transmit several infections to dog owners. The most common causes Lyme disease, which can result in enlarged lymph glands, joint inflammation, and pain.
• **Rabies:** this is the most dangerous disease that can be transmitted by dogs. In regions where rabies is endemic, humans are at risk if bitten by any dog that has not been vaccinated. Once the disease is fully established, in dogs and in humans, there is no cure.
• **Migrating roundworms (toxocariasis or visceral larva migrans):** canine roundworms are a potential human health hazard. If a person accidentally swallows roundworm eggs, the resulting larvae migrate through the body. This can cause blurred vision if

an eye is affected, and in some children, may trigger an allergic response. Toxocariasis should not be confused with an infection in cats called toxoplasmosis or "toxo" – a disease that can cause brain damage and blindness to an unborn child if contracted by a woman during the first trimester of her pregnancy.
• **Hydatid disease (echinococcosis):** if a dog eats raw, infected sheep offal, it can pick up hydatid tapeworm and pass this nasty parasite to humans. Once contracted, by dogs or by us, this can be an untreatable disease. In areas where this disease is present, precautions should be taken to prevent it: dogs should be wormed every six weeks, and prevented from eating raw offal. Children should be taught never to play with untreated dogs.
• **Ringworm:** this superficial fungal infection causes circular skin lesions in humans. It is most commonly carried by Persian cats, but can also be carried and transmitted by dogs. Affected dogs are treated with topical antifungal medication combined with oral antibiotics *(see also p.233)*.

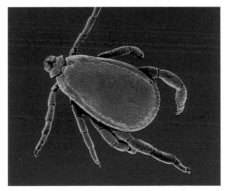

Sheep and deer ticks can jump into your dog's fur, and then on to you. Ticks can carry a range of bacteria, some of which can cause disease in us.

Giving medicines

- Be fast and efficient
- Use bribery when possible
- Always complete full treatments

Giving a pill

Drop the pill as far as possible into your dog's mouth, over the hump of the tongue

1 Command your dog to sit. Open its mouth with one hand and, holding its head upwards, drop the tablet into the back of its throat.

Gently stroke your dog's throat until it swallows

2 Hold your dog's head up slightly, close its mouth and massage its throat. When it swallows and licks its lips, you know the pill has gone down. Praise your dog for good behaviour.

The simplest way to give medicine to your dog is to hide it in food. Hollow dog treats – made exactly for this purpose – are commercially available, but hiding a tablet in a piece of meat or bread, especially if coated with peanut butter, works just as well. Always check with your vet first, however, since some foods should not be given with certain types of medicine.

If these sneaky methods do not work with your dog, you will have to give the pill directly by mouth. Do not try this if you think your dog may bite. If you have a boisterous dog, you may need to hold it between your legs, with your knees behind its shoulders.

If giving the pill directly proves impossible – which it can be, especially with some smaller breeds – contact your vet: the medication may be available in liquid form, and can be syringed into your dog's mouth.

Giving liquid medicines

Administering liquids requires a different technique to giving a pill:
- Hold the upper jaw as you would for giving a pill, but keep the head level, rather than tilting it upwards;
- Tip or squirt the medicine into the side of the mouth between the teeth, never into the back the throat, because it could go down the windpipe;
- Close your dog's mouth and rub its throat until it swallows.

Applying ear medicines

No sensible dog enjoys being treated with ear drops or ointment. Try to make the procedure as non-threatening and as comfortable as possible. Before you start, roll the tube of ointment or drops in your hands to warm the cold medication.

1 Clean away excess wax from under the ear flap, especially from the hole at the bottom, which is the opening of the ear canal.

2 Holding the head still, insert the nozzle into the ear hole, pointing the tip of the nozzle towards the tip of the nose. Squeeze the bottle gently.

3 Drop the ear flap back into position and, without letting your dog shake its head, gently massage the area below the ear canal opening.

Eye medicines

Certain conditions may require you to administer medicines into a dog's eyes. To apply eye drops:

• Remove any sticky eye discharge from the eye and surrounding skin using a cotton pad soaked in warm water or eye wash solution;

• Hold your dog gently with one hand, and, with the other, bring the drops or ointment towards its eye from behind;

• Squeeze the medicine into the eye from above, making sure that the container does not touch the eye;

• After applying ointment, hold the eye closed for a few seconds – your dog's body temperature will warm the ointment, helping it to disperse.

Giving an injection

In certain circumstances, you may need to give injections at home. Giving injections should only be attempted after discussing the procedure fully with your vet. Although it sounds daunting, giving an injection is quite straightforward – simpler in many ways than giving medicines by mouth. To give an injection to your dog, follow these steps:

• Draw the medicine into the syringe, tap it until any air bubbles rise to the top, and then expel the air by squeezing the syringe until the first drop of medicine emerges from the needle;

• Hold your dog and, while speaking calmly to it, grasp the relatively insensitive fold of skin on the neck between the shoulder blades;

• Insert the needle through the skin into the tissue just underneath, but above the underlying muscle;

• Carefully expel the contents of the syringe, and remove the needle.

When accidents happen

- Stay calm
- Protect yourself first, then attend to your dog
- Monitor your dog's vital signs

In the unlikely event that your dog is seriously injured, your prompt action could save its life. First assess the situation: you may need to move the dog if it is still at risk, making sure you do not put yourself in danger. Restrain your dog, and check its heart and breathing: if these vital systems have failed, you will need to perform artificial respiration or heart massage. Check carefully for signs of shock (see p.225). If all of these systems are in order, arrange for care for physical injuries such as lacerations or broken bones. Always have an injured dog examined as soon as possible by a vet: a dog may appear normal after an accident but may have potentially life-threatening internal injuries.

Shock is a lethal, hidden danger. After an accident, check your dog for signs of shock, such as pale gums, even if it appears unharmed.

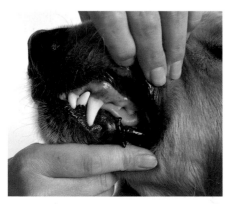

Accident procedures

In the event of an accident, follow these simple guidelines:

1 Calmly approach the dog. Talk to it reassuringly and avoid intimidating eye contact. Watch how it responds to you, and check its expression to determine how much pain your dog is in and how frightened it is.

2 Stroke the relaxed dog under its chin, and then slip a lead around its neck. If a dog lead is not available, improvise with a tie or belt looped over the dog's neck.

3 If the dog is large, wrap your arm as far as possible around the neck, leaving your other hand free to examine the dog. With small dogs, gently but firmly grip the muzzle. Apply a little pressure against the dog's body with the elbow of your free hand while you carry out your examination.

4 An injured dog is likely to be frightened and irrritable. To prevent injuries to yourself and others in attendance, it is advisable to apply a muzzle. A simple muzzle can be improvised at the scene of the accident from a length of gauze or other strong material. Do not muzzle a dog that is having difficulty breathing.

Monitor breathing

Check that an injured dog is breathing by watching for the movement of its chest. If the dog has stopped breathing, artificial respiration should be performed immediately (see p.223).

Monitor the breathing of an injured dog until it can be seen by a vet – an increased rate can indicate pain, shock, or lung and heart problems. Dogs will normally breathe in and out between 20 and 30 times per minute, but this

Improvising a muzzle

You should muzzle an injured dog if it looks frightened or has an obvious painful injury. Use gauze bandage, a tie, torn cotton sheet, or other soft material. Only use rope or other materials that may injure the dog in extreme emergencies.

① To improvise a muzzle, you need a 50–75 cm (2–3 ft) length of material. Make a loop large enough to fit over the dog's muzzle. Reassure your dog as you quickly slip the loop over the muzzle, and tighten. Do not tie a knot.

② Cross the tie under the muzzle and wrap behind the dog's ears. Tie a secure bow. If the dog is short-muzzled or very small, wrap a towel around its neck – this can be secured with a pin while you proceed with your examination.

varies between breeds. When assessing your dog, it is important to distinguish between breathing and panting. Panting – the natural way for your dog to eliminate excess heat – will increase with exercise, anxiety, and pain. To ensure that you monitor breathing rather than panting, watch the rise and fall of your dog's chest.

Check heart rate

A dog's normal heart rate can vary from 50 beats per minute in large breeds, to 160 beats per minute in small individuals, and up to 200 times a minute in a puppy. If your dog has been involved in an accident, monitor its heart rate carefully – an increased rate could indicate fever, pain, heart conditions, or the first stages of shock.

If a dog is unconscious, determine if the heart is beating *(see p.222)*; if it is not, your immediate priority is CPR *(see p.223)*. If it is, monitor the rate: on a large dog, press the fingers of your hand firmly against the left side of the chest just behind the elbow. On smaller dogs, grasp the chest on both sides, just behind the elbows, and squeeze gently until you feel heartbeats. This may be difficult to do on fat dogs. Alternatively, feel for a pulse by placing your fingers inside the hind leg where it meets the groin; a large artery passes this point close to the surface of the skin.

Clear the airway

If an injured dog is unconscious but breathing, straighten its neck, open its mouth to remove any debris, and gently pull the tongue forward. This is most important in breeds with flat faces, in which the tongue can obstruct the dog's breathing.

Life-saving first aid

- Think ABC – Airway, Breathing, Circulation
- Give first aid then get professional help
- Never underestimate shock

Brain cells have an enormous need for oxygen; if they are deprived, even for a few minutes, they are quickly damaged and can die completely. If a dog's heart has stopped beating, oxygen is no longer being supplied to the brain. The heart must be restarted within a few minutes if a dog is to survive.

If you act quickly you can save a dog's life: giving heart massage can restart a stopped heart, and artificial respiration can transfer the oxygen you breathe out into your dog's lungs, until it starts breathing again. The combination of heart massage and artificial respiration is known as cardiopulmonary resuscitation or CPR.

Life-threatening situations
CPR may be needed in any of the following circumstances:
- Blood loss;
- Choking;
- Concussion;
- Diabetic coma;
- Electric shock;
- Heart failure;
- Near-drowning;
- Poisoning;
- Shock;
- Smoke inhalation.

When to give CPR
If your dog is unconscious, quickly assess whether the heart is still beating *(see below)*. If it has stopped, CPR

Know your ABC
In case of accidents, it's as easy as ABC to remember what you should check for in your dog. **A** is for airway: Is the airway open? If not, clear any debris and pull the tongue forward. **B** is for breathing: Is the dog breathing? If not, give artificial respiration *(see opposite)*. **C** is for circulation: Is there a heartbeat or pulse? If not, give heart massage *(see opposite)*.

should be performed immediately *(see opposite)*. If the heart is beating but the dog is not breathing, give artificial respiration *(see opposite)*.

How to check if the heart is beating
Only give heart massage if your dog's heart is not beating. There are several ways to check if the heart has stopped. Feel or listen for a heartbeat or pulse. Check the eyes: they dilate when the heart is no longer beating. Check the gums: if, when you press your finger against normal pink gums, they blanch then return to pink, the heart is still beating. If the gums do not refill with blood, the heart has stopped.

How to check if a dog is breathing
Artificial respiration should only be performed if a dog is not breathing. An unconscious dog sometimes breathes so gently it is difficult to see. If you are not sure, hold a mirror close to your dog's nose and look for condensation: this is visible either as fogging or tiny water

Giving artificial respiration

If a dog has stopped breathing, but its heart is still beating, give artificial respiration until the dog starts breathing again or until veterinary help arrives.

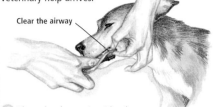

Clear the airway

① Place the dog on its side, clear any debris from its nose and mouth and pull the tongue forward. Close its mouth and, with the neck in a straight line, place your mouth over the dog's nose and blow in until you see the chest expand. If you find this offensive, use your hand to form an airtight cylinder between your mouth and the dog's nose, and blow through this.

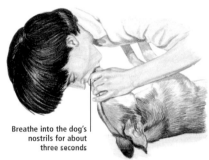

Breathe into the dog's nostrils for about three seconds

② Take your mouth away. The dog's lungs will naturally deflate. Repeat this procedure 10 to 20 times a minute until it breathes on its own.

Keep checking for a heartbeat

③ Check the pulse every 15 seconds to ensure the heart is still beating. If it stops, integrate heart massage with artificial respiration *(see right)*. Get emergency veterinary help as soon as possible.

Giving CPR

CPR is the combination of heart massage and artificial respiration. If you have a medium or large dog, use the procedure below; you will need a different technique if your dog is small *(see over)*. Do not worry about bruising a rib or applying too much pressure when giving heart massage to a large dog – this is a life-or-death situation.

① If a dog is not breathing, press your ear firmly to its chest: if the heart is still beating, start to give artificial respiration *(see left)*. If you cannot hear the heart, start to give heart massage immediately.

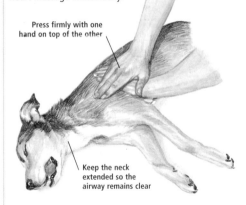

Press firmly with one hand on top of the other

Keep the neck extended so the airway remains clear

② Place the dog on its side, if possible with its head lower than the rest of its body. Put the heel of one hand on the dog's chest just behind its left elbow, then the heel of the other on your first hand. Press downward and forward at a rate of 100 times a minute, pushing towards the neck.

③ After 15 seconds of heart massage, give artificial respiration *(see left)* for 10 seconds. Continue alternating until a pulse returns, then give artificial respiration alone. If two people are present, one gives heart massage for five seconds, then the other a breath of artificial respiration. Seek immediate emergency veterinary attention.

droplets on the surface of the mirror. If this is present, your dog is breathing. Alternatively, hold a small piece of tissue or cotton wool in front of the dog's nostrils and watch carefully – any movement indicates shallow breathing.

CPR for small dogs

If you have a small dog, you will need to use a slightly different technique to perform CPR:
• Place your dog on its side, if possible with the head lower than the rest of its body. Grasp its chest, behind the elbows, between your fingers and thumb. Support the dog's back with your other hand.
• Squeeze firmly, compressing the rib cage, squeezing up towards the neck; repeat this action using quick, firm pumps at a rate of 120 times a minute.
• After 15 seconds of heart massage, give artificial respiration for 10 seconds. Continue alternating until a pulse returns, then give artificial respiration alone. Get immediate emergency veterinary attention.

When bleeding occurs

Heavy bleeding or slow, continuous, lighter bleeding can lead to dangerous clinical shock. While internal bleeding is difficult to manage, external bleeding can often be controlled by applying pressure *(see right)*.

If blood is spurting from a wound, an artery has been damaged; this type of bleeding will be more difficult to stop because arteries carry blood at a higher pressure (carrying blood away from the heart) than do veins (carrying blood back to the heart). Watch carefully for any signs of shock *(see opposite)* and treat if necessary.

Stopping bleeding

If a dog is bleeding, firm pressure needs to be applied to stop the flow. Seek veterinary assistance as soon as possible.

1 If first aid material is available, apply pressure with a non-stick gauze pad. Otherwise, use any clean absorbent material, such as kitchen paper towel, a pad of toilet paper or facial tissue, or a clean tea cloth. Apply pressure for at least two minutes.

Apply pressure gently but firmly

2 Do not remove the blood-soaked material – it helps with clotting. Leave removal to your veterinarian. Secure the area with a bandage, and get immediate veterinary attention.

Apply more absorbent material if soaked through

Shock

Shock is a silent killer: a dog may look fine after an accident, then die a few hours later of clinical shock. Treating shock takes precedence over treatment for other non-life-threatening injuries.

The colour of a dog's gums gives a good clue to shock. Normal gums are a healthy pink, but during shock they

Anaphylactic shock

Insect bites, certain drugs, and, in rare circumstances, some types of food can cause a dog to go into "anaphylactic" shock. Early signs are facial swelling, retching, vomiting, staggering, and sudden diarrhoea. Later signs are blue gums, gurgling lung sounds, and distressed breathing. If you hear distressed gurgling sounds, suspend the dog by its hind legs for ten seconds to try to clear the airway, and get immediate veterinary help.

What to do if your dog is in shock

If your dog shows signs of shock do not let it wander about or give it anything to eat or drink, and do the following:

1 Stop any bleeding and give heart massage or artificial respiration as necessary *(see pp.222–3)*.

2 Wrap the dog in a blanket to prevent further heat loss.

3 Use pillows or towels to elevate the dog's hindquarters – this ensures maximum blood flow to the brain.

4 Keep the dog's head extended, and seek the assistance of your nearest vet immediately.

become dull pink or even white. In healthy dogs, if you press your finger against the gums, blood is squeezed out of tiny blood vessels called capillaries. The gums whiten, but the capillaries immediately refill when you remove the finger. As shock advances, the time the the capillaries take to refill increases.

If you have a dog with black pigmented gums, such as a Chow Chow or Shar Pei, it is difficult to assess shock in this way. In these breeds, examine the inner lining of the vagina of a female dog – a pale colour indicates shock. For a male, retract the prepuce and examine the colour of the penis.

Signs of early shock
The signs of early shock include:
• Faster than normal breathing;
• Faster than normal heart rate;

• Pale gums;
• Anxiety or restlessness;
• Lethargy and weakness;
• Subnormal rectal temperature;
• Capillaries in the gums take more than two seconds to refill.

Signs of late shock
Signs of late shock include:
• Shallow, irregular breathing;
• Irregular heart beat;
• Very pale or blue gums;
• Extreme weakness or unconsciousness;
• Very cool body temperature – less than 98°F (36.7°C);
• Capillaries in the gums take more than four seconds to refill.

Conserve body heat in a dog suffering from shock with blankets and a warm hot water bottle.

Wounds and injuries

- Always suspect hidden damage
- Bandages protect and reduce pain
- Move an injured dog carefully

Traffic accidents, dogfights, and unexpected traumatic injuries are the most common causes of bleeding wounds. An injured dog may be in considerable pain, and must be treated with great care to minimize discomfort and reduce the danger of biting.

Closed wounds

Do not underestimate a closed wound. Because the skin is unbroken, there may appear to be little damage beneath, but dramatic internal injuries and fractures may have occurred. The full extent of these injuries may not be apparent for several days, so even if wounds look minor, you should call your vet for professional advice.

Closed wounds are typically accompanied by some or all of the following symptoms: swelling; pain; discolouration caused by bruising under the skin; increased heat in a specific location; and superficial damage, such as scratches to the skin. To treat a closed wound, apply a cool compress and seek veterinary attention.

Open wounds

Serious open wounds require urgent attention from a vet, but even with a minor injury the first priority is to stop the bleeding *(see p.224)*. Open wounds are accompanied by some or all of the following symptoms: broken skin, sometimes only a puncture; pain;

Bandaging

When bandaging, first place a nonstick absorbent pad over the cleaned, dried, disinfected wound. Wrap it with gauze so that the absorbent pad does not slip. Do not stretch the gauze tightly when wrapping an injury; this cuts off blood supply to the area. Apply a final stretchy or adhesive layer, placing two fingers under it as you start to wrap to prevent you from applying the tape too tightly. It should be secure enough not to fall or be pulled off but not so tight that it cuts off the circulation. Wounds often swell, and a seemingly well-applied bandage might restict blood flow a few hours later. Do not let the bandage get wet, and prevent the dog from chewing it. Never leave a bandage on for more than 24 hours unless explicitly instructed by your vet.

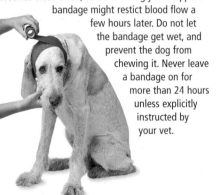

bleeding; and increased licking or attention to a specific area.

To treat an open wound, first flush with 3% hydrogen peroxide, tepid salt water, or clean bottled or tap water. Using tweezers or fingers, remove any obvious dirt, gravel, splinters, or other material from the wound. Do not pull penetrating objects, such as arrows or pieces of wood or metal, from a wound, because this could cause uncontrollable bleeding. If there is hair in the wound, apply water-soluble jelly to a pair of scissors and then cut the hair, which will adhere to the scissors. Do not use petroleum jelly.

Splints and bandages

If your dog is bleeding, bandage the wound to keep it dry and protect the dog from further injuries, including self-inflicted damage from chewing and excessive licking. Bandaging also provides constant mild pressure to control pain or bleeding and to prevent pockets of serum from building up under the skin.

If your dog has a suspected fracture, apply a splint to reduce pain and further injury during transport to the vet. Never try to straighten leg fractures – splint them as they are, wrapping the leg in plenty of cotton wool (winding the roll around the leg) or torn strips of blanket or sheeting. Wrapping a rolled newspaper or magazine into the fabric adds rigidity.

Tourniquets are dangerous

A tourniquet should only be used in cases of profuse and life-threatening bleeding. Improper or prolonged use cuts off the blood supply and can lead to the loss of an entire limb. To apply a tourniquet, wrap a tie or strip of torn sheet above the bleeding wound and tie it with a releasable knot. Slip a pen, pencil, or stick into the knot and twist until bleeding stops. Hold or tie this down in place for no more than 10 minutes. Loosen every few minutes while you transport the dog to the veterinary clinic. Do not use a tourniquet

if your dog has been bitten by a venomous snake, because it will increase any inflammation. Instead, immobilize the bitten area and apply an ice pack to reduce the size of local blood vessels while you get urgent veterinary attention.

Moving an injured dog

When lifting and transporting an injured dog, avoid bending or twisting because this can cause further injury. Small dogs can be wrapped in a bulky blanket. An ironing board or removable shelving makes a useful temporary stretcher for bigger dogs. Secure the dog to the stretcher with neckties, torn sheeting, or rope. Make sure that the dog's neck is extended so that breathing is not obstructed.

Frozen peas make an ideal compress as they thaw quickly and wrap to the contour of the injured area.

Poisoning

- Keep household chemicals in dog-proof containers
- Secure areas where vermin bait is used
- Watch where your dog walks

Poisons can enter the body through the skin, by being inhaled, or by being eaten. As inveterate scavengers, dogs are most prone to swallowing poisons, but fortunately, most ingested chemicals are vomited straight back up. Nevertheless, vets still deal with too many needless accidents caused by not keeping dangerous substances safely stored out of a curious dog's reach.

Contact poisons

Never apply any substance to a dog's coat, even if it is safe for humans, unless you know it will not cause harm to your dog. If a dog's coat is

Essential oils can be deadly

Don't dab even a drop of any essential oil on your dog's hair. A single drop of a concentrated product, even one that may have therapeutic properties for humans, can be harmful for a dog.

Clean harmful chemicals from your dog's coat as soon as possible; it may ingest them while grooming.

contaminated with paint, tar, or motor oil, never use paint remover, concentrated biological detergent, methylated spirit, or any similar product to clean it off; these substances are highly toxic if ingested. The simplest treatment is to cut away the affected hair. If this is not possible, treat in the following way:

- If the substance is soft, wearing rubber gloves, rub in plenty of vegetable oil, then wash with soapy water – dog or baby shampoo is safe – and rinse thoroughly with fresh water;
- If contamination is extensive, rub powdered starch or flour in with the vegetable oil to absorb the poison, removing the mixture with a wide-toothed comb;
- If the coat is contaminated by something other than paint, tar, petroleum products, or motor oil, flush the region for at least five minutes with clean water, concentrating on the eyes, armpits, and groin.

Inhaled poisons

If a dog has inhaled a poisonous substance, this will most often result in breathing difficulties, but may also cause neurological problems, such as twitching and salivating. Do not put yourself at risk by entering an environment containing dangerous toxic fumes. To treat your dog:

• Watch for signs of shock and treat if needed, keep the airway open, assist breathing, and give CPR if necessary (see pp.222–5);
• If the dog is convulsing, wrap it in a blanket and seek immediate veterinary assistance;
• Do not underestimate the damage caused by inhaling smoke or other irritant fumes like tear gas: serious and potentially fatal swelling may affect the air passages hours later;
• After any serious inhalation accident, seek urgent veterinary assistance.

Swallowed poisons

Dogs will eat anything, and this puts them at risk from poisoning caused by a number of chemicals used in our

Poisons in the home and garden

Many common household chemicals and drugs should be kept away from your dog. These include: alkaline cleaners; solvents or paintstripper; antifreeze; aspirin; sedatives or anti-depressants; flea repellents; lead from old paint or pipes; slug and snail bait; wood preservatives.

ASPIRIN

Many garden plants are toxic and should be kept out of reach: castor bean seeds; cherry laurel wood and branches; dumb cane leaves; foxglove stems and flowers; jimsonweed or thorn apple; laburnum bark, flowers, seeds, and leaves; mistletoe berries; oleander bark, stem, and leaves; yew bark, needles, and seeds.

YEW BERRIES

Poisoning by caustic agents

Many common household chemicals are caustic, causing irritation and burning, and destroying tissue. If your dog has swallowed a caustic poison, do not induce vomiting, but treat in the following way:

Household acids: limescale remover; wood preservatives; rust remover; toilet bowl cleaners; car battery fluid; metal cleaners	Give egg white, bicarbonate of soda, charcoal powder or vegetable oil by mouth. Apply a paste of bicarbonate of soda to any burns in the mouth. If the dog also has skin burns, flush these for at least 15 minutes with fresh water.
Household alkalis: chlorine bleach; oven cleaners; swimming pool chlorinating agents; caustic soda; paint stripper	Give egg white or small amounts of citrus fruit juice or vinegar. Carefully apply dilute vinegar to any mouth or skin burns, and get immediate veterinary help.

homes and gardens (see box), and in public areas. Keep poisonous substances out of your dog's reach. Become familiar with any lawn or vermin chemicals used in your local parks; signs of their use may be posted. If your dog has eaten a poisonous substance, treat in the following way:

• If you know that poison, such as slug bait, rodenticide, or herbicide, has been swallowed in the last two hours, induce vomiting in the conscious dog by giving a large crystal of washing soda, concentrated salt, or 3% hydrogen peroxide – one teaspoon every 15 minutes until vomiting occurs (see pp.218–19);
• Give one to two teaspoons of a slurry of activated charcoal in water – this will help to absorb any remaining poison;
• Telephone your vet for advice, and if vomiting has occurred, keep a sample to take to the surgery;
• If the swallowed poison is caustic (acid or alkali), or is petroleum-based, do not induce vomiting;
• If the poison is unknown, see your vet as soon as possible.

Skin and coat conditions

■ A common reason for veterinary visits
■ Fleas are not the only cause of itchiness
■ Routine grooming prevents skin problems

Skin problems account for around 40 per cent of visits to the vet. The reason is obvious: it is easy to see when something is wrong. Parasites, and particularly the flea, are responsible for the majority of irritating skin conditions. You may never see it, but a single flea can lead to inflammation, scratching, licking, scaling, bleeding or crusting skin, erosions, ulcers, lumps, and hair loss. Your vet, however, may diagnose many other possible causes for these skin changes.

Persistent scratching can damage the skin, resulting in bacterial skin infections.

Making a diagnosis
Your vet will carry out a thorough examination and use a number of methods to help diagnose the specific cause of skin disease. The simplest way to do this is to see if a particular treatment works.

Alternatively, your vet may want to examine the dog's skin with an ultraviolet light to check for ringworm, take a smear or culture for bacteria or yeast, a scrape for parasites, or a biopsy for cellular changes. Skin and blood tests, and diet and environment changes may also be used to diagnose allergic skin disorders.

Signs of skin disease
There are many basic signs that indicate that a dog is suffering from skin disease. These include scratching, hair loss, pigment changes, visible lumps, inflammation, scurfy, dry scales and crusts, and wet erosions and ulcers. Most forms of skin disease have a variety of these clinical signs.

Itchy skin
There is always a good reason for a dog scratching, but sometimes it is frustratingly difficult

Ask the vet

Q: Can food allergies cause skin disease?
A: Allergies to food can sometimes cause an itchy skin condition. Feed a unique "exclusion diet" that a dog has never had before, for at least six weeks: if the itchiness and any associated problems diminish, this is diagnostic of a food allergy.

Common causes of itchy skin

Parasites	Fleas; scabies; harvest mites; ear mites; fly-bites; lice; ticks; *Cheyletiella*; maggots.
Infection	Bacteria; fungi including *Malassezia*.
Allergies	Flea allergy dermatitis; food allergy dermatitis; atopic dermatitis; contact allergy dermatitis; hives.

to determine exactly what that reason is. A consequence is that the "itching" gets treated rather than its underlying causes. As well as scratching, dogs respond to itchy skin by licking, nibbling or chewing, biting, rubbing, and rolling. Itchy skin may also lead to personality changes, including loss of tolerance, irritability, and aggression.

Allergies and parasites, especially fleas, are the most common triggers for scratching. Many dogs are irritated by the minute amount of anti-coagulant saliva that a flea leaves when it takes a meal. Excessive scratching can then lead to the skin becoming infected *(see below)*. The skin's oil glands may also become overactive causing a crusty, smelly condition. If one of your pets has fleas, mites, or ticks, examine and treat all of your dogs and cats *(see pp.214–15)*. Treat your home too, to eliminate immature or resting parasites.

Pimples and erosions

Skin disease caused by bacteria (pyoderma) usually occurs when the surface of the skin is damaged – through allergy, for example – allowing bacteria to multiply. Skin infections can cause pustules and papules to form: a pustule is a small, elevated, pus-filled pimple, while a papule is a small, elevated pimple filled solidly with inflammatory cells.

When pimples are damaged or burst they are called erosions, and if an erosion breaks through the full thickness of skin, it forms an ulcer. Erosions and ulcers can result from:
• Acute moist dermatitis (wet eczema, summer dermatitis, hot spot) – infection that causes the surface of the skin to become moist and oozing;
• Skin fold pyoderma – bacterial growth between folds of skin – common in Cocker Spaniel lip folds;
• Puppy acne and puppy impetigo;
• Cellulitis from a penetrating wound;
• Furunculosis *(see over)*.

Scaling and crusting skin

If the surface of the skin becomes scaly, it can flake off as particles of dandruff, or remain, building up as calluses. Scaling is often associated with seborrhoea, a condition that results

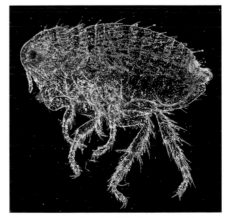

Fleas are tiny and can be difficult to spot – if you suspect your dog may be infested, look for tell-tale, sooty, black droppings in its coat and bedding.

Loss of large patches of hair can be a sign of a more serious underlying disease; if you notice changes to your dog's coat, consult your vet.

Irish Wolfhounds are prone to fluid-filled lumps called bursas – these develop after repeated trauma to the bony part of the elbow.

from increased activity of the skin's oil-producing sebaceous glands. Crusts are masses of serum, blood, and inflammatory cells, produced as a consequence of skin inflammation. There are several possible causes of scaling and crusting, including:
• Bacterial skin infection (pyoderma);
• *Malassezia* dermatitis;
• Sarcoptic mange (scabies), resulting from infestation with sarcoptic mites *(see p.215)*;
• Acne or "folliculitis";
• *Cheyletiella* mange, resulting from infection with *Cheyletiella* mites *(see p.215)*;
• Leishmaniasis – an infection of the blood caused by the pathogenic protozoa *Leishmania*;
• Hereditary seborrhoea (as in the Cocker Spaniel);

Anal furunculosis

Furunculosis is a very uncomfortable condition that affects the hairless skin around a dog's anus. It is most common in the German Shepherd, and is probably caused by an immune disorder, complicated by deep infection. Chronic treatment with anti-inflammatories and antibiotics is needed, and in some cases surgery is required.

• Ringworm *(see opposite)*;
• Elbow calluses;
• Heat, chemical, or sun burns;
• Cancer;
• Immune-mediated disorders such as pemphigus foliaceus.

Shedding and losing hair

A dog's coat often sheds during warm weather and regrows during cooler weather. Central heating in our homes can upset this natural rhythm, with the result that many dogs shed their coats all year round. Shedding varies between breeds: Poodles, for example, have coats that constantly grow, shedding little, while Yorkshire Terriers shed little because they have rather thin, long topcoats and negligible undercoats. Females often shed more after a season, during pregnancy, and while lactating.

Hair loss, or alopecia, is different from shedding because it causes local or partial baldness in a dog. It occurs because hair fails to grow, is scratched or licked out, or spontaneously falls out. Alopecia can have any of the following causes:
• **Hormonal disorders:** sex hormone imbalance; underactive thyroid gland

(hypothyroidism); overactive adrenal gland (hyperadrenocorticism or Cushing's syndrome) *(see pp.242–3)*.

• **Parasitic and fungal conditions:** Demodectic mange caused by infestation with *Demodex* mites *(see p.215)*; ringworm *(see below)*.

• **Environmental:** pressure sores; elbow calluses; burns; reactions at the site of an injection; clipping of the coat (in a spitz breed).

• **Inherited conditions:** pattern baldness in Dachshunds; colour-dilution alopecia in breeds selectively bred for unusual coat colour; sebaceous adenitis in Standard Poodles; zinc-responsive dermatosis in Nordic breeds.

• **Behavioural:** persistent licking of an area, often caused by boredom or stress, resulting in lick dermatitis (lick granuloma or acral dermatitis).

Skin lumps and bumps

Dogs can exhibit a wide variety of skin lumps. An accurate diagnosis is essential, as some types, such as warts, cysts, and tumours, require removal by a vet. Cysts feel like hard lumps just under the skin. Warts are pink, mottled, crusty around their roots, and may be pigmented. They are most common in elderly dogs.

Older dogs can sometimes develop slow-growing, soft, fluctuating, egg-shaped masses under the skin – these are often benign tumours. Lumps in older dogs should always be examined by a veterinary surgeon, however, because they could be cancerous *(see pp.272–3)*.

Ringworm

Ringworm is a highly contagious condition caused when a hair follicle is infected by a ringworm fungus *(below)*, and this spreads to other hairs. It is more common in puppies than in adults. Ringworm does not usually cause itchiness, but secondary bacterial infection can produce crusts in the skin, with consequent licking and scratching.

Ringworm can be transmitted to humans *(see p.217)*, so early treatment is vital. This involves use of antifungal shampoos, creams, or lotions, often enilconazole or ketoconazole. A dog is treated for at least two weeks after clinical signs have disappeared or fungal culture is negative. In more severe cases, your vet will dispense oral antibiotics, usually griseofulvin, given for at least four weeks.

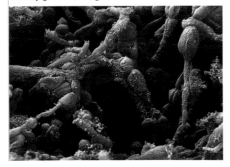

A glossary of lumps and bumps

TYPE	DESCRIPTION
Cyst	A simple, sac-like cavity that develops within the skin.
Abscess	A deep infection, walled off in a pocket of tissue under the skin.
Haematoma	An accumulation of blood under the skin, especially in the ear flaps. Skin becomes hot and reddened, but is rarely painful.
Granuloma	A connective tissue response to anything that penetrates the outer layer of the skin.
Lipoma	A tumour of fat cells. Occurs anywhere on the body, especially in older individuals.
Melanoma	A pigmented skin tumour (although there are also unpigmented melanomas).
Histiocytoma	A button-like raised lump anywhere on the body.
Papilloma or wart	A cauliflower-like growth protruding from the skin.
Perianal adenoma or hepatoid adenoma	A discrete swelling in the tissue around the anus in older male dogs.
Mast cell, basal cell, or squamous cell tumour	Common tumours arising from skin cells. They can be either benign or malignant.

Respiratory disorders

- Laboured breathing is a serious concern
- Always check for signs of shock
- The cause may lie outside the respiratory system

Problems may occur anywhere in the respiratory system – from a tickle in the nose producing a sneeze, to trauma in the chest causing laboured breathing and clinical shock. Infections and disorders can occur in either the upper respiratory system, including the nose and windpipe, or in the chest and lungs – the lower respiratory tract. Irrespective of the cause, virtually all conditions of the respiratory system cause obvious changes in your dog's regular breathing pattern.

Pugs and other flat-faced breeds are prone to a range of upper respiratory problems, such as narrow nostrils, dangerously narrowed windpipe, and susceptibility to heat stress.

Panting
Normal panting, which is shallow, rapid, open-mouthed breathing, is not a medical problem. It is what hot, nervous, excited, or exhausted dogs do. Pain also induces panting, as will exercise or even medications such as corticosteroids. Don't mistake laboured breathing for normal panting – any breathing difficulties require veterinary attention.

Sneezing
Sneezing and discharges from the nose may be caused by minor conditions like hay fever, by more significant problems, such as a foreign object lodged in a nostril, or by major problems like nasal tumours. Sneezing itself is not an illness, but a reflex action that rids the nasal passages of something the body considers to be irritating.

Treating a nosebleed
If sneezing is particularly intense, this can lead to a nosebleed. Follow these guidelines if your dog's nose is bleeding:
- Keep your dog quiet and confined;
- Apply a cold compress, such as a bag of frozen peas, to the top of the nose between the eyes and nostrils, and hold in place for five minutes;
- Cover the bleeding nostril with absorbent material;
- Do not muzzle your dog;
- Do not tilt your dog's head back to prevent blood dripping;

• Do not pack the bleeding nostril with anything, because this can stimulate further bouts of sneezing.

Coughing

Coughing is often triggered by inflammation or damage to the lining of the air passages, and it removes unwanted material from the windpipe and bronchi. Coughing is commonly caused by allergy, pollution, infection, or foreign material in the air passages. Other less common causes include inhalation or ingestion of poisonous substances, fluid in the chest cavity, worms, heart conditions, chest diseases or injuries, tumours, or a collapsed windpipe. If your dog has been coughing for more than a day, or if the cough recurs, contact your veterinary surgeon for advice.

Canine cough

The most common and serious cause of contagious coughing in dogs is infection by the bacterium *Bordetella bronchiseptica*, resulting in a condition known as canine cough (kennel cough or laryngotracheitis). Affected dogs develop a harsh, dry cough about five days after contact with a carrier of the disease. Spasms of coughing can be triggered in affected individuals by the mildest pressure of a collar on the

Canine cough is caused by an infection that can spread quickly wherever many dogs meet, such as boarding kennels, parks, or dog shows.

inflamed windpipe. Canine cough is most serious in the debilitated and the very young, causing a loss of appetite, depression, and in some cases, nasal discharge. If your dog is visiting an area where there is a high risk of contracting canine cough, talk to your vet about vaccinating your dog against *Bordetella* with an aerosol intranasal vaccine.

Foreign object in the nose

If you can see a foreign object, such as a blade of grass, lodged in your dog's nose, carefully remove it with tweezers. If you cannot remove the object get immediate veterinary help to do so.

Breathing problems

There are a variety of reasons why a dog may be suffering from breathing difficulties. The majority are serious and require prompt action. They include: physical obstructions preventing air intake, chest injury, pneumonia, tumours, trauma, heart failure, poisoning, an allergic reaction, pain, smoke inhalation, heatstroke, a collapsed windpipe or lung, or a torn diaphragm.

If a respiratory problem involves the windpipe or lungs, the cause may be obvious, but if the disorder is associated with a heart condition, for example, it may develop more insidiously. The early stages of heart failure – causing a "throat-clearing" cough and slightly more laboured breathing – are easy to dismiss as relatively unimportant, so any breathing problem should be reported to your vet. Common types of breathing problems include:

• **Rapid, shallow breathing:** dogs breathe faster after exercise, but also in response to dangerous conditions, such as shock, poisoning, heatstroke, or pain. Contact your vet immediately if your dog's breathing rate has suddenly increased without exercise.

• **Laboured breathing:** breathing difficulties are always a cause for concern, and are usually accompanied by rapid breathing. Possible triggers include heart failure, lung disease, a

Swallowing small pieces of stick, bone, or other items, which then become lodged in the windpipe, is a common cause of choking.

build-up of fluid in the chest (pleural effusion), trauma (such as a torn diaphragm), and tumours. If your dog is having difficulty breathing, contact your vet immediately.

• **Noisy breathing:** noisy breathing sounds are always significant, and may be caused by obstructions, such as foreign bodies, affecting the upper respiratory tract, or paralysis of the vocal cords. If your dog is breathing noisily, contact your vet the same day.

• **Wheezing:** this is not as common in dogs as it is in people or cats. When it does occur, it usually indicates a lung problem; an inflammation to the bronchi of the lungs (bronchitis) caused by allergy or infection. Wheezing dogs should receive veterinary attention within 24 hours.

• **Choking:** this is an immediate emergency and should be differentiated from gagging, which may look similar but is not life-threatening. If your dog is choking, do not wait for veterinary help. Safely try to remove the cause of

Snoring

Dogs with flattened faces – Pugs, Pekingese, Boston Terriers, and Boxers – have loose, slack, soft palates, and, when they are relaxed, are inclined to snore. This is also common in Cavalier King Charles Spaniels. The intensity and frequency of snoring increases with age. If your pup snores intensely, discuss this with your vet, as simple surgery to reduce excess soft palate tissue may be beneficial to reduce later complications.

choking (see below), but take great care – a choking dog is likely to be in great distress, and is liable to bite.

Swallowing objects is not the only cause of choking. An allergic reaction to an insect bite or sting in the mouth may cause the tongue to swell. Physical injuries to the neck or throat may cause swelling, blocking the airway. A dog may also choke on its own vomit. If you suspect any of these causes of choking, seek urgent veterinary help.

Try to minimize your dog's risk of choking. Dogs, and especially pups, chew anything as a natural method of investigation, to relieve boredom, to exercise the teeth and gums, or simply just for the fun of it. Never leave small chewable articles where dogs can reach them. Pups in particular may swallow small objects, and are at risk of choking on them. Never give chicken bones to your dog, and be careful to remove any bones from fish – small bones can become lodged in a dog's throat, causing the dog to choke.

How to treat choking and gagging

If a dog is making choking sounds, is greatly agitated or in distress, and has a blue tongue and bulging eyes, check whether it is conscious, then treat for choking. If the dog is pawing at its mouth and gagging but with no breathing difficulties, is in mild distress, and rubbing its face on the ground, look for an object stuck in the mouth.

CHOKING: CONSCIOUS

1 To treat a large dog, put your arms around the dog's belly, make a fist and squeeze firmly up and forward just behind the ribcage. This is a canine variation of the Heimlich manoeuvre.

2 If the dog is small, place your hands on either side of its belly and squeeze firmly up and forward to expel the blockage

CHOKING: UNCONSCIOUS

1 With the dog on its side, place the heels of both of your hands just behind the back ribs.

2 Press sharply to expel the blockage.

3 Use your finger to sweep debris from the mouth.

4 Give CPR if necessary (see p.222–3), and seek immediate veterinary assistance.

GAGGING: OBJECT IN MOUTH

1 Restrain your dog without a muzzle.

2 Open the dog's mouth with one hand, grasping the upper jaw and the pressing upper lips over the upper teeth.

3 Use your other hand to open the lower jaw.

4 With a spoon handle, remove the object; it may be stuck in the teeth or in the roof of the mouth.

Common terms

Your vet may use any of the following words to describe the respiratory problems your dog is suffering from:

Rhinitis or sinusitis	Inflammation of the nasal passages or sinuses. Usually caused by allergy or irritation.
Cleft palate	A congenital non-union at the midline of the hard palate seen in newborn puppies. Usually needs surgical correction.
Laryngitis	Inflammation of the voicebox, often caused by infection, but also by excess barking.
Laryngeal paralysis	Paralysis of the vocal cords, causing a throaty cough. Mainly seen in mature Labradors.
Canine cough	A word used to describe a variety of transmissible infections causing inflammation of the windpipe and voice box.
Collapsed trachea	Condition where the windpipe flattens on itself. Most common in Yorkshire Terriers.
Bronchitis	Inflammation of the bronchi – the major air passages of the lungs.
Chronic obstructive pulmonary disease or COPD	Describes chronic lung conditions, often with an allergic component.
Pleurisy or pleuritis	Inflammation of the lining of the chest cavity.
Pleural effusion	Fluid around the lungs.
Pulmonary edema	Fluid build-up in the lungs.

Blood and circulation

■ Clinical problems can mimic signs of natural aging
■ Some breeds are more at risk than others
■ Early treatment prolongs life expectancy

Heart disease is more common in dogs than in any other domestic species. The most common form damages the heart's valves; this occurs primarily in small dogs, from middle age onwards. Congenital heart defects and heart attacks are less common. A wide variety of medications, developed to treat human heart conditions, are used to successfully delay the progression of heart failure.

Heart valve problems

Valvular heart disease is caused when the heart valves do not close properly, causing blood to back up into the lungs or liver (congestion). The earliest signs of heart failure – reduced activity and exercise tolerance – are often mistaken for natural age-related changes. Soon, a dry, non-productive cough develops, initially after exercise and at night. Eventually dogs lose weight, breathe more rapidly, and develop swollen

Diagnostic aids

Your vet can diagnose some forms of heart disease simply by listening to the heart with a stethoscope, but in most circumstances, other tests are needed, such as analysis with X-rays or electrocardiography (ECG) – assessment of the electrical impulses in the heart. Ultrasound or "echocardiography" is used to assess heart structure and function, and is at the core of accurate assessments. Blood pressure or other blood tests may also be required.

abdomens. Dogs suffering from congestive heart failure are treated with ACE inhibitors such as enalapril, and diuretics such as frusemide are used to eliminate excess fluid.

Dilated cardiomyopathy (DCM)

Cardiomyopathy usually affects dogs under seven years old, and involves dilation or enlargement of the bottom of the heart and thinning of the heart muscle, leading to congestive heart failure. It occurs mostly in medium to large breeds, especially the Doberman, and affects more males than females. Affected dogs lose weight, are lethargic, and tire easily from routine exercise. As heart failure progresses, fluid builds up in the lungs and the belly. Affected individuals are treated for congestive heart failure.

Valvular heart disease
is the most common heart problem in Cavalier King Charles Spaniels.

Heartworms

Heartworms, *Dirofilaria immitis*, spread through

How valves work

Blood moves through arteries and the chambers of the heart through one-way valves that prevent blood from flowing in the wrong direction. The valves consist of flaps or leaflets made of a tough, elastic protein called collagen.

① Blood at high pressure pushes the leaflets of the valve open. As the blood on the other side of the valve is at a lower pressure, the blood flows through the valve.

Blood flows through the valve

Valve leaflets open

High-pressure blood forces valve open

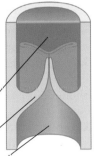

② Movement of blood through the valve results in an increase in pressure on the other side of the valve. This causes the valve to close, preventing blood from flowing back.

High-pressure blood closes valve

Closed valve

Blood at low pressure

mosquito bites and grow in the upper chambers of the heart, causing lack of energy, a moist cough, and heart failure. This parasite is a problem in the Americas, the affected region stretching from the Gulf Coast and Eastern seaboard of North America, especially at low elevations, into Quebec and Ontario. In Europe they occur throughout the Mediterranean region.

Your veterinary surgeon will advise you on the use of effective heartworm prevention and treatments during the mosquito season in any region of the world where heartworm is endemic (see also p.214).

Anaemia

Anaemia is a deficiency in red blood cells resulting from a lack of production or loss of blood cells, or their destruction. It causes lethargy and weakness, and can result from obvious external bleeding but also from internal bleeding from ulcers, tumours, parasites, or bowel disease. Some drugs and rodent baits cause also anaemia, and a heavy flea infestation can cause severe anaemia in puppies. The most common form of anaemia diagnosed in clinical practice is called immune-mediated haemolytic anaemia (IMHA). In this condition, the body's immune system turns upon and destroys its own red blood cells.

To treat anaemia, the source of blood loss is found and further loss is controlled. Blood transfusions are given when needed. For IMHA, the outlook is less promising. Even with rapid diagnosis and treatment with high doses of corticosteroids and other immune suppressing drugs, fatal relapses are frustratingly common.

Your vet may use ultrasound to look for weak contractions or heart valve problems in your dog.

Brain disorders

- Seizures vary from mild to severe
- A seizure can be mistaken for a heart condition
- Brain scans may reveal unexpected brain tumours

The brain, through its connections with the spinal cord and peripheral nerves, coordinates all activities, thoughts, senses, feelings, emotions, movement, and body functions *(see pp.28–9)*. If the brain is damaged, this can lead to behaviour changes, seizures, loss of coordination, paralysis, or coma.

Brain injuries
Brain injuries are frequently caused by physical injuries, especially as a result of road traffic accidents; they can also result from poisoning with certain substances, such as snake venom and organophosphate insecticides.

Injury to the brain can also be caused by meningitis – inflammation of the tissue around the brain – and encephalitis – inflammation of the brain itself. Causes of encephalitis include distemper and rabies – diseases that are preventable through routine inoculation *(see pp.212–13)*.

Dogs with brain injuries behave and move differently; there may be seizure, stupor,

If you notice a sudden, dramatic change in your dog's behaviour, consult your vet – it could be due to a brain disorder.

Only dreaming

Dogs dream the same way we do. During deep or "activated" sleep dogs may have rapid eye movements (REMs), paddle with their feet, twitch their lips and noses, sometimes even bark. This behaviour is perfectly normal, and should not be confused with the signs of a brain disorder.

coma, or paralysis. Treatment varies with the cause of the injury. See a vet immediately after a road traffic accident, before signs of brain injury develop, for the best chance of successful treatment.

Coma
A coma may be caused by a physical injury, such as a concussion, or by heart failure, heatstroke, or very high fever. Kidney or liver failure, high or low blood sugar, lack of oxygen to the brain, and many infections and toxins can also result in coma.

Initially, an affected dog appears confused, but this evolves through a state of stupor until consciousness is finally lost. The unconscious dog cannot be roused and is insensitive to pain. If your dog is in a coma, seek urgent veterinary attention.

Seizures or fits

A seizure may be stunningly dramatic or so subtle it is easily dismissed as a momentary loss of concentration.

In general, seizures may involve loss of consciousness, accompanied by involuntary muscle contractions, dilation of the pupils, paddling with the limbs, trembling, and face twitching. During a seizure, dogs also frequently salivate, urinate, and defecate. Seizures can be mild, occur in clusters, or be prolonged, lasting more than five minutes.

Some dogs have an inherited predisposition for seizures, but they can also be caused by a number of other conditions, including:

- Epilepsy;
- Brain injury;
- Scar tissue on the brain;
- Brain tumour;
- Low blood calcium;
- Low blood sugar;
- Heatstroke;
- Migrating intestinal worm larvae;
- Hydrocephalus – increased fluid in the brain;
- Post-distemper encephalitis;
- Poisoning.

Brain tumours

Brain tumours are rare; they occur in only around 1 in 6,500 dogs. Clinical signs associated with this type of cancer include behaviour and temperament changes, seizures, circling, changes in movement and gait, blindness, and altered mental abilities, senses, and facial nerve control. With the increasing availability of brain scans, tumours are being diagnosed more frequently.

As with other types of cancer *(see pp.272–3)*, initial treatment for an affected dog is aimed at controlling clinical signs and improving a dog's quality of life. This often includes the use of anticonvulsants and corticosteroids. The second objective of treatment is to prolong good quality life; this may involve radiation therapy, surgery, or a combination of both.

What to do if your dog has a seizure

1. Protect yourself: during a seizure, a dog may unintentionally bite.

2. Protect your dog: pull it away from danger by the scruff of the neck, and place something soft, like cushions, around and under its head.

3. During and after a seizure, comfort your dog with soothing words and a gentle touch.

4. If a seizure lasts for more than six minutes, see your vet the same day.

5. After a seizure, allow your dog to drink.

6. If your dog is disorientated after a seizure, confine it, but stay near and comfort it.

7. Note the length of seizure and any abnormal behaviour to help your vet diagnose the problem.

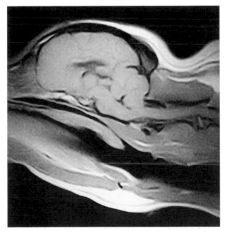

Your vet may examine a Magnetic Resonance Imaging (MRI) scan of your dog's brain, like this one of a normal brain, to look for abnormalities.

Hormonal disorders

- Increased drinking can indicate a hormonal problem
- Skin and hair changes may suggest thyroid disease
- An immune disorder is often involved

Hormones are chemical messengers that influence the activity of cells and tissues all round the body. The first hormones to be identified were those produced by discrete, visible glands, such as the thyroid and the pituitary. Later, scientists discovered other messengers, including the brain biochemicals dopamine and serotonin, and trace chemicals called cytokines. New cytokines are being discovered almost monthly, and this is an area where some of the most exciting advances in therapy are being made.

Pituitary disorders

The pituitary is the "master gland" at the base of the brain, and it controls much of the hormonal, or endocrine, system. The most common clinical pituitary disorder is diabetes insipidus (unrelated to sugar diabetes, or diabetes mellitus). This condition is due to lack of production of antidiuretic hormone (ADH) – a hormone that instructs the kidneys to concentrate urine. An affected dog will drink and urinate in excess. The disease can be treated with synthetic ADH hormone (called DDAVP), given as eye drops or tablets.

Thyroid disorders

Thyroid hormone regulates the body's metabolic activity. Its activities are highly diverse, so clinical signs of thyroid disease vary enormously.

Underactivity of the thyroid gland, or hypothyroidism, is a greatly underdiagnosed condition, and may in fact be the most common hormonal problem in dogs. In four out of five cases, the condition is thought to be triggered by an infectious disease, resulting in an overreaction by the immune system, producing antibodies that attack and destroy thyroid cells.

Common signs of the condition include weight gain, reduced exercise tolerance, thinning hair, and lethargy. Affected individuals can also develop skin infections, poor hair quality, weakness, increased skin pigmentation, and a "tragic" facial expression.

Treatment with the thyroid supplement L-thyroxine is extremely effective. A treated dog will quickly become more alert and willing to exercise. Weight loss is obvious within

Cocker Spaniels are prone to underactive thyroid problems.

Thyroid and parathyroid glands

The thyroid consists of two separate lobes, located on each side of the windpipe just below the larynx. It produces the hormones T4 (thyroxine) and T3 (triiodothyronine), collectively known as thyroid hormone. The parathyroids consist of four tiny masses that sit on the thyroid like caps, or even lie within thyroid tissue.

Parathyroid hormone is necessary to extract calcium from bone and transport it around the body, where it plays an important role in muscle contraction.

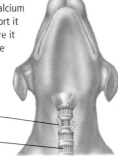

The thyroid gland is controlled by the pituitary

Windpipe

weeks but coat changes take much longer, perhaps up to 12 weeks.

If the thyroid gland is overactive, the rare condition of hyperthyroidism develops. The affected dog has a voracious appetite but loses weight, and usually drinks and urinates more. Hyperthyroidism is usually caused by a hormone-producing thyroid tumour.

Adrenal gland disorders

The adrenal glands – located beside each kidney – produce the hormone cortisol, vital for life-sustaining metabolic activities. Overactivity of these glands causes Cushing's disease (hyperadrenocorticism). Small terriers, Poodles, Cavalier King Charles Spaniels, and Boxers are particularly prone to this condition. An affected dog drinks and urinates excessively and is constantly hungry. It can develop a potbellied appearance and lose hair from its body, but not from its head or legs. The dog will

pant more and become weaker and more lethargic. Skin infection (pyoderma) is also not uncommon.

Treatment for Cushing's disease varies depending on the cause of the disorder. Affected dogs are usually treated with trilostene or ketoconazole to reduce the overproduction of hormone, but if the condition has been caused by an adrenal tumour, surgical removal of the tumour may be the most appropriate treatment.

If the adrenal gland is underactive, this causes hypoadrenocorticism, or Addison's disease. This condition often develops when the dog's immune system destroys adrenal gland tissue.

Common signs are loss of appetite, lethargy, depression, weight loss, and weakness; however, the illness is intermittent, and because it comes and goes, it is difficult to diagnose. The breed most predisposed to Addison's disease is the Leonberger. Affected dogs are generally treated by replacing the hormones in which they are deficient.

Excessive drinking can be a sign that your dog has a hormonal disorder.

Muscles, bones, and joints

■ Some conditions are part inherited
■ Lameness is a common indicator of problems
■ Rest is the most important part of any treatment

Dogs are highly active animals, and their skeletons and muscles are subject to great stresses. Injuries are fairly common, but muscle and bone tissues have a remarkable capacity for self-repair. Other problems can result from diseases of the joints or bones.

The most common sign of muscle, bone, or joint disorders is lameness, usually, but not always, caused by pain. If your dog becomes lame, you should seek immediate veterinary attention and ensure that your dog rests the injured limb. Adequate rest is vital; any physical activity could turn minor lameness into a chronic, major injury.

Diagnostic procedures

Finding the cause of lameness is often a challenge. Your vet might take X-rays, do blood tests, analyse joint fluid, conduct an MRI scan, take a biopsy, or conduct an "arthroscopic" exam of a joint using a fine fibre optic endoscope. A technique called nuclear scintigraphy, to scan bone and surrounding tissue, may also be useful. The most common muscle, bone, and joint disorders are described below.

Inherited joint diseases

Some dogs are born with an inherited predisposition to joint diseases, such as

Common causes of lameness

CONDITION	CLINICAL SIGNS
Cut pads	Licking of the affected area may or may not occur.
Grass seed and other foreign body penetration between the toes	Persistent licking of the affected foot usually occurs. An abscess forms at the site of foreign body penetration. Lameness progressively worsens until the abscess bursts.
Bite wounds and secondary infections	Licking of the wound occurs. Lameness worsens as swelling and infection increase.
Sprains and strains	Lameness is sudden, sometimes accompanied by swelling or bruising. May last between a few days and several weeks.
Degenerative joint diseases	Most common in older dogs. Worst upon awakening, but improves with exercise.
Inherited joint diseases	Common in younger dogs. Seldom involves associated swelling. Worsens over time.
Ligament tears	Lameness is sudden, and pain usually minimal. Lameness becomes chronic over time, accompanied by only a minimal capacity to bear weight.
Fractures and dislocations	Lameness is sudden, and pain is severe. Accompanied by swelling and inability to bear weight.
Bone tumours	Single leg limp in older dogs. Painful swelling may be felt through muscles. Worsens with time. Does not respond to rest.
Spinal cord damage	Sudden in small dogs; can sometimes have a gradual onset in larger breeds. Moderate to severe pain. Can often result in symmetrical lameness.
Degenerative nerve diseases	Mostly in German Shepherds. Gradual onset in middle aged dogs. No pain or swelling. Hind paws buckle over.

Ask the vet

Q: My arthritic dog has improved since we began a course of acupuncture treatment. How does sticking needles in its back reduce pain?
A: Acupuncture, and some other complementary therapies, certainly make some dogs with joint problems more comfortable. The exact reason why remains elusive but therapies such as acupuncture, acupressure, shiatsu, chiropractice, osteopathy, and massage, all involve touch. This may somehow trigger a dog's endorphins – its natural painkillers.

hip dysplasia, elbow dysplasia, or avascular necrosis. If you want to avoid problems, steer clear of those breeds that are most susceptible. Always buy your pups from a reputable source, and check that they have been bred to minimize the chances of joint disorders. Do not allow your puppy to become overweight, and avoid physical stress on developing limbs. Feed your dog with a diet specially formulated for fast-growing breeds prone to joint problems. The most common inherited joint diseases include:

• **Hip dysplasia:** this painful condition causes lameness in one or both hind legs. The term "dysplasia" means abnormal development, and in hip dysplasia, it is the head of the thigh bone (femur) that does not develop properly. The result is that the femur no longer fits into the socket of the hip, causing wear and tear, and leading to pain and lameness. While genetics plays a role in the onset of this condition, other factors, such as overfeeding during puppyhood, may be equally important. Mild cases of hip dysplasia generally respond well to medication, but more severe problems require surgical correction.

• **Elbow dysplasia:** most frequently seen in Bernese Mountain Dogs, Labrador and Golden Retrievers, and Rottweilers, elbow dysplasia is really a constellation of different elbow problems including osteochondrosis (see below). Cartilage in the dog's joints develops abnormally, and can interfere with the movement of the elbow joint. Elbow dysplasia generally occurs during a pup's growth period between four to ten months of age, causing lameness that worsens with exercise. In most cases, treatment will involve surgery to repair the affected joint.

• **Osteochondrosis (OC):** also known as osteochondrosis dessicans (OCD), this condition affects growing puppies. Pieces of poorly developing cartilage flake within a dog's joints and interfere with smooth joint function. This commonly occurs in the shoulders, but also in the elbows, stifles, and hocks. It is often seen in heavy, fast-growing dogs fed high-energy diets.

Simple rest is sufficient treatment for some affected individuals, but other dogs benefit from having the floating chips of cartilage removed surgically.

Lameness caused by hip dysplasia is common in large, fast-growing breeds.

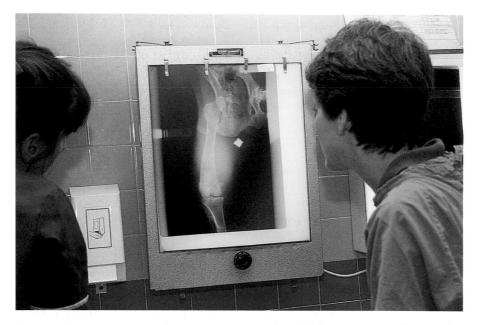

Your veterinary surgeon may use X-rays to identify damage in your dog's painful joints.

• **Avascular necrosis:** in toy breeds, such as the Poodle and the West Highland White Terrier, the blood vessels serving the head of the femur are prone to injury. If these vessels are damaged, the head of the femur effectively dies, causing lameness. Also known as aseptic necrosis or Perthe's disease, this condition usually occurs between 4 and 12 months of age.

Surgery is the only treatment for avascular necrosis: the dead head of the femur must be surgically removed to eliminate pain. In the months following the operation, a "false" fibrous joint develops that is surprisingly efficient.

Degenerative joint disease (DJD)

Cartilage is the tough gristly tissue that coats the moving surfaces of joints, acting as both lubricant and shock absorber. When cartilage degenerates,

or when it fails to repair itself normally after damage, this results in DJD. Regardless of its cause, the progress of DJD is similar in any joint. The first sign is a reduced ability to physically accomplish activities that previously were possible. As DJD progresses, overt stiffness or lameness develops, which is at first intermittent but eventually becomes permanent. DJD is sometimes inaccurately referred to as "arthritis" – a far broader term for any type of joint inflammation.

Treatment for DJD involves controlling the dog's weight and exercise regimen, and minimizing pain. A dog's weight should be reduced to

Slipping kneecaps

Patellar luxations – slipped kneecaps – are common in toy breeds, particularly the Yorkshire Terrier. The kneecap painlessly slips off, causing the dog to hobble on that leg. Most dogs need no treatment at all, but occasionally a lateral knee ligament may be torn, requiring surgical correction.

within the normal range for its breed and sex. Discuss a suitable calorie-controlled diet with your vet. Moderate, sensible exercise, such as walking or swimming, is necessary to maintain good muscle tone, but avoid strenuous exercise, such as running and retrieving games. Pain is controlled with non-steroid anti-inflammatories, such as meloxicam and carprofen. Both are licensed for chronic use when kidney and liver function is monitored.

There are many commercial nutritional supplements that claim to protect joint cartilage. The most widely available of these are glucosamine and chondroitin. When used regularly over a period of time, these appear to be beneficial. Feeding essential fatty acids (EFAs) found in marine fish oil or linseed oil may also be effective – in some individuals this seems to reduce the need for drugs to control joint pain.

Polyarthritis

In this rare condition, inflammation affects many joints in the dog's body. It can be triggered by autoimmune diseases, infection, or hypersensitivity to drugs, especially some of the older antibiotics, such as trimethoprin sulfa. Affected dogs may develop a fever, skin rash, and swollen lymph nodes, as well as inflammation. This disorder usually resolves when use of the offending drug is discontinued.

Older German Shepherds

Chronic degenerative myelopathy (CDM or CDRM) affects many German Shepherds. The disease causes a progressive loss of the use of the hind legs, so that the dogs walk with a drunken gait. This is a painless degenerative nerve disease for which, regrettably, there is no cure.

Ask the vet

Q: Do dogs get rheumatism?
A: Many dog owners tell me their dogs are "rheumatic" or have "rheumatism". While the autoimmune condition rheumatoid arthritis is common in humans, it remains rare in dogs, occurring mainly in the foot joints (carpal and tarsal joints) in toy or small breeds between one and eight years old.

Joint and bone infections

Occasionally, bacteria can get into a dog's joints through penetrating wounds or via the bloodstream. *Borrelia burgdorferi*, the organism that causes Lyme disease, and other tick-borne infections such as *Rickettsia* and *Ehrlichia* can all reach joint cavities. Infections of the joints will cause lameness, but can be easily treated with a prolonged course of antibiotics.

Bones are quite resistant to infection, but they are occasionally affected by bacteria like *Staphylococcus*, which enter from wounds, bites, and foreign bodies, as well as from distant locations via the bloodstream. Acute infection is accompanied by fever, loss of appetite and weight, lethargy, and heat and swelling in the muscles surrounding the site of infection. Bone infection, or osteomyelitis, is treated with six-week courses of antibiotics that specifically act in bone tissue.

Bone tumours

Dogs develop a variety of bone tumours, the most common of which is osteosarcoma. This highly malignant cancer is most likely to occur in the long bones of middle-aged, or older, large and giant breeds.

The first sign of a bone tumour is usually lameness and pain. Unfortunately, this type of cancer

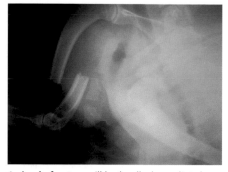

A **simple fracture** will heal well when splinted or set in a cast, but more complex breaks may require internal fixation with pins, plates, or screws.

Swimming is ideal gentle exercise for a dog suffering with a joint disorder, because it tones muscles while relieving pressure on the joints.

spreads very easily *(see pp.272–3)*, and by the time a tumour has been found, there is a 90 per cent chance that the cancer will have spread to other parts of the body, such as the lungs and liver.

Removal of the tumour, which usually involves amputation of the limb, remains the treatment of choice for tumours in long bones. This is combined with medication for pain relief. With dramatic intervention, around half of dogs with this form of cancer survive for a year or more.

Broken bones

If your dog sustains a fracture, it is likely to be the result of an accident. Before treating the fracture, it is important to remove the dog and yourself from danger, attend to shock, and if necessary, perform life-saving first aid *(see pp.222–5)*.

Fractures can be open – when broken bone protrudes through the skin – or closed. In a closed fracture, the break is not visible but also causes pain and swelling. Greenstick fractures, common in the bones of young dogs, occur when a bone "bends" – cracking on one side only, and compressing on the

other. Fractures of long bones are the most evident, because the dog cannot bear weight on the affected limb.

Joint dislocations

A complete dislocation, or luxation, occurs if the joint surfaces of two bones become separated; a subluxation is a partial dislocation in which the joint surfaces are only partly separated. Subluxations can often be difficult to diagnose, even with X-rays. In some cases, if a dog is seen shortly after an injury, the dislocated bones can be manually replaced under general anaesthesia. However, if left for too long, a surgical procedure may be necessary to repair the joint.

Ask the vet

Q: Do dogs ever need mineral supplements?
A: Only if they are ill or elderly. Contrary to what many breeders believe, fast-growing pups do not need, and should not be given, calcium supplements. Research carried out over 25 years ago revealed that too much calcium can actually be harmful to joint development. Diets formulated by the major pet food makers contain balanced amounts of vitamins and minerals to ensure healthy growth. The best also contain high levels of beneficial antioxidants *(see pp.198–201)*.

Torn ligaments

By far the most common ligament injury is to the anterior cruciate (knee) ligament, which is most likely to tear in middle-aged, overweight dogs. The treatment varies according to weight: for dogs of less than 7 kg (15 lb), it may be sufficient to rest the injured leg. In three months, fibrous tissue develops in the joint, effectively repairing it. If this is not successful, and for larger dogs, a surgical repair is usually necessary.

Bruised and torn muscles

Muscular problems in dogs occur most often where muscle fibres meet nerves, or in the nerves that supply the muscle. Strains, bruising, and tearing are overwhelmingly the most common muscle problems. Bruised, stretched, or torn muscle fibres are difficult to see, especially in dogs with full coats of hair. These forms of damage may be caused by injuries from falling and collision, and also by excessive work or exercise: racing Greyhounds are particularly prone to muscle tears. Minor injuries produce local sensitivity and tenderness, while major damage causes more swelling and greater pain.

Parting the hair may reveal reddening caused by muscle damage below. To treat bruised or torn muscles, rest is vital. If the damage is severe, at least three weeks rest may be required. A cold compress, applied to the affected area, can help to reduce inflammation and will minimize pain.

Muscle problems

Myasthenia gravis is a congenital, or acquired, deficiency in a chemical called acetylcholine (ACh) that transfers information from a nerve

Common terms	
Your vet may use any of these words to describe the cause of your dog's lameness.	
Strain	A strain means damage to muscle fibres and tendons. Strains are often accompanied by slight bleeding and bruising.
Sprain	A sprain is an injury caused by the wrenching of a joint, resulting in overstretching of the ligaments. It causes lameness similar to a muscle strain.
Cramp	Painful cramp occurs when muscle filaments, the components of muscle fibres, remain permanently contracted. This occurs most frequently in canine athletes such as Greyhounds.
Tear	Ligaments, tendons, whole muscles, or parts of muscles can tear.
Fracture	The most common fractures cause the two or more parts of broken bone to separate. These are called "complete" fractures. Less common fractures split or compress bone without separation. These are more difficult to diagnose.
Dislocation or luxation	A bone that separates from its adjoining bone at a joint has been dislocated. Dislocations often involve ligament tears. A partial separation is a subluxation.

fibre to a muscle fibre. Signs of this condition include physical weakness and low exercise tolerance. Infection by the bacterium *Clostridium botulinum* (botulism) and tick paralysis can prevent ACh from being released by nerve fibres at their junction with muscle fibres, and can result in paralysis. Fortunately, muscle conditions such as these are very rare.

Natural wear and tear

Over time your dog's muscles naturally shrink and lose their power. Metabolic disorders elsewhere in the body may affect muscle mass by reducing the amount of nutrients muscles need or producing toxins that damage muscle fibre. If your dog is losing muscle mass for no apparent reason, you should seek the advice of your vet.

Spinal disorders

■ Rest is essential for all types of spinal damage
■ Immediate surgery is vital when paralysis occurs
■ Some breeds, large and small, are at increased risk

Damage to the spinal cord, whether it occurs spontaneously or results from an accident, can cause loss of voluntary muscle movement, changes in spinal reflexes or muscle tone, muscle shrinkage, and loss of touch and pain sensations. This damage may be irreparable.

Paralysis

Paralysis is often caused by traumatic spinal cord injury from road traffic accidents or falls, gunshot wounds, or from intervertebral disc disease *(see opposite)*. Partial paralysis affecting the hindquarters is more common than complete paralysis. Traumatic paralysis is treated with methylprednisolone intravenously, but, in most cases, surgery will also be necessary.

Damage to a peripheral nerve, caused by a car accident or any other trauma in which a leg is jerked away from the body, can bring about loss of sensation in the muscles served by that nerve, and

Handling a dog with back injuries

If your dog has suffered a back injury, first check for signs of other life-threatening injuries, and if necessary, give CPR or treat the dog for shock *(see p.222–5)*. Handle the dog as described below, and seek veterinary assistance as soon as possible.

❶ Keep the back as straight as possible during handling. Muzzle the dog if necessary.

❷ Find a hard, flat surface, such as a piece of plywood, that can be used as a stretcher. It should be small enough to fit in a vehicle. Place this along the back of the injured dog.

❸ With the help of others, if they are available, and speaking soothingly to the dog, grasp the skin over the hips and the shoulder blades, and gently pull the dog on to the make-shift stretcher.

❹ Secure the dog to the stretcher using heavy-duty tape or similar material over the hips and shoulders. Prevent neck movement if there are neck injuries.

❺ If you have been unable to find any hard material to make a stretcher, fold over a large blanket so that it is thick and firm and draw the dog on to it. Secure the dog with heavy-duty tape, and lift the blanket from both ends.

The spinal cord in the neck of this Doberman is compressed in several places where the discs in the intervertebral spaces have slipped.

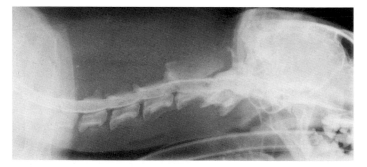

Slipped discs

A dog's delicate spinal cord is protected by the movable, bony vertebrae of the spine. Gelatinous discs, coated with fibrous tissue, act as shock absorbers between adjacent vertebrae. If a disc "slips" and pushes on the spinal cord, this can cause pain, paralysis, and loss of muscle function.

Intervertebral discs consist of a gelatinous material encased in a fibrous outer coating. The spinal cord runs between these discs and the vertebrae of the spine.

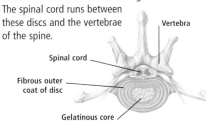

Vertebra

Spinal cord

Fibrous outer coat of disc

Gelatinous core

If the disc protrudes into the spinal canal, the spinal cord can become compressed, causing pain. Protrusions can be the result of a sudden rupture of the disc, or a slow bulging that presses on to the spinal cord.

Ruptured disc presses on the spinal cord

eventual paralysis. While in some cases it may be necessary to amputate the injured limb, a surgical procedure to transpose muscle attachments and produce a stiff, straight leg is sometimes a successful alternative.

Intervertebral disc disease

The fibrous tissue that separates the intervertebral discs from the spinal cord (see above) can degenerate and rupture, causing pain and paralysis. For most dogs, corticosteroids are beneficial when given on the same day that injury occurs. After that, the most important part of treatment is rest, usually for at least two weeks.

Wobbler syndrome

This serious condition, also known as cervical spondylomyelopathy, occurs most frequently in young Great Danes and young to middle-aged Dobermans. It causes progressive loss of coordination in the hind legs, caused by instability of the vertebrae in the neck that results in compression and damage to the spinal cord. If untreated, partial paralysis may spread to the front legs. Wobbler syndrome responds best to early surgical correction.

Chronic myelopathy

Primarily affecting German Shepherd dogs, although it does occur in other large breeds, chronic degenerative radiculomyelopathy (CDRM) is a debilitating disease that causes partial paralysis. Starting as early as six years of age, an affected dog slowly develops a painless lack of coordination of the hind legs. Over the following years, weakness evolves into partial paralysis, but pain perception and voluntary control over urinating and defecating remain intact. Unfortunately, while many treatments have been attempted, none have been discovered yet that slow down or reverse CDRM. Weight control and routine daily exercise are valuable, however, to ensure the best possible muscle tone.

Breeds with long backs and short legs, like the Dachshund, are prone to intervertebral disc disease.

Mouth and teeth

- Gum disease is the most common medical problem
- Chewing on sticks and stones is dangerous
- Prevent problems by brushing your dog's teeth

Dogs use their mouth and teeth not only for eating, but also for defence, for grooming, for showing affection to others, or simply to explore, taste, play, and amuse. As a consequence there is a wide variety of potential problems.

Mouth infections

Infection or inflammation in the mouth – stomatitis – can be caused by cuts, burns, foreign bodies stuck in the mouth, and diseases of the gums and the structures that support the teeth (periodontal disease). Metabolic diseases such as kidney failure can also cause painful stomatitis. Stick injuries are common and potentially serious, especially those in the back of the mouth. To treat stomatitis, the cause is addressed: physical injuries are treated, foreign objects are removed, dental conditions are corrected, and any underlying metabolic disorders are controlled to prevent recurrence.

Secondary bacterial infection is common, so appropriate antibiotics are almost always used.

Foreign bodies in the mouth

Chewing on sticks, stones, bones, and other hard materials is fun for your dog, but also potentially dangerous: sticks can cause damage to the mouth and can also crack teeth, especially molars. This may lead to tooth-pulp exposure and infection. If your dog has a foreign body stuck in its mouth, gently restrain the dog and carefully remove the object with a spoon handle (see p.237).

Foreign bodies in the throat

Sticks can lodge in the back of the throat, too far for easy removal with a spoon handle. A dog with something in its throat gags, paws anxiously at its mouth, and may drool or vomit. This is a potentially life-threatening situation.

Common mouth and dental problems

PROBLEM	POSSIBLE CAUSES	SEE VET
Slow or selective eating	Any mouth condition that causes pain.	Within 24 hours.
Eating with head tilted, or dropping food, then eating it	Pain on one side of the mouth.	Within 24 hours.
Difficulty opening the mouth	Inherited or acquired head, jaw, or neck disorder; tumour; abscess; penetrating foreign body.	Same day.
Drooling saliva	Mouth and gum disease; foreign object in the mouth; rabies; excess heat; tumour; salivary "cyst"; heat injury.	Same day.
Gagging	Foreign object; tumour.	Immediately.
Bad breath	Periodontal disease; lip fold disease; foreign object; tumour; stomach condition; metabolic disease.	Within 24 hours.

Dealing with foreign bodies

OBJECT	SIGNS	TREATMENT
Stick or bone in roof of mouth	Pawing at face.	Pry out with spoon handle.
Stick or bone wedged in teeth	Pawing and drooling.	Pry out with spoon handle.
Fish hook in lips	Visible.	Push through, cut off barb with pliers, then pull out.
Fish hook in mouth or swallowed	Pawing; dog seems depressed.	Immediate veterinary attention.
String or elastic around tongue	Dribbling; string or elastic may be visible.	Immediate veterinary attention.
Porcupine quills in lips	Visible.	Pull out with pliers or seek veterinary attention.
Porcupine quills in mouth	Pawing and dribbling.	Immediate veterinary attention.
Anything penetrating tongue	Pawing and dribbling; open mouth; swelling under tongue.	Immediate veterinary attention.

A foreign body in the throat may cause swelling that interferes with breathing. If the object blocks the voice box, the dog chokes and faints. Treat the dog immediately for choking (see p.237).

Periodontal disease
Virtually every dog will develop periodontal disease during its lifetime. Poor dental hygiene is the prime cause, and dogs with periodontal disease commonly have bad breath (halitosis).

Periodontal disease is preventable: the best way is to regularly brush your dog's teeth (see p.197); chewing on dry food, even dry food formulated to clean teeth, will not on its own prevent periodontal disease. Check your dog's mouth for a red line bordering the teeth: this is the first sign of gum inflammation (gingivitis). Treatment at this stage prevents gingivitis from developing into periodontal disease.

Mouth tumours
Tumours are uncommon but can occur on the gums, tongue, or roof of mouth, or in the salivary glands. When possible they are surgically removed, followed by radiation therapy or chemotherapy.

Your vet can treat your dog's inflamed gums to eliminate pain and infection, and prolong the use and function of the teeth.

Stomach problems

- Vomiting has causes inside and outside the stomach
- Withhold food and water from vomiting dogs
- Bloat is a life-threatening emergency

Vomiting and diarrhoea are two of the most common problems seen by vets. Their causes are often trivial, but in some cases they can be life threatening. Knowing a little about the different types of vomiting will help you decide if your dog needs veterinary attention.

• **Acute vomiting:** dogs "cure" themselves of their scavenging indiscretions by vomiting back foods and foreign bodies that should not be in the stomach. Worms might also be removed this way. Acute vomiting also occurs as a result of motion sickness. With otherwise healthy dogs, simply withhold food and water for two hours after a single vomiting episode.

• **Intermittent vomiting:** this may be caused by food allergies or more serious conditions, such as metabolic diseases, ulcers, or tumours. See your vet within two days if vomiting occurs intermittently over several days.

• **Repeated vomiting:** can result from a simple stomach irritation or a life-threatening obstruction, so warrants immediate veterinary attention.

• **Projectile vomiting:** often caused by an obstruction that prevents food from leaving the stomach or by neurological conditions that affect the brain's control centre. See a vet the same day.

• **Vomiting blood:** suggests stomach or small intestine ulceration, poisoning, foreign bodies, tumours, or serious infection. See your vet the same day.

• **Vomiting bile:** this may be a form of mild allergy. Affected dogs vomit bile, often at the same time each day, but are otherwise healthy. Vomiting is usually controlled with anti-nausea drugs until any diet change is effective.

Principal causes of vomiting

TYPE	UNDERLYING CAUSES
Dietary	Scavenging; overeating; food intolerance; true allergy.
Gastric disorders	Inflammation (gastritis); parasites; ulcers; foreign bodies; tumours; bloat (dilatation-volvulus); motility problems.
Intestinal disorders	Inflammation (inflammatory bowel disease, colitis); parasites; foreign bodies; tumours; infections (parvovirus, distemper); bacterial overgrowth (small intestine bacterial overgrowth or SIBO); telescoping of intestines (intussusception); constipation.
Other abdominal disorders	Inflamed pancreas (pancreatitis); inflamed peritoneum (peritonitis); abdominal tumours.
Metabolic and hormonal conditions	Kidney failure; liver diseases; diabetes; underactive adrenal gland (hypoadrenocorticism); overactive thyroid (hyperthyroidism); blood poisoning (septicaemia, endotoxaemia); electrolyte and acid–base upsets; anxiety, fears, phobias.
Poisons and drugs	Lead; antifreeze (ethylene glycol); strychnine; heart medications (digitalis); non-steroid anti-inflammatories; chemotherapy drugs; some antibiotics.

Treatment for vomiting dogs

Withhold food after the vomiting episode for 2–24 hours, depending upon the severity of the vomiting and the age and fitness of the individual.

Regularly give the dog small amounts of water or ice cubes. Dissolving rehydration salts in the water is beneficial, and soda water can help to neutralize the build-up of acid in vomiting dogs. Reintroduce food gradually, starting with frequent, small portions of low-fat, low-protein, soft food. A good home-made diet is one part low-fat cottage cheese and two parts boiled rice. This avoids stretching the stomach and will help food pass into the intestines.

Regurgitating food

Regurgitation occurs when food in the oesophagus is expelled back almost effortlessly through the mouth. The most common cause is an enlarged oesophagus – likely to be diagnosed when pups move from milk to solid food. Affected dogs are treated with frequent, small, high-calorie meals. The meal is put on an elevated platform, allowing gravity to assist the food through the oesophagus. Drugs that stimulate the movement of food from the oesophagus to the stomach may also be used.

Drug awareness

Corticosteroids and non-steroid anti-inflammatories (NSAIDs) can occasionally cause stomach ulcers. If your dog is on these drugs and vomits intermittently, appears unhappy, and loses weight, see your vet. When using NSAIDs, only use those licensed for veterinary use. They are safer for dogs than many NSAIDs licensed for use in people.

Bloat: a life threatening condition

If your dog's belly swells and it seems uncomfortable, see a vet immediately. Bloat (gastric dilatation-volvulus) is one of the most serious of all medical emergencies. The causes of this condition are not clear, although in young dogs, it may result from overeating. The dog's stomach becomes bloated due to a build up of fluids and gas. This may be accompanied by drooling, retching, restless wandering, listlessness, signs of pain, and attempts to vomit; signs of shock develop fast (see pp.224–5). Urgent veterinary attention is required to release the trapped gas and treat the dog for shock. However, bloat is an acute condition and has a high fatality rate even for dogs that receive immediate surgical intervention. The risk of bloat runs in families: middle-aged individuals of large or giant breeds with deep, narrow chests are particularly at risk: these include the Great Dane, Weimaraner, Standard Poodle, Irish Wolfhound, Irish and Gordon Setters, and Doberman. To minimize the risk of bloat, limit water consumption for an hour before or after each meal. Give both water and food often but in small quantities, and prevent your dog from rolling or taking exercise after meals.

Some dogs chew on grass to settle an upset stomach.

Digestive disorders

- Diarrhoea may be trivial or life-threatening
- Bowel problems can originate in other parts of the body
- The liver and pancreas are vital for digestion

Diarrhoea, the most common medical condition associated with the intestines, can occur as a result of damage to the digestive system, but may simply be your dog's way of coping with an ingested irritant.

Diarrhoea may be accompanied by vomiting, tummy rumbles, pain, burping, or passing wind, and it may contain mucus or blood. Get immediate veterinary attention if your dog is lethargic, has a fever, or passes blood, or if the bout of diarrhoea is persistent or explosive, because these symptoms could indicate a potentially serious condition.

In some cases, diarrhoea can be associated with an increase or loss of appetite or severe lethargy. Examination of the characteristics of a dog's diarrhoea and observation of any changes in behaviour can help to identify the problem (see opposite).

Loss of appetite can stem from problems inside or outside the digestive system.

General causes include the following:
- Dietary indiscretion;
- Dietary allergy or sensitivity;
- Food poisoning;
- Parasites, such as *Giardia* or *Trichuris*;
- Viruses, such as parvovirus or distemper;
- Bacteria, such as *Campylobacter*;
- A reaction to some drugs.

Treatment for diarrhoea

A dog with persistent diarrhoea should always be examined by a vet. Acute diarrhoea is treated symptomatically; where the cause is known, such as with diet, drug, toxin, or parasite problems, these are eliminated. Antibiotics are seldom used unless bacterial infection is suspected.

A dog with diarrhoea can become dehydrated, so even if you are withholding food from your dog, encourage it to drink plenty of fresh water. Many experts recommend that you avoid changing the dog's diet after a bout of diarrhoea; its regular diet provides familiar food to the gut flora.

Acute bloody vomiting and diarrhoea

This life-threatening condition occurs most frequently in small, middle-aged dogs like Miniature Poodles, Miniature Schnauzers, and Dachshunds. A dog with these symptoms needs emergency help – it may require hospitalization and aggressive fluid therapy.

Types of diarrhoea

CHARACTERISTIC	DESCRIPTION	CAUSE
Consistency	Watery.	Rapid transit through gut.
	Covered in jelly (mucus).	Large intestine condition (colitis).
	Oily or greasy.	Malabsorption condition (fat).
	Bubbly.	Gas-forming bacteria in intestines.
Colour	Tarry and black.	Bleeding from upper digestive tract.
	Clots or bright red.	Bleeding from lower digestive tract or anus.
	Clay-like and glistening.	Poor digestion/absorption (pancreas disease).
	Pasty and light.	Lack of bile from liver.
	Yellow-green.	Rapid transit through the gut.
Frequency and quantity	Small amounts very frequently.	Irritation to colon.
	Large amounts 3–4 times daily.	Digestion/malabsorption condition in small intestine.
Odour	Normal.	Rapid transit/malabsorption.
	Unpleasant.	Bacterial action (fermentation), blood.
Other signs	Vomiting.	Gastroenteritis.
	Weight loss.	Malabsorption.
	No weight loss; good appetite.	Large intestine condition.

Inflammatory bowel disease (colitis)

The term "colitis" refers to a range of immune-mediated diseases that involve inflammation of the large intestine or colon. Affected dogs have chronic diarrhoea, pass stools more frequently, experience pain when they pass stools, lose weight, look malnourished, and are often anaemic. The German Shepherd has a high incidence of colitis and other bowel disorders. Your vet will recommend a "hypoallergenic diet", and immune-suppressing drugs such as corticosteroids are routinely used.

Constipation

Constipation is not uncommon and is usually self-limiting, lasting only a day or two. Serious causes include eating indigestible material, nerve disorders, obstructions, pain, and dehydration.

In older dogs, inactivity and poor muscle tone can cause constipation. If your dog is suffering from age-related constipation, follow these guidelines:
• Soak dry food in equal parts of water and leave 20 minutes for it to be fully absorbed, to increase fluid intake;
• Let your older dog out frequently, increasing opportunities to defecate;
• Give your dog cow's milk – a natural laxative – or use a mild product such as lactulose, as instructed by your vet.

Rectal obstructions

Obstructions that affect the rectum can cause constipation or ribbon-like stool. An enlarged prostate gland, for example, can interfere with the normal passage of stool. A perineal hernia occurs when a weakness in the walls of the rectum causes a bulge; stool can build up in the bulge, diverting the course of the rectum and dilating it, resulting in a rectal obstruction.

The objective of treatment is to remove the obstruction. Dogs with

Ask the vet

Q: Does milk cause diarrhoea?
A: Any change in diet can potentially cause diarrhoea, but milk can be a particular problem for dogs that no longer produce sufficient amounts of the enzyme lactase, as they did as pups. If your dog likes milk but suffers from diarrhoea when it is consumed, try feeding lactose-free milk.

A **dog scoots** to relieve irritation under the tail, but excessive scooting can aggravate the underlying problem and should be discouraged.

enlarged prostates are given drugs to shrink the prostate, or are neutered. Hernias are often surgically repaired.

Scooting

Dogs scoot by dragging their bottoms along the ground, preferably on an abrasive surface such as grass or carpet. Although irritation from worms causes some dogs to scoot, anal sac irritation is a more common cause. Some dogs with anal sac problems simply jump up from a resting position as if they have had a fright or felt a sudden pain. Uncomplicated blocked anal sacs can be emptied by gentle external pressure *(see p.197)*. If the anals sacs are infected, the sac swells and bursts through the skin on either side of the anus, producing a painful draining abscess. Treatment for infected anal sacs will involve antibiotics.

A distended belly

There are a number of causes of a distended abdomen, but obesity is the most common. In unneutered females, pregnancy and exaggerated phantom pregnancies are also normal causes of a distended abdomen. A dog's belly can become enlarged, however, for a number of clinical reasons that involve serious medical conditions; see your vet immediately if your dog's abdomen suddenly and unexpectedly enlarges.

Flatulence

Burping and flatulence may be caused by swallowing air when eating quickly, but also by eating highly fermentable foods such as soya (tofu) and undigestible carbohydrate as in uncooked greens. To minimize these problems, feed several small meals of easy-to-digest, low-fibre food daily. Activated charcoal and the over-the-counter product simethicone may be useful to absorb intestinal gas.

Pancreas disorders

The pancreas secretes digestive enzymes into the intestines to digest food. Not enough digestive enzymes leads to malabsorption conditions. Seepage of enzyme anywhere other than directly into the intestine causes intense and painful inflammation. The pancreas has additional hormonal roles: it secretes a variety of hormones, including insulin, into the bloodstream. Common pancreas disorders include:
• **Acute pancreatitis:** in this extremely painful condition, the pancreas becomes inflamed. Affected dogs tuck up their bellies, vomit, and develop signs of shock. In less severe instances, a dog with pancreatitis may appear uncomfortable; it may drop its front half into a resting position but is reluctant to drop its hind quarters,

assuming a "prayer position". To treat, pain control and overcoming shock are vital. Food is withheld to reduce pancreatic activity. When stability returns, a low-fat maintenance diet is given, usually in small, frequent meals.

• **Exocrine pancreatic insufficiency:** the pancreas can lose its ability to manufacture digestive enzymes when the immune system malfunctions and attacks and destroys the part of the pancreas that secretes these enzymes. Affected individuals eat voraciously, but lose weight. They scavenge, and pass copious quantities of grey, cow-manure-like diarrhoea. This condition can be treated with pancreas enzyme capsules, given before meals.

Diabetes mellitus

Insulin, produced by the pancreas, helps body cells absorb glucose. In diabetes mellitus (or "sugar diabetes"), the immune system mistakenly destroys the pancreas's insulin-manufacturing capacity. A resulting lack of insulin causes blood sugar to increase after eating. Breeds more likely to suffer from sugar diabetes include Dachshunds, Poodles, and small terriers.

A diabetic dog requires daily insulin injections (see p.219), and your vet will also recommend a high fibre diet.

Liver disorders

The liver's digestive responsibilities include metabolizing or detoxifying substances from the intestines. Common liver problems include:

• **Liver disease (hepatitis):** acute hepatitis involves sudden and severe inflammation of the liver. It can be caused by infections such as infectious canine hepatitis (ICH) and leptospirosis, trauma from accidents, advanced heatstroke, or poisoning from plants, chemicals, or drugs.

Early signs of liver disease include vomiting, lethargy, increased drinking and urinating, and weight loss. By the time that jaundice (yellow staining to the body) develops, over 80 per cent of liver function has been lost. Treatment involves correcting the underlying cause; diet management eases the work of the liver while that is done.

• **Liver shunt:** blood vessels from the intestines sometimes bypass the liver; toxic substances are not removed, and brain inflammation can result. Affected dogs may stagger, twitch, act lethargically, or have seizures. This condition may require surgery.

A dog assumes the "prayer position" to ease the pain of pancreatitis.

Urinary tract disorders

■ Chronic kidney disease is usually insidious
■ Increased drinking is always significant
■ Pain accompanies many bladder problems

Changes in a dog's normal urinary functions, and particularly in the quantity, colour, or consistency of urine, warrant immediate investigation by a vet because they can indicate serious, even life-threatening disease.

Urine changes

The amount and quality of urine gives excellent clues to problems in the kidneys or lower urinary tract. Increased urinating can be caused by any of the following conditions:
• Kidney disease;
• Sugar diabetes or diabetes mellitus *(see p.259)*;
• Pituitary diabetes or ADH deficiency diabetes *(see p.242)*;
• Liver disease or hepatic insufficiency *(see p.259)*;
• Womb infection or pyometra *(see p.264–5)*;
• Overactive adrenal gland or hyperadrenocorticism *(see p.243)*;
• Underactive adrenal gland or hypoadrenocorticism *(see p.243)*;
• Underactive thyroid gland or hypothyroidism *(see p.242)*;
• Drugs or diet;
• Pain, fever, or altered behaviour.

Blood in the urine

If you notice blood in your dog's urine (haematuria), see your vet the same day – this could indicate a potentially serious condition. Medical reasons for haematuria include:
• Trauma;
• Severe inflammatory urinary tract disease;
• Bladder or kidney stones;
• Poisoning from a "coumarin" rodenticide such as warfarin;
• Autoimmune haemolytic anaemia;
• Tumours in the genital tract.

Acute kidney failure

Kidney failure occurs when more than three-quarters of kidney function has been lost. It may result from injury, disease, from an immune disorder, or simply from advancing years. Kidney

Urinary disorders
become far more
common in a
dog's later years.

Ask the vet

Q: What is uraemia?

A: Uraemia occurs at a late stage in kidney failure, when waste products that are normally eliminated in the urine, such as urea, enter the bloodstream. If the uraemia is advanced, the prognosis is grave. Typical signs of uraemia include excess thirst and drinking, loss of appetite, weight loss, lethargy or apathy, ammonia breath, pale gums and mouth ulcers, vomiting, and diarrhoea.

Dogs love the taste of antifreeze that may leak from your car radiator, but it is extremely poisonous and can result in kidney failure and coma.

failure can occur suddenly (acute kidney failure) but more often it is slow or "chronic" *(see below)*.

Acute kidney failure is a life-threatening event usually caused by a condition outside the urinary tract, such as heart failure, shock, severe infection, or systemic diseases such as advanced tumours. Certain poisons, such as ethylene glycol (antifreeze), can also result in sudden kidney failure. An affected dog may lose its appetite, become weak and lethargic and collapse, and there may be vomiting and diarrhoea. Any dog showing the above signs should be seen by a vet as quickly as possible, because intensive care with immediate intravenous fluid therapy is vital for survival.

Chronic kidney failure

This is a slow, insidious disease that usually, but not always, affects older dogs. General signs begin with increased drinking and urinating, and a slight slowing down. Eventually, fatigue and increasing listlessness develop, and the dog loses interest in its surroundings. Left untreated, mild retching begins, followed by vomiting froth or meals. Body tremors or loss of fine balance develop, and the dog suffers mild seizures. Diet management is the primary treatment for chronic

kidney failure *(see below)*. Fluids may be given intravenously, although in some circumstances it is necessary to deliver them under the skin (subcutaneously). High blood pressure is managed with ACE inhibitors, such as enalapril. Many drugs are cleared from the body by the kidneys, so if a dog is diagnosed with chronic kidney failure, the dose of all drugs it is receiving should be reevaluated.

Diet and chronic kidney failure

Once a dog has developed chronic kidney disease, the condition cannot be reversed. However, a carefully formulated diet can help to slow the progression of the disease and manage the symptoms to allow the best possible quality of life. Your vet will advise you on a suitable diet for your dog based on how far the disease has progressed. The primary objectives in making changes to the dog's diet are to:

• **Reduce phosphorus:** restricting phosphorus levels in the diet has been shown to slow the progression of kidney failure.

• **Reduce sodium:** this helps to control high blood pressure.

Reducing risks of kidney disease

Follow these steps to reduce risk and increase early detection of kidney disease.

1 Accurately weigh your mature dog every three months. Report any weight loss of five per cent or more to your vet.

2 Prevent gum disease. It could lead to bacteria in the blood damaging the kidneys.

3 During annual health checks for your mature dog, ask your vet to perform a routine blood test to assess your dog's kidney function.

4 In breeds known to suffer from inherited juvenile kidney failure, such as Cocker Spaniels, ensure the breeding stock is genetically free from this dangerous condition.

Inherited juvenile kidney failure

Some breeds of dogs inherit a genetic predisposition towards juvenile kidney failure. In the Cocker Spaniel, Samoyed, and Shar Pei, kidney disease can develop very early, with some individuals not surviving into adulthood. Only with careful selective breeding will these fatal inherited conditions be eliminated.

- **Increase fat intake:** a high level of fat in the diet helps to stimulate appetite and increase calorie consumption.
- **Give adequate high-quality protein:** a moderate level of high-quality protein in the diet is beneficial to maintain muscle mass and normal activity levels.
- **Increase vitamin intake:** dogs with chronic kidney failure are prone to deficiencies in certain vitamins, so these should be added to the diet.
- **Increase antioxidants:** these scavenge free radicals – naturally occurring reactive molecules that can damage kidney cell walls. Most dog food manufacturers add antioxidants to their speciality diets (see pp.198–201).
- **Give plenty of water:** ensure that a dog with kidney failure always has a supply of fresh, clean water.
- **Consider supplements:** Omega-3 polyunsaturated fatty acids (Omega-3 PUFA) appear to protect the kidneys and possibly also lower blood pressure. Diets already containing these fatty acids or Omega-3 PUFA supplements may be an effective therapy for dogs with kidney failure.

Lower urinary tract disorders

Bladder and associated urethral conditions affect dogs of all ages. Cystitis, an inflammation of the lining to the bladder, and urethritis, an inflammation of the urethra, can result from bacterial infection, mineral deposit, injuries, tumours, and even stress. Some of these conditions can be very painful. An affected dog's urine appears cloudy or has a sour smell, and when analysed, may be found to contain crystals, blood, bacteria, or other substances.

Bladder sediment and stones

Dogs of all ages and breeds can develop mineral sediment ("crystals") or stones ("uroliths") in any part of the urinary tract. They usually form in the bladder and pass down into the urethra. If a stone blocks the urinary tract, this can be a painful and potentially life-threatening condition. Treatment for bladder stones involves eliminating the underlying cause and reducing the quantity of sediment or preventing its recurrence though diet management.

Antibiotics are given when infection is the source of the condition. Dogs are also encouraged to drink more water; the simplest way to do this with dogs that eat dry food is to switch them over to wet food diets.

If stones are very large, they can be felt on abdominal examination, while others are revealed by X-ray or ultrasound. Large stones or those causing urethral blockages are surgically removed.

Urinary tract obstruction

A dog with an obstruction in the urinary tract is in obvious pain. It strains, cries, is restless, and cannot pass any urine. Left untreated, clinical shock rapidly develops. This is a life-threatening condition; if your dog displays symptoms of urinary tract obstruction, you should seek urgent veterinary assistance. Most blockages are caused by stones. Urethral stones lodged behind the bone in the penis (the os penis) are the most common cause, but urinary retention can also result from prostate conditions, tumours, and spinal cord injuries.

Using a catheter, your vet will try to push the stone back into the bladder. If this is not possible, the distended bladder is reduced by drawing off retained urine via a needle inserted through the abdominal wall. In some cases, surgery will be required to remove the blockage.

Incontinence

There are several possible causes of involuntary urination, or incontinence, from within the urinary tract; these include chronic lower urinary tract inflammation, bladder distension,

kidney failure, and age-related loss of urethra sphincter mechanism (USM) control. Other causes of incontinence are the result of hormone imbalances in older males and females and in spayed females, especially Dobermans and Bearded Collies. Fortunately, there are specific and effective drug therapies for both USM and hormone imbalance forms of incontinence.

Bladder stone formation

Minerals in the urine sometimes crystallize into granules, creating bladder stones. The mineral deposit irritates the lining of the bladder, causing straining and frequent passing of urine, sometimes with blood. Formation of bladder stones can ultimately be controlled by diet.

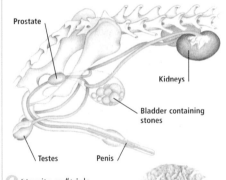

Prostate

Kidneys

Bladder containing stones

Testes   Penis

① Struvite or "triple phosphate" stones are the most common canine bladder and urethra stone. They are usually triggered by infection, so treatment will involve antibiotics.

② Calcium oxalate stones are the second most common type of stone. They cannot be dissolved by dietary means and, if they are large, may require surgical removal.

③ Cystine stones are not common, but are seen occasionally in Dachshunds and Bulldogs. Treatment may involve surgery.

The reproductive tract

- Many conditions are life-threatening in females
- Infection is most likely to occur after oestrus
- Prostate conditions are common and painful

Many of the medical conditions affecting a female dog's reproductive tract are extremely serious and can even be fatal, although risk of these disorders can be reduced by spaying. In contrast, few reproductive disorders affecting the male are life-threatening.

False pregnancy – pseudocyesis

False pregnancy is a normal phenomenon (*see p.140*). The female dog exhibits behaviour changes and her mammary glands enlarge. Unless your dog is physically or psychologically uncomfortable, there is no need for treatment, but if treatment is undertaken, prolactin inhibitors are given orally.

Dangers during birth

There are several risks to a female dog when giving birth. If she fails to have successful contractions or has difficult labour, the pups may need to be delivered by Caesarean section. After birth, there is a risk of haemorrhage, infection, prolapse or rupture of the uterus, or eclampsia – a life-threatening loss of calcium from the body. If your dog has difficulties during or after birth, seek urgent veterinary help.

Infertility

Male infertility can occur as a consequence of prostatic or testicular disease, an underactive thyroid, or even a prolonged high fever. Female infertility is difficult to assess, although hormonal blood tests during oestrus may be useful. Each female has her own idiosyncratic oestrous cycle, however, and the most common reason for unsuccessful mating is miscalculation of the correct time for mating.

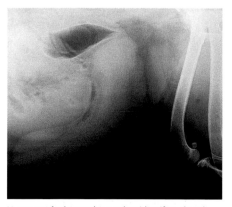

X-ray analysis may be used to identify a closed pyometra; this dangerous condition, caused when pus builds up in the womb, requires urgent surgery.

Routine examination for mammary lumps is vital in older dogs, as tumours must be identified early if treatment is to be successful.

Female reproductive tract disorders

CONDITION	SYMPTOMS AND TREATMENT
Womb infection or pyometra	This is potentially life threatening, and usually occurs after an oestrous cycle. Bacteria multiply in the womb and create pus. If the cervix remains open, the pus escapes through the vagina and out of the vulva. This is known as an "open pyometra", and is relatively easily diagnosed and treated. If the cervix is tight, however, pus builds up in the womb; this is called a "closed pyometra" and clinical signs develop quickly. A dog with pyometra has increased thirst and a decreased appetite. She rests more and may or may not have a vaginal discharge. Untreated, this leads to collapse and shock. If a dog has a closed pyometra, immediate surgery is needed to remove the womb.
Vaginitis and juvenile vaginitis	Vaginitis (inflammation of the vagina) in adult female dogs causes discomfort, and affected dogs persistently lick their vulva. Some young pups develop a sticky, green-yellow vaginal discharge that dries into a hard crusty wick in the hair on the tip of the vulva. This condition, known as juvenile vaginitis, almost always spontaneously clears when a pup has her first season. If your pup is affected, postpone spaying until three months after her first season.
Mammary tumours	In most cases, mammary tumours appear as hard, pebble-like mobile masses under the skin near teats, but the most aggressive form causes rapid, painful swelling in breasts in the groin area. Removal and examination of a lump is the only guaranteed way of diagnosing mammary tumours. Neutering a female dog can reduce the risk of mammary tumours: if bitches are spayed before their first season, the risk is negligible, and even spaying after the first season still reduces the risk by over 99 per cent. However, spaying a female dog after she has had about six oestrous cycles has no effect on the risk of her developing mammary tumours.

Male reproductive tract disorders

CONDITION	SYMPTOMS AND TREATMENT
Discharge from the sheath, (balanoposthitis)	A male dog normally produces a cream-yellow coloured lubricant in the sheath (smegma). Injury or infection to the sheath or penis can cause increased redness, excessive drip that may be foul-smelling, and licking. To treat, the sheath is flushed with warm saline or dilute antiseptic – this reduces the quantity of discharge. If the problem is due to bacterial infection, the dog is treated with antibiotics.
Penis stuck out of sheath (paraphimosis)	During an erection, the bulbourethral gland on a dog's penis can swell so much it is too wide to retract into the sheath. If the erection is prolonged, the penis becomes dry and cannot be withdrawn. To treat this condition, lubricate the penis with water-soluble jelly and slide it back in its sheath. If this is not possible, keep it moistened with lubricant and get veterinary help.
Undescended testicles	There is a high incidence of cancer in undescended testicles. Abdominal testicles may be surgically removed. Partly descended testicles that have passed through the inguinal ring should be monitored for changes in texture or size, and removed if and when necessary. Because this condition is inherited, dogs with partly or completely undescended testicles should not be used for breeding.
Scrotal or testicular enlargement	The most likely cause of testicle enlargement is a testicular tumour. To treat, tumours are surgically removed and identified by a pathologist. Malignancy is very rare. Infection or injury from dog bites, frostbite, or contact with corrosive chemicals can also cause painful enlargement. A moist scrotal skin infection causes weeping skin damage that heals into a hard, carapace-like scab, giving the impression of testicle enlargement. Penetrating injuries are treated with pain killers and antibiotics.
Prostate problems	The prostate may become infected when there is either bladder or urethra infection. All prostates increase in size with time, reaching maximum size usually between six and ten years of age. This swelling pushes upon the floor of the rectum, causing a bottleneck for stool to pass through. Initial signs of "benign hyperplasia" include difficulty passing stools. In rare instances hyperplasia can produce small to enormous prostatic cysts that can cause rectal obstruction (see pp.257–8). Prostate tumours are uncommon. A dog may be treated with injections of delmadinone, but if severe, hyperplasia is reduced by castration.

Eye disorders

- Inherited conditions can lead to blindness
- Flat-faced breeds are most at risk of eye injury
- Many dogs cope very well with blindness

Eye disorders account for a large number of visits to the clinic because they are amongst the easiest problems to recognize and always appear potentially worrisome.

Understanding the signs

Check with your vet if you notice any of the symptoms below: they may simply indicate an allergy, but can also be caused by more serious concerns, such as corneal damage.

- Squinting;
- Discharge and cloudiness;
- Redness or inflammation;
- Visible third eyelid;

Most eye problems can be simply treated with a course of eyedrops or ointment.

Eye discharges

The colour and consistency of the eye discharge gives good clues to the cause of the problem.

Watery and colourless	Usually indicates an allergic or irritating condition.
Jelly-like protective mucus	Suggests irritation or an infection.
Yellow-green pus	Indicates a bacterial infection that demands treatment.
Staining to the hair below the eyes	Indicates that tear drainage is blocked. This is called epiphora and is most common in small Poodles and flat-faced breeds such as Pugs.

- Tear overflow;
- Bulging or sunken eye;
- Crust or inflammation around eye;
- Deterioration or loss of vision;
- Increased irritability and pain.

Corneal injuries

Damage to the eye, through fighting or due to an accident, is one of the most common reasons for blindness, especially in flat-faced breeds like the Pekingese, in which the eye is not deeply recessed. Damage to the cornea – the outermost layer of the eye – causes swelling and produces a cloudy appearance, and corneal abrasions can develop into ulcers. Your vet will clean the eyes and treat with appropriate antibiotics, but in extreme cases, surgery may be needed.

Cataracts

A cataract is the loss of transparency to part or all of the lens, and is another common cause of blindness. Cataracts in one eye only can be triggered by physical injury, but if they appear in both eyes, the most likely explanation is late-diagnosed sugar diabetes or a genetic predisposition (especially in Labradors and Cocker Spaniels). Cataracts can be surgically removed, but only when they cause complete blindness and there is no associated degeneration of the retina.

Careful breeding is the only way to reduce the risk of inherited cataracts. The condition may not develop until a dog is six years of age, so before breeding from a dog, check that its parents, grandparents, and great-grandparents are known to be free from hereditary cataracts.

In youth, the lenses of the eye are flexible and clear, but with aging they become hardened, hazy, and blue-grey, and can begin to resemble cataracts. This natural change, called "sclerosis", is seen in dogs over nine years of age, and does not require treatment.

Progressive retinal atrophy (PRA)

This inherited eye condition is recognized in over 90 breeds. Symptoms of the disorder usually begin with night blindness, and progress to lack of confidence when jumping or

A complete cataract creates a crystalline yellow-white lens. Removal of the cataract by surgery can partly restore vision to the eye.

walking down stairs. Complete blindness is usually inevitable and there is no treatment. As with hereditary cataracts, there are examination schemes to certify that breeding individuals are free from PRA. DNA tests are available for breeding stock in breeds including Labradors, Cocker Spaniels, and Poodles.

Other eye conditions

Reduced tear production causes "dry eye" or keratoconjunctivitis sicca. The most common cause, particularly in West Highland White Terriers, is an immune-mediated disease. Eyes lose their lustre and there is often an accompanying purulent conjunctivitis. The condition responds well to cyclosporin ointment.

The iris and front chamber of the eye can be affected by infectious diseases, such as leptospirosis. The iris of an affected dog becomes inflamed (uveitis), and the pupils may constrict. Other signs include red eyes, squinting, avoidance of light, and excess tear production. In severe cases, blindness can result. Treatment is generally with antibiotics and corticosteroids.

Something in the eye

If you see foreign material in the eye, use your thumb to retract the eyelid and flush it out out with tepid water. Alternatively, moisten a cotton swab and ease the irritant out of the eye. If you can't remove it, protect the eye and seek immediate veterinary attention.

Hearing disorders

- Ear problems are very common
- Some conditions can cause loss of balance
- Deafness is inherited in some breeds

The ear is a vulnerable part of a dog's body. The outer ear flap is easily damaged, while the ear canal encourages the accumulation of wax, debris, and water, and provides an access point for a variety of infections.

Common indicators

Dogs with ear problems may show any of the following clinical signs:
- Head and ear shaking;
- Scratching one or both ears;
- Unpleasant odour from ears;
- Yellow or brown ear discharge;
- Inflammation to the ear flap or opening of ear canal;
- Yelping or other indication of pain when touched around the ears;
- Head tilted to one side;
- Apparent loss of hearing.

Outer ear problems

Many cases of ear inflammation, or otitis, are caused by white, pinhead-sized mites, *Otodectes cyanotis*. They can be killed by treatment with an effective product for at least three weeks. All pets that have been in

contact with the affected dog should be treated too: these mites spread easily. Some reside outside the ears, providing a ready source for infestation.

Infection of the external ear is often caused by a yeast, *Malassezia pachydermatis*, which takes advantage of the damage inflicted by mite infestations, allergies, or other ear canal inflammations. Untreated external ear infection may lead to a ruptured eardrum and middle or inner ear infection with associated head tilt and loss of balance. Your vet will prescribe a suitable ear medicine: for example, if the ear drum is ruptured, certain drugs,

Ear problems should always be seen by a vet – do not try to treat your dog at home.

Grass seeds

Plant awns, or foxtails, can enter a dog's ear and work their way down the ear canal. Your dog will usually shake its head vigorously when this happens. Do not attempt to remove the seed yourself – a dog's ears are delicate and easily damaged. Seek veterinary attention.

such as the antibiotics gentamycin and neomycin, might not be used because they may cause nerve deafness.

Certain breeds, including Labrador and Golden Retrievers, seem predisposed to haematomas – hot, soft, fluctuating swellings to the ear flap. These occur when a blood vessel breaks and blood accumulates between the skin and the cartilage of the ear. A vet will drain and stitch the haematoma to prevent the ear from refilling with blood, and corticosteroids may also be used.

The tips of the ears, especially those with little hair cover, are at risk from frostbite. If your dog has been exposed to prolonged cold, pad the ears with lukewarm water. Do not rub them: it will only make them itch more.

In hot weather, ears can be affected by sunburn, especially in breeds with white coats. Apply sunblock with a protection factor (SPF) of 30 or more before letting your dog out in direct sunshine for prolonged periods.

Balance and deafness
Middle or inner ear problems may lead to loss of balance, especially in older dogs. Signs include head tilt, a ticking movement of the eyes, loss of coordination and appetite, and vomiting. This suite of symptoms – known as canine vestibular syndrome – can sometimes be mistaken for a stroke. Its exact cause is not known, and it can often diminish within a week, and disappear entirely within a month of first appearance of the symptoms, although there may be some residual head tilt. Symptomatic treatment is given to control the dog's

Dalmatians are particularly prone to congenital deafness.

nausea and prevent accidental injuries.

Temporary deafness can be caused by excess production of ear wax or by seborrhoea, a condition that also affects the skin. These problems are easily treated with appropriate medication from your vet. Impaired hearing and eventual deafness can develop insidiously in older dogs, and may be hereditary in some breeds. For an accurate diagnosis, a specialist vet is able to carry out a brain stem auditory evoked response (BAER) test.

Handling a deaf dog can be demanding. However, with patience, good food rewards, and simple but flamboyant hand signals, an affected dog can be obedience trained. Keep a dog with hearing difficulties on its leash at all times.

Ask the vet

Q: Do my Cocker Spaniel's ears need special attention?
A: Reduce the weight of thickly haired droopy ears. Routinely clip or shave the hair from the inside surfaces. This permits better air circulation and minimizes the risk of ear infections.

Immune-system disorders

- Allergies are a growing problem
- Avoidance is the best treatment
- Vets can alter the immune system

The function of the immune system is to recognize and destroy invading microbes and renegade body cells that have become cancerous. If the immune system is oversensitive or fails to switch off properly, this results in allergies or autoimmune diseases; these conditions are being diagnosed with increasing frequency in dogs.

Antibodies and immunity

Antibodies are proteins manufactured by specialized white blood cells. They act like markers or tags, identifying bacterial proteins (antigens), chemicals, and cells to be dealt with by other parts of the immune

Certain forms of heart disease in breeds such as the Doberman may be due to immune-mediated problems.

system. Mothers pass antibodies to their young in the first milk the pups consume (colostrum) as temporary protection *(see p.44–5)*. These maternal antibodies drop to low levels by the time a pup is 10–12 weeks old.

Managing the immune system

Vets manipulate the immune system in two different ways. By administering vaccines to a dog, they can stimulate the immune system to produce new antibodies, protecting the dog against a specific germ *(see p.212)*. Vets can also suppress a dog's immune system when it becomes overactive, such as in autoimmune conditions or allergic reactions.

Autoimmune disorders

Autoimmune or "immune-mediated" problems occur when a dog's immune system malfunctions, losing the ability to differentiate between dangerous particles, such as invading bacteria, and the normal cells in a dog's body; the immune system then targets and destroys these cells or tissues. For example, underactive thyroid problems in dogs can be caused by the immune system attacking the thyroid glands *(see p.242–3)*. Autoimmune haemolytic anaemia (AIHA), a rare blood disease, is caused when the immune system destroys red blood cells.

Allergic reactions

An allergic reaction occurs when the immune system overreacts to harmless substances – known as allergens – that a dog inhales, eats, or otherwise comes into contact with. Allergic responses can affect a dog's skin, causing itchiness; the lining of the air passages, causing sneezing, coughing, or difficulty with breathing; or the lining of the gastrointestinal system, causing vomiting or diarrhoea. Dogs are not born with allergies, but can develop them after being exposed to an allergen over a period of time.

1 In an allergic reaction, the immune system manufactures antibodies to a specific allergen, such as pollen. If exposure to the allergen is repeated, these antibodies bind to the surface of "mast cells", found in the skin, the gastrointestinal system, and the nasal passages.

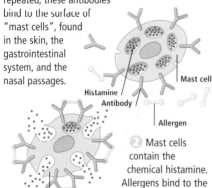

Histamine
Antibody
Mast cell
Allergen
Mast cell is destroyed

2 Mast cells contain the chemical histamine. Allergens bind to the antibodies on the mast cell and link them together, causing the cell to break open. This releases the store of histamine, causing inflammation of tissues and resulting in the symptoms of allergy.

Chemicals in insect bites, certain foods, drugs, plants and herbs, dust mites, plant pollens, fungal spores, and even your own shedding skin, can cause an allergic reaction in your dog. Just as allergy runs in human families, there is a breed predisposition in dogs too. For example, breeds with predominantly white coats – such as West Highland White Terriers, Bull Terriers, and English Setters – are predisposed to skin allergies; Westies and Golden Retrievers have a higher than normal incidence of gastrointestinal allergies.

Plant pollen is a common allergen

Immune complex diseases

Antibodies sometimes combine with antigens producing "antibody–antigen complexes". These are also known as "immune complexes", and are normally filtered out of the general blood circulation. However, they are sometimes deposited and build up in joint capsules, in kidneys, or in the walls of blood vessels, where they attract the attention of other parts of the immune system, leading to local inflammation and tissue damage. The most common form of immune complex disease is immune-mediated arthritis in joints.

Diagnosing and treating allergy

Vets identify allergies by examining breeding history, using skin and blood tests, implementing altered or novel diets, or by temporarily removing a dog from its normal environment. Yet finding specific causes for allergies is frustratingly difficult. For immediate relief from the symptoms, vets will prescribe drugs such as antihistamines, and may recommend essential fatty acid (EFA) supplements.

Allergic conditions

Skin condition	Contact dermatitis. Inhalant allergic dermatitis. Food allergy. Hives (urticaria).
Respiratory conditions	Hay fever (allergic rhinitis). Allergic bronchitis. Allergic pneumonitis – pulmonary infiltrate with eosinophils (PIE).
Gastrointestinal conditions	Allergic gastritis. Allergic enteritis. Eosinophilic enteritis. Allergic colitis.
Autoimmune skin conditions	Collie nose (nasal solar dermatitis). Discoid lupus erythematosus. Pemphigus. Systemic lupus erythematosus.

Cancer

- Genetics plays a central role in cancer
- Many cancers are found during routine examinations
- Therapies are constantly improving

Cancers are diseases that occur when a cell in a dog's body starts to replicate uncontrollably, forming clumps of abnormal or cancerous cells called tumours. These cancer cells escape detection and trick the natural killer cells of the body's immune system into not attacking and destroying them. Having eluded the body's defences, cancer cells embark upon an eternal life of producing countless generations of descendant cancer cells.

Genes and cancer

Some individuals carry genes that predispose them to certain cancers. The Bernese Mountain Dog, for example, has a 60 per cent chance of dying as a result of cancerous tumours. In other breeds, the genetic link can be much

Afghan Hounds are amongst a group of breeds with a higher than average incidence of cancers.

Ask the vet

Q: Can stress cause cancer?
A: Social stress does not cause cancer, but it has been shown in cats and rats that stress can increase the speed at which a cancer grows, especially cancers caused by viruses. Stress appears to decrease the numbers and efficiency of natural killer cells, the cells that normally spot cancer cells and coordinate their destruction (see p.45).

more complicated. Individuals may inherit a cancer-producing gene but also a cancer-suppressing gene, and even another gene that suppresses the cancer-suppressing gene. In addition, these genes can be turned on and off by a host of environmental factors including ultraviolet light, radiation, and various chemicals.

Names are important

Cancers are classified according to the part of the body in which they originate. Carcinomas, for example, arise from the tissues that line the internal and external surfaces of a dog's skin and organs, while sarcomas arise from within tissues such as muscles, blood vessels, and bones.

Diagnosing cancer

While sophisticated diagnostics, including body scans, can help to identify potential tumours, a sample of tissue from the suspected area is necessary for an accurate diagnosis of cancer. Small tumours may simply be removed, but for larger ones, your vet may either take a small piece of suspect tissue (a biopsy), or use a needle and syringe to withdraw a sample of cells to be analysed.

Cancers generally occur later in life, but can also affect younger individuals. Early diagnosis is vital, and dogs over seven years old should have yearly preventative veterinary examinations. Common signs of cancer include:
• Abnormal swellings that persist or continue to grow;
• Sores that do not heal;
• Weight loss;
• Loss of appetite;
• Bleeding or unusual discharge from any body opening;

Regular examination for abnormal lumps can help to identify problems as early as possible, allowing the best possible chance of recovery.

• Offensive odour;
• Difficulty eating or swallowing;
• Hesitation to exercise or lack of stamina when exercising;
• Persistent lameness or stiffness;
• Difficulty in breathing, urinating, or defecating.

How cancer spreads

In the later stages of cancer, a process known as metastasis can result in the spread of cancerous cells around the body and subsequent formation of secondary tumours at new sites. Cancer can spread via both the lymphatic and blood systems.

❶ Cancer spreads via the bloodstream when a rapidly dividing tumour ruptures a nearby blood vessel. This allows cancerous cells to enter the blood vessel and travel in the blood to other parts of the body.

Tumour cell ruptures blood vessel

Cancerous cell

❷ Cancerous cells travel throughout the body, and may find their way into tiny blood vessels called capillaries *(see p.37)*, where they pass through the thin capillary walls and start to invade the local tissues.

Normal tissue

Cancer cell divides, forming secondary tumour

Capillary

Cancer treatments

Surgery is usually the most effective treatment for cancer, but if it is impossible to completely remove the tumour or if the cancer has spread to other parts of the body, radiation therapy and chemotherapy may be used. New treatments for cancer have also been developed that may prove very effective; these include drugs that selectively cut off the blood supply to the cancer, or that stimulate a dog's immune system to attack the tumour. Gene therapy allows cancerous cells to be specifically targeted and destroyed.

In some cases, however, you and your vet may make the difficult decision that, rather than embarking on a potentially distressing course of treatment, it may be preferable to go for a good quality of life for your dog, even if this will inevitably mean a shorter life expectancy.

Emotional disorders

- Emotion is chemically controlled
- Some vets feel unsure how to approach problems
- Drugs alone are not sufficient treatment

Feelings like anxiety evolved to protect dogs from danger. The cortex of the dog's brain recognizes a threat or a stress and communicates with the rest of the brain through the limbic system, triggering a cascade of chemical changes that affect the entire body. But if these changes last too long, or get triggered too easily by inappropriate stimuli, then emotional disorders may result. The sustained release of stress chemicals can cause long-term damage; and when this happens to older dogs, there is an Alzheimer's-like deterioration in brain function.

The role of brain chemistry

The eloquent American neurologist Robert Sapolsky wrote, "People with chronic depressions are those whose cortex habitually whispers sad things to the rest of the brain." In people and in dogs, this whispering takes place in the limbic system of the brain, where mind and body meet.

The limbic system is a spider's web of interconnections in the dog's brain that orchestrates instincts and emotions through its production of chemical messengers called neurotransmitters.

These brain chemicals, such as serotonin, have a great influence on mood, and in humans decreased serotonin levels are linked with depression. Some research in dogs suggests that serotonin is also related to confidence: top dogs have high levels of serotonin, while underdogs may produce less. In humans, levels of mood-altering neurotransmitters can be controlled by drugs and through psychotherapy and counselling. In dogs, techniques such as obedience training, desensitizing, counter-conditioning, and exercise all affect neurotransmitter levels, behaviour, and emotions.

Phobias and anxiety

A phobia is an irrational fear of an object or a situation. Dogs develop rational fears – of veterinary clinics, for example – but also irrational

Teething, anxiety, boredom, or insufficient exercise may cause destructive chewing behaviour.

In their wild state, dogs are rarely separated from other members of the pack. In the home, separation may lead to anxiety and depression.

fears, of thunder, or men wearing hats or carrying umbrellas. Dogs may also become irrationally anxious when, for example, their owner leaves the room.

Phobias and anxiety lead to panic attacks, in which a dog hyperventilates and his muscles become tense. They can also lead to compulsive behaviour, in which a dog ritually performs a certain activity, such as pacing back and forth. An inability to relax or to sleep is an extreme form of canine anxiety.

Depression may manifest itself in decreased or, rarely, increased appetite, clinging, or "remote" behaviour, irritability and lethargy.

Diagnosis and treatment

Phobias, anxieties, depression, and grieving have not been considered an integral part of veterinary medicine until recently, and many vets are still uncomfortable in applying these terms to dogs. If you suspect that your dog has psychological problems, seek out a veterinary surgeon with advanced training in behavioural medicine.

Dealing with behavioural problems usually involves a combination of drug treatment and therapy. Sedatives such as acepromazine may be used to tranquillize anxious dogs. Anti-anxiety drugs such as diazepam may be prescribed for short-term anxiety, such as that associated with travel.

Increasingly, veterinary surgeons are treating canine emotional disorders with a combination of environmental enhancement, desensitizing or counter-conditioning training, and newer mood-altering drugs, such as clomipramine and amitriptyline, which work on neurotransmitters in the brain.

Age-related behaviour problems

The term "canine cognitive dysfunction" (CCD) is often used to describe the deteriorating behaviour patterns associated with old age. The term "senile dementia" is also used in the same context. Dogs exhibit most of the signs of senile dementia that are seen in humans – standing at the wrong place by the door when wanting to go out, for example. Some dogs bark absently; others seemingly forget why they are where they are.

Some aspects of aging are irreversible but others can be delayed, or even reversed, with effective use of licensed medication. The drug selegeline, used for delaying the development of advanced symptoms of Parkinson's disease, is licensed for use in dogs. All older dogs benefit from routine, daily mental stimulation.

Geriatric conditions

- Each type of body cell has a specific life expectancy
- Aging is a natural occurrence, not a disease
- Age-related changes can be slowed, sometimes arrested

Aging is not an illness. With age, a dog's body simply does not work as well as it once did. And just like us, older dogs get both wiser and sillier.

When is a dog old?

Disease control, good nutrition, and successful veterinary intervention mean that dogs are living longer now than ever before. Fully one third of the dogs seen by vets can be considered "geriatrics". Lifespans vary considerably from breed to breed, however, and what is old in one breed is not necessarily old in another. Certain breeds have a shorter than average life expectancy because they are prone to inherited disorders: the Doberman, for example, has a much lower average life span than a Miniature Poodle, because the breed is prone to kidney failure and heart disease. Mixed breeds, and smaller dogs in general, tend to live longer than many larger pure-bred dogs.

Preventative checkups

With any age-related condition, the earlier a problem is diagnosed, the easier and cheaper it will be to treat. For this reason, yearly or even twice yearly health examinations are vital for an older dog. At some time between six and ten years of age, depending on your breed of dog, you should also arrange for a full "senior citizen" preventative health checkup.

Common age-related problems

Old age brings with it a variety of medical conditions, most of which have already been described on the preceding pages, but some of which are specifically related to aging. Many of these are caused by a drop in the efficiency with which the dog's cells and tissues can repair themselves.

- **Diminished sight and hearing:** every dog over nine years old develops sclerosis *(see p.267)* – an affected dog sees movement, especially at a distance, but has poor vision at close range. Impaired hearing is also common in older dogs, and full hearing loss may occur rapidly over a relatively short period.

Reduced vision in old age may make your dog feel less secure, and it will often rest more as a result.

Immune system changes

As a dog gets older, the efficiency of its immune system gradually diminishes. It may occasionally fail to detect and destroy germs, leading to a greater incidence of infections, or it may fail to detect abnormal cells that then develop into a cancerous tumour. The immune system of an older dog is more also likely react inappropriately, destroying the dog's normal cells (see p.270).

- **Behaviour changes:** senile dementia and other, less dramatic, behavioural changes typify old age. Older dogs sleep more and take more time to remember who, what, and where, when they wake up. They hate changes in routine. Age-related deterioration of the senses and behaviour can be slowed down by creating new, attractive mental activities for your dog.
- **Doggy smell:** older dogs groom themselves less than young dogs. This is because they are not as supple and find grooming more difficult, and perhaps also because they simply can't be bothered. They therefore need more frequent attention from you.
- **Bad breath:** gum infections and associated bad breath will eventually occur in almost every dog, but toy breeds are particularly affected. With serious infection, there is an associated risk that bacteria will enter the bloodstream. Minimize problems through routine dental hygiene: brush your older dog's teeth and gums regularly (see p.197), and give it rock-hard biscuits or enzyme-treated rawhide to chew.

- **Constipation and gas:** older dogs are more likely to become constipated and pass more wind. They benefit from changes to their diet: a balanced fibre diet that promotes the growth of beneficial non-gas-forming bacteria will help. Ensure your dog exercises and drinks plenty of water.
- **Painful joints:** the incidence of painful degenerative joint disease (DJD) increases with time (see pp.246–7). Medication will help, but weight reduction and routine exercise are vital.
- **Lack of strength:** many natural changes associated with aging mean that less nourishment reaches the muscles, making dogs more lethargic and easily tired. These effects can be offset by feeding a highly digestible diet with added vitamins and antioxidants. Talk to your vet about medicines that increase oxygen in the bloodstream.
- **Incontinence:** urinary incontinence occurs in aging males but more often in older females (see also p.263). Your vet can prescribe medication that increases sphincter muscle tone or overcomes hormonal imbalance.

Older dogs may experience joint discomfort. Gently massaging stiff joints after sleep will help.

The end of a dog's life

- Make informed decisions on your dog's behalf
- It is normal to grieve
- Other dogs are waiting to fill the emotional void

Elderly dogs do what humans find so difficult, if not impossible – they don't look back on what they once could do, but rather concentrate on what they're now capable of doing. No matter how healthy your dog is, however, decline is inevitable, and there will come a time when you will face tough decisions about the future.

Euthanasia: a release from suffering

Euthanasia means voluntarily ending the life of a dog suffering from a terminal or incurable condition. In my experience, the following are valid reasons for euthanasia:

- Irreversible disease that has progressed to a point where distress or discomfort cannot be controlled;
- Old age wear and tear that permanently affects the "quality of life";
- Physical injury, disease, or wear and tear resulting in permanent loss of control of body functions;
- Uncorrectable aggressiveness, with risk to children, owners, or others;
- The carrying of untreatable disease dangerous to humans.

The emotional pain we feel when our dogs die is not to be underestimated.

Making a decision

To help you decide what is in your elderly dog's best interests, ask yourself the following questions:

- Is the condition no longer responding to therapy?

• Is it no longer possible to alleviate the pain or suffering?
• If your dog recovers, is it likely to be chronically ill, an invalid, or unable to care for itself?
• If your dog recovers, will there be severe personality changes?
• Will providing any necessary care create serious problems for myself and my family?
• Will the cost of treatment be unbearably expensive?

If the answer to these questions is "yes", then euthanasia is the honest, simple, and humane option. Remember that your dog is a member of your family, and as such, any difficult decisions should be agreed upon by all his human "relatives". I think I speak for virtually all vets, however, when I say that I receive far more letters of thanks in a single year for ending lives properly than I have had in over 30 years for saving lives.

How euthanasia is performed

The anaesthetic drug phenobarb is the most commonly used agent in euthanasia. Within seconds, the dog loses consciousness, and within another few seconds the heart stops. Depending on the circumstances, a sedative may be given before the phenobarb, and then a cannula put in a vein to ensure that all goes smoothly.

While brain death occurs within seconds, continuing electrical activity in muscles may cause muscle twitches. If the respiratory muscles are affected there can be a reflex "gasp" occurring up to ten minutes after death. Where I practice, all bodies are routinely cremated unless owners prefer burial. Bodies are kept in cold storage until they are collected. If you bury a dog, as I have done with all of mine, make sure it is enclosed in biodegradable, not synthetic, material. A grave should be deep enough so that wild animals cannot dig it up.

Grieving is normal

Feelings of bereavement when a dog dies are normal. If you are an average dog owner, the stages of grief – from disbelief through to resolution – typically evolve for almost a year.

The universal value of dogs is that what we enjoyed about living with our previous dog is there in all others: honesty, constancy, fidelity, companionship, and a unalloyed glee in doing things that deep down inside we would really like to do too. And if your previous dog's looks, conformation, and temperament fitted your family's needs and it was a purebred, it is even easier to find a dog to fill the void. Each dog is unique, but when a canine gap opens in your home, there are countless individuals, little and large, capable, willing, and eager to fill it.

Don't assume that all changes in your old dog's behaviour are caused by aging: if in any doubt, consult your vet.

Glossary of medical terms

Abscess A localized pocket of infection in body tissues

Anaemia Reduced red blood cells or reduction in oxygen-carrying pigment (haemoglobin)

Anaphylactic shock An exaggerated, life-threatening allergic response to foreign protein or other substances

Antibody Protein produced by specialized white blood cells in response to certain antigens. Antibody binds to antigen, a fundamental act of immunity

Antigen Any agent capable of inducing a specific immune response

Ataxia A lack of muscle coordination

Atrophy Wasting

Autoimmune disease Any condition in which the body's immune system erroneously attacks normal body parts

Aversion therapy Treatment of a behaviour problem involving the use of mild physical or mental discomfort

Bloat Dilation of the stomach, usually with gas or air

Brachycephalic Having a shortened muzzle and a wide head

Caesarean section The surgical opening of the uterus to deliver full-term puppies

Canine cognitive dysfunction (CCD) Another term for canine senile dementia

Castration Usually refers to the surgical removal of the testicles in males (in law it may refer to the sterilization of both male and female)

Cataract Crystalline cloudiness in the lens of the eye

Chronic degenerative radiculomyopathy (CDRM) An inherited progressive deterioration to spinal transmission of signals, especially in the German Shepherd Dog

Chronic obstructive pulmonary disease (COPD) A condition in which the structures within the lungs are inflamed or damaged, resulting in shortness of breath

Clinical signs What you observe your dog doing

Clinical symptoms How your dog is feeling

Colitis Inflammation to the large intestine (the colon)

Colostrum The first milk produced just after birth, containing passive protection against a variety of infectious diseases

Congenital A condition present at birth; congenital conditions may or may not be hereditary

Corticosteroid Any of the hormones produced by the adrenal cortex (outer layer of the adrenal gland)

Cramp The involuntary contraction of muscle filaments (the components of muscle fibres), occurring most frequently in canine athletes

Cryosurgery Destruction of cells through freezing

CT scan Computed tomography using X-rays to scan the body

Cytology Examination of body cells under a microscope

Degenerative joint disease (DJD) An inability to maintain healthy joint tissue or repair it after damage; often called "arthritis" or "osteoarthritis"

Dehydration Loss of the natural level of liquid in body tissue

Diabetes insipidus Deficiency in a pituitary hormone (anti-diuretic hormone or ADH) that controls urine concentration in the kidneys

Diabetes mellitus or sugar diabetes High blood sugar, either because of a lack of insulin production or because body tissue cannot absorb circulating insulin

Dislocation The separation of a bone from its adjoining bone at a joint, often involving ligament tears

Echocardiography Imaging of the heart using sound waves bounced off the interior and exterior of the heart, then visualized on a monitor

Electrocardiogram (ECG) Record of the electrical activity in the heart

Elisa testing A test used to detect or measure levels of an antigen or antibody

Emphysema Pathological accumulation of air in tissues

Endocrine gland A gland that manufactures hormones and secretes them directly into the bloodstream

Endorphin Naturally occurring brain chemical that diminishes pain perception

Endoscope An instrument for viewing the inside of an area of the body

Epilepsy A disturbance in electrical activity in the brain that causes a seizure

Essential fatty acids Fatty acids that cannot be synthesized by the body and must be acquired from the diet

Euthanasia The painless termination of life; may be active (by giving a substance that causes death) or passive (by withdrawing medical support that sustains life)

Exclusion diet A diet that excludes all components of any previous diet, usually consisting of novel sources of protein, fat, and carbohydrate

Exudate Fluid that has escaped from blood vessels and deposited either in or on tissues

Free radicals Naturally occurring atoms that destroy cells

Genetic disease A medical condition known to be transmitted to an animal in a parent's genes

Gingivitis Inflammation of the gums

Glaucoma Increased fluid pressure inside the eye

Granuloma A benign connective tissue tumour associated with irritation or inflammation

Haematoma A blood-filled swelling under the skin

Haematuria Blood in urine

Hernia The protrusion of a body part out of the cavity in which it is normally located

Hip dysplasia An abnormal development of hip joint tissue, usually leading to arthritis; in part a hereditary condition

Hypersensitivity An exaggerated immune response to a foreign agent

Hyperthermia Unusually high body temperature

Hypoglycaemia Reduction in blood sugar

Idiopathic disease A condition of which the cause is unknown

Immune-mediated disease A condition caused by an overreaction of the immune system

Incontinence Uncontrolled dribbling of urine, especially when lying down; more common in older and neutered females

Incubation period The time between exposure to a disease-producing agent and the development of clinical signs of disease

Inflammatory bowel disease (IBD) A group of intestinal diseases, each characterized by an increase in a specific type of inflammatory cell

-itis An inflammation; for example, nephritis is an inflammation of the kidneys

Jaundice A yellow pigmentation of the mucous membranes or skin, usually associated with liver disease

Keratoconjunctivitis Inflamed cornea and conjunctiva

Laparotomy The surgical opening of the abdominal cavity

Laser Light amplification by stimulated emission of radiation; a concentrated beam of light used as a tool in surgery

Lipoma A benign tumour of fat, particularly common in older, overweight large breeds

Macrophages Large white blood cells that consume debris

Magnetic resonance imaging (MRI) Diagnostic imaging showing detailed cross-sections of the internal anatomy of structures such as joints or the brain; particularly useful for brain scans

Malabsorption A condition in which insufficient amounts of nutrients are absorbed into the circulation from the small intestines

Melaena Black, tarry diarrhoea containing old blood

Malignant tumour A tumour that has the capacity either to invade the tissue that surrounds it or to spread via the blood or lymphatic circulation to other parts of the body, such as the lungs or the liver

Metastasis Spread of cancer cells from the area of origin to other parts of the body

Metritis Inflammation of the uterus (womb)

Mucus Clear, lubricating secretion produced by cells in mucous membranes

Myelogram X-ray of the spinal cord after the injection of contrast material (a substance opaque to X-rays)

Myocarditis Inflammation of the heart muscle

Necrosis Cell death

Neoplasia Cancerous cell growth, which may be benign or malignant

Nephritis Inflammation of the kidneys

Nictitating membrane Third eyelid

NSAID Non-steroidal anti-inflammatory drug; this group of drugs includes aspirin, carprofen, and meloxicam

Oedema Excessive accumulation of fluid in body tissue; swelling

Oestrous cycle The reproductive cycle in females

Osteochondrosis Disease involving abnormal development or growth of cartilage

Ovariohysterectomy Removal of the ovaries and uterus, the normal "spaying" procedure

Oxalate Mineral sediment of stones produced in the bladder, as in "calcium oxalate"

Palliative treatment Therapy that improves comfort but does not cure

Perianal Around the anus, as in "perianal adenomas"

Perineal Referring to the area between the anus and the genitals

Periodontal Around or near the teeth

Peritonitis Inflammation of the lining of the abdominal cavity

Pinna The ear flap

Pituitary gland The "master gland" at the base of the brain, controlling all other hormone-producing glands and controlled by the hypothalamus (an area at the base of the brain)

Pseudocyesis False or phantom hormonal pregnancy

Psychogenic Originating in the mind, as in "psychogenic polydypsia"

Regurgitation Backward flow: for example, regurgitated food comes from the oesophagus (as distinct from vomit, which comes from the stomach); regurgitated blood flows back from the heart's ventricles to the atria

Sclerosis Hardening of tissue, as a consequence of age or inflammation

Scooting Dragging the bottom on the ground

Sebaceous gland Oil-producing skin gland that adds water-proofing to the coat

Seborrhoea An increased activity of the skin's oil-producing sebaceous glands

Seizure Abnormal electrical activity in the brain, causing unusual nervous responses; also known as a "fit" or "convulsion"

Separation anxiety An emotional problem resulting in destructive behaviour, barking or howling, urinating, or defaecating when left alone

Septicaemia Bacterial infection in the blood circulation

Shock A life-threatening emergency in which the cardiovascular system fails, causing physical collapse, rapid pulse, and pale mucous membranes

Small intestine bacterial overgrowth (SIBO) An intestinal condition in which,

for a variety of reasons, a pure culture of bacteria increases and displaces other beneficial bacteria

Sprain An injury caused by over-stretching a ligament, resulting in lameness

Stomatitis Inflammation of the mucosa of the mouth

Strain Damage to muscle fibres and tendons, often accompanied by slight bleeding and bruising

Struvite A mineral sand or sediment, otherwise called triple phosphate or magnesium ammonium phosphate hexahydrate, found in the bladder

Synovial fluid Lubricating joint fluid

Testosterone Male sex hormone

Thyroid gland The largest endocrine glands in the dog's body, producing hormones vital for growth and metabolism

Tumour Also called a neoplasm; a lump or bump, caused by multiplying cells, which can be benign or malignant

Ulcer A lesion where surface tissue has been lost through damage or disease

Uraemia Build-up of waste in the blood as a consequence of kidney failure

Uroliths Stones in the bladder

Wobbler syndrome Ataxia caused by compression of the cervical spinal cord due to vertebral instability

Zoonoses Diseases transmissible between animals and humans

Useful contacts

General veterinary associations

British Small Animal Veterinary Association
Dog care and the practice of veterinary medicine
Woodrow House, 1 Telford Way,
Waterwells Business Park,
Quedgeley, Gloucester GL2 4AB
Tel: 01452 726700
Fax: 01452 726701
Web: www.bsava.com

Royal College of Veterinary Surgeons
The registering and disciplinary body for UK vets
Web: www.rcvs.org.uk

Federation of European Companion Animal Veterinary Associations
40 rue de Berri, 75008 Paris, France
Tel: (33) 1 5383 9160
Fax: (33) 1 5383 9169
Web: www.fecava.org

Irish Veterinary Asociation
53 Lansdowne Road, Ballsbridge,
Dublin 4, Ireland
Tel: (353) 1 668 5263
Fax: (353) 1 660 4345

Australian Vet Association
PO Box 371, Artarmon NSW 1570,
Australia
Tel: (61) 2 9411 2733
Web: www.ava.com.au

Veterinary Cancer Society
Up-to-date information on cancer treatments
Web: www.vetcancersociety.org

Breed registries

The Kennel Club
1–5 Clarges Street, London
W1J 8AB
Tel: 0870 606 6750
Web: www.the-kennel-club.org.uk

The Irish Kennel Club
Web: www.ikc.ie

Federation Cynologique Internationale (FCI)
Place Albert 1er, 13,
B-6530 Thuin, Belgium
Tel: (32) 71 591 238
Fax: (32) 71 592 229
Web: www.fci.be

Australian National Kennel Council
5 Costin Street, Fortitude Valley,
Queensland 4006
Tel: (61) 7 3257 1035
Web: www.ankc.aust.com

Training

Association of Pet Behaviour Counsellors
For behaviour problems
Web: www.apbc.org.uk

Association of Pet Dog Trainers
For basic training
Web: www.apdt.co.uk

Welfare, research, and special interest

National Canine Defence League
Information on the peculiarities of "recycled" dogs and dog training
Web: www.ncdl.org.uk

RSPCA – Royal Society for the Prevention of Cruelty to Animals
Wilberforce Way, Southwater,
Horsham, West Sussex RH13 9RS
Tel: 0870 333 5999
Fax: 0870 7530 284
Web: www.rspca.org.uk

SSPCA – Scottish Society for the Prevention of Cruelty to Animals
Braehead Mains, 603 Queensferry
Road, Edinburgh, EH4 6EA,
Scotland
Tel: 0131 339 0222
Fax: 0131 339 4777
Web: www.scottishspca.org

USPCA – Ulster Society for the Prevention of Cruelty to Animals
PO Box 103, Belfast BT6 8US,
Northern Ireland
Animal Helpline: 08000 280 010
Web: www.uspca.co.uk

ISPCA – Irish Society for the Prevention of Cruelty to Animals
300 Lower Rathmines Road,
Dublin 6, Ireland
Tel: (353) 1 4977 874
Fax: (353) 1 4977 940
Web: www.ispca.ie

Royal Society for the Protection of Animals – Australia
PO Box 265, Deakin West,
Australian Capital Territory 2600,
Australia
Tel: (61) 2 6282 8300
Web: www.rspca.org.au

Petlog
National Microchip Register
PO Box 2037
London W1A 1GP
Tel: 020 7518 1000
Fax: 020 7518 1014
Web: www.petlog.org.uk

Animal Aunts
Britain's largest pet- (and house-) sitting agency
Web: www.animalaunts.co.uk

Dogs in the news
Current news stories involving dogs
Web: www.dogsinthenews.com

For dog information and links to other websites:
Web: www.lib.uoguelph.ca/
veterinary/vetfile

For information on microchips and the Pet Travel Scheme:
Web: www.identichip.co.uk

Index

A

abdomen, distended 258
accidents 220–9
adrenal glands 31, 233, 243
afterbirth 142–3
aggression 159, 192–3
aging 158–9, 200–1, 275, 276–9
Airedale Terrier 84
Akita 121
Alaskan Malamute 125
allergies 164–5, 231, 237, 271
anaemia 239, 270
anal sacs 152, 153, 157, 197, 258
anaphylactic shock 225
antibodies 45, 141, 270, 271
antioxidants 199, 201, 262, 277
anxiety 275
arteries 37, 224
arthritis 245, 246, 271
artificial respiration 222–4
Australian Shepherd 108
autoimmune disorders 270
avascular necrosis 246

B

babies, safety 202
back injuries 250
bad breath 196–7, 252, 253, 277
bandages 226, 227
barking 46, 135, 170, 178, 189, 190
Basset Hound 102
bathing 194
Beagle 89
Bearded Collie 105
bedding 169
behaviour problems 188–93, 275
Bichon Frise 64
bile 40, 41, 44, 254
biological clock 149, 158
birth 142–3
biting 165, 193, 216

bladder 29, 43, 262–3
bleeding 224, 227, 234–5
blindness 267
bloat 200, 255
blood 36–7, 44–5, 239, 260
Bloodhound 118
boarding kennels 202–3
body language 46, 47, 148–9, 155, 180
body odour 153, 277
bones 26–7, 244–8
chewing 176, 200
Border Collie 91
Border Terrier 76
Bordetella 212, 213, 235
boredom 188, 189, 191, 233
Boston Terrier 74
Boxer 114
brain 28–9, 141, 145, 159, 222, 240–1, 274
breathing 37, 220–1, 222–4, 235–6
breed standards 49, 54
breeders 166–7
breeding 42–3, 138–45
Brittany 88
brushing 195–6
Bull Terrier 83
Bullmastiff 123
burying bones 151

C

Cairn Terrier 77
cancer 241, 247–8, 272–3
canine cough 235
canned food 168, 199–200
car travel 203
cardiopulmonary resuscitation (CPR) 222–4
cartilage 245, 246
cataracts 267
cats 172, 202
Cavalier King Charles Spaniel 65
chemical poisons 228–9
Chesapeake Bay Retriever 100
chewing 151, 176–7, 189,

191, 200, 237, 252
Chihuahua 58
choking 236–7
choosing a dog 164–7
Chow Chow 113
circulatory system 36–7
clicker training 180
clipping 195
coat 24–5, 133, 210, 211
contamination 228
grooming 156–7, 194–6
hair loss 25, 232–3
coats, winter 169
Cocker Spaniel 85–6
colitis 257
collars 168–9, 183
colour, coat 133
coma 240
communication 46–7, 147, 148–9, 152–3
competitions 204–5
constipation 257, 277
Corgi, Pembroke Welsh 92
costs 164
coughing 235
courtship 138, 139
crates 54, 170–1, 202, 203

D

Dachshund 68
Dalmatian 111
deafness 269
death 278–9
depression 274, 275
diabetes 259, 267
diarrhoea 200, 254, 256–7
digestive system 38–41, 150, 254–9
digging 191
dilated cardiomyopathy (DCM) 238
disabled people 56–7
discipline 180, 181
discs, slipped 251
diseases 212–13, 217
dislocation, joints 248
distemper 212, 213
DNA 136–7

Doberman 116
dog walkers 179
domestication 22–3
dominance 135, 192, 193
dorsal tail glands 153
dreams 240
droppings, scavenging
150–1, 259
drugs 218–19, 255
dry dog food 199

E
ears 34, 197, 219, 268–9
cropping 49, 209
eggs 43, 139
elbow dysplasia 245
emergencies 220–9
emotions 161, 274–5
endocrine system 30–1,
242–3
equipment 168–9, 195
euthanasia 278–9
evolution 22
examining a dog 210–11
excitement 191
eyes 32–3, 197, 219, 266–7,
276

F
faeces 41, 152, 174–5, 178
false pregnancy 140–1, 258,
264
female dogs 133, 165
neutering 216–17
reproductive system 42,
43, 138–43, 264–5
scent marking 152–3
feral dogs 129
fibre, in diet 39, 198, 201,
277
first aid 222–9
flatulence 258, 277
fleas 195, 215, 230, 231
food 38–41, 147, 150–1,
198 201
foreign bodies 235, 252–3,
267
Fox Terrier 80
fractures 227, 248
furunculosis 232

G
gagging 237, 252
gardens 179, 229
genetics 49, 136–7, 272
German Shepherd Dog 119
Giardia 214, 215
Golden Retriever 93
Great Dane 126
Greyhound 104
grooming 156–7, 194–6
guide dogs 56

H
hair see coat
harnesses 169, 203
head 211
head halters 187
hearing 34, 268–9, 276
hearing dogs 56–7
heart 36–7, 221
heart disease 238–9
heart massage 222–4
heartworms 214, 238–9
hepatitis 212, 213, 259
hip dysplasia 245
history of dogs 22–3
holidays 149, 202–3
home, dog-proofing 178–9
hookworms 214
hormones 25, 30–1, 133,
139, 140, 141, 201, 232–3,
242–3
house training 171, 174–5
howling 46, 190
Hungarian Vizsla 101
hunting 52
Husky, Siberian 115
hydatid disease 217
hypothalamus 30, 158

I
identification 169, 203
immune system 44–5, 165,
198, 201, 212, 239, 242,
270–1, 272, 277
incontinence 263, 277
injections 219
injuries 226–7
instincts 28, 145
insulin 259
insurance 165, 178, 209
intelligence 145, 149

intestines 38, 40–1, 198,
256–7
itchy skin 230–1

J
Jack Russell Terrier 75
joints 27, 244–7, 248, 271,
277
jumping fences 191

K
kennel clubs 53
kennel cough 212, 213, 235
kennels, outdoor 171
kidneys 42–3, 260–2

L
Labrador Retriever 94
lameness 244–9
laws 165, 178
learning 146–7
leashes 168, 169, 183, 186,
190
leg problems 227, 244–9
leptospirosis 212, 213, 267
Lhasa Apso 72
lice 215
licking 156, 233
life expectancy 276
ligaments 27, 249
limbic system 28, 35, 274
liver 41, 259
living with dogs 160–1
lost dogs 203
lungs 37, 236
Lyme disease 217, 247

M
male dogs 133, 165
neutering 133, 193,
216–17
reproductive system 42,
43, 138–9, 265
scent marking 152
Maltese Terrier 59
mating 43, 138–9
meat 39, 198, 201
medicines see drugs
microchips 169, 203
milk 31, 143, 144, 257, 270
minerals 201, 248
mites 215, 231, 268

mixed breed dogs 128–9, 166
mouth 39–40, 196–7, 252–3, 277
movement 27
muscles 26, 27, 244, 249, 277
muzzles 221
myelopathy, chronic 251

N

nails 25, 157, 196
names 173
nervous system 28–9
neutering 133, 165, 193, 201, 216–17, 264
Newfoundland 127
nibbling 156
nipping 191
nipples 140, 143
Norfolk Terrier 81
nose bleeds 234–5

O

obesity 201, 258
oestrus see season
Old English Sheepdog 106
older dogs 158–9, 200–1, 275, 276–9
osteochondrosis (OC) 245
ovaries 43, 139, 140

P

pack behaviour 134–5, 145, 149, 150
pancreas 258–9
panting 221, 234
Papillon 67
parainfluenza 212, 213
paralysis 250–1
parasites 165, 214–15, 217, 230, 231, 238–9
parathyroid glands 243
parvovirus 212, 213
paws 25
pedigree dogs 53, 128, 166–7
Pekingese 66
periodontal disease 253
pheromones 47, 152
phobias 274–5
Pinscher, Miniature 60
pituitary gland 30, 31, 43, 242

plants, poisonous 229
play 31, 154–5
Pointer 97
German 95
poisons 228–9, 240
polyarthritis 247
Pomeranian 61
Poodle 70, 110
pregnancy 43, 140–1, 201, 258
progressive retinal atrophy (PRA) 267
protein 199, 201, 262
Pug 62
pulling on the lead 190
puppies: birth 142–3
choosing 166
first few weeks 144–5, 172–3
immunity 45
parasites 214
play 31, 154–5
socialization 135, 146–7, 155
training 170–1, 182–7
vaccinations 213
in the womb 141
Pyrenees, Great 120

R

rabies 212, 213, 217
random-bred dogs 128–9, 166
rectal obstructions 257–8
regurgitation 151, 255
reproductive system 42–3, 264–5
rescue dogs 129, 167
respiratory system 36, 37, 234–7
responsible ownership 216–17
rewards 147, 180–1, 186–7, 188
Rhodesian Ridgeback 103
ringworm 217, 230, 233
rolling 157
Rottweiler 122
Rough Collie 107
roundworms 214, 215, 217
rubbing 157

S

St. Bernard 124
Samoyed 109
scavenging 150–1, 228, 254, 259
scent marking 47, 152–3
scenting ability 35
Schnauzer 73
scooting 157, 258
Scottish Terrier 78
scratching 157, 230–1
search and rescue dogs 57
season 43, 138–9, 140
seizures 241
selective breeding 23, 48–9, 52–3, 132, 137
senses 29, 32–5
Setter: English 99
Irish 96
shaking 157
Shar Pei 112
Shetland Sheepdog 69
Shih Tzu 71
shock 220, 224–5, 255
shows 52–3, 54–5, 204
sight 32–3, 276
skeleton 26–7
skin 24, 44, 211, 230–3
sleep 158, 172–3, 240, 277
smell, sense of 29, 35, 47
sneezing 234
snoring 236
social behaviour 134–5, 146–7, 155
sperm 42, 43, 139
spinal cord 29, 250–1
splints 227
Springer Spaniel, English 87
Staffordshire Bull Terrier 82
stain removers 175
stomach 38, 40, 44, 254–5
stress 272, 274
stroking 161
submission 175

T

tails, docking 49, 209
tapetum lucidum 33
tapeworms 157, 214, 215, 217
taste, sense of 35

teeth 39, 196–7, 200, 253, 277
temperature 210
territory 47, 134, 135, 152–3, 193
therapy dogs 57
thermometers 210
throat, foreign bodies in 252–3
thyroid gland 31, 242–3, 270
ticks 215, 217, 231, 247
"tie" 139
tongue, taste buds 35
touch, sense of 29, 57, 153
tourniquets 227
toxocariasis 217
toys 176–7, 181
training 31, 54, 149, 170, 180–7
travel 203
tumours 233, 241, 247–8, 253, 265, 272–3

U
unconsciousness 221, 237, 240
urinary system 42–3, 260–3
urine 29, 43, 277
    house training 174–5
    scent marking 47, 152–3

V
vaccinations 141, 212–13, 270
vegetarian diets 200
veins 37, 224
vets 147, 208–9
vision 32–3, 276
vitamins 201, 262, 277
voice 46, 147, 148, 180
vomeronasal organ 35
vomiting 38, 151, 228, 254–5, 256

W
walking, training 186
water, drinking 41, 256, 262
weight 38, 201, 210–11, 216
Weimaraner 98
West Highland White Terrier 79
wheezing 236
Whippet 90
whipworms 214
wobbler syndrome 251
Wolfhound, Irish 117
wolves 22–3, 27, 134–5
womb 141, 142, 265
working dogs 56–7, 205
worms 214, 215, 217, 238–9, 254
wounds 224, 226–7

Y
Yorkshire Terrier 63

Acknowledgments

Author's acknowledgments

"She's just like you!", my wife explained, looking at our young Golden Retriever, Macy, lying at my feet as I wrote this book. "She pretends she's relaxed and content to dream dog dreams but she really wants to investigate every scent, tree, and squirrel, and socialize with every dog, person, or goose, for that matter, that she meets. Neither of you can or want to sit still."

Julia's right, about both Macy and me. We've both inherited a natural curiosity about the world we live in. This can be fun to observe in a dog but I suspect it might be less appealing in a human. So thanks Julia, for putting up with my weekends buried in canine trivia, my absence at meetings, and my absence when staring at a computer screen. Its good to know you get pleasure from the end result too.

This book has been wonderful to write because the editorial team has been so knowledgeable, affable, and professional. Thanks to Marek Walisiewicz, Paul Reid, and Kati Dye at Cobalt id for being dog lovers as well as superb editors.

Publisher's acknowledgments

Cobalt id would like to thank Dr Kim Bryan for proofreading, Hilary Bird for indexing, Debbie Maizels for illustration, and the following for help with content and images: Dr Jane Dobson and Lizza Baines at Queen's Veterinary School Hospital, University of Cambridge; Paula Oldham at Iams UK; Prof Dr A Hesse at Universitätsklinikum, Bonn; Reinhard Forberger at Boehringer Ingelheim; Portman Veterinary Clinic; Anne Readings at Silverstream Kennels; and Logan, Arthur, Megan, and Josie.

Picture credits

The publisher would like to thank the following for their kind permission to reproduce their photographs: (Abbreviations key: t=top, b=bottom, r=right, l=left, c=centre)

1: Getty Images/Morgan Mazzoni; 2: Corbis/Paul Barton (tl); 2–3: Getty Images/Sean Ellis; 4: Getty Images/Paul Harris (bl); 4–5: Getty Images/Ted Wood; 6: Getty Images/Karl Hentz (bl); 6–7: Getty Images/Chip Simons; 8: Masterfile UK/Valerie Simmons; 9: Getty Images/Michelangelo Gratton (br); 10–11: Getty Images/VCL/Chris Tubbs; 12–13: Getty Images/Gary Randall; 13: RSPCA/Angela Hampton (tl); 14: NHPA/E. A. Janes; 18: Getty Images/Gary Randall; 21: Digital Vision; 37: Science Photo Library/NIBSC (cr); 37: Getty Images/Peter Cade (tl); 43: Science Photo Library/J Walsh (cr); 45: Science Photo Library/Biology Media (br); 51: National Geographic Society/James L Stanfield; 57: Corbis/Jim Craigmyle (tr); 57: Pictor International (tl); 129: Marek Walisiewicz (cl); 131: Getty Images/Lorentz Gullachsen; 141: Portman Veterinary Clinic (br); 163: Getty Images/Ron Chapple; 167: RSPCA/Tim Sambrook (br); 187: Getty Images/Lori Adamski Peek (br); 203: Marek Walisiewicz (tr); 207: Getty Images/Christian Michaels; 209: Sylvia Cordaiy Photo Library Ltd/Monika Smith (br); 215: Science Photo Library/Sinclair Stammers (tr); 217: Science Photo Library/K H Kjeldsen; 231: Science Photo Library/Alfred Pasieka (br); 232: RSPCA/Angela Hampton (tl); Cheryl A Ertelt (tr); 233: Science Photo Library/Eye of Science (bl); 235: RSPCA (tr); 236: RSPCA/Angela Hampton (tr); 241: Queen's Veterinary School Hospital, University of Cambridge (br); 246: RSPCA/Ms Marina Imperi (t); 248: FLPA – Images of nature/Martin B Withers (tl); 248: Sally Anne Thompson (tr); 250: Portman Veterinary Clinic (br); 258: Warren Photographic/Kim Taylor (tl); 259: Warren Photographic/Jane Burton (br); 261: Marek Walisiewicz (tr); 263: Prof Dr A Hesse, Univeritätsklinikum, Bonn (br,1), (br,2), (br, 3); 264: Queen's Veterinary School Hospital, University of Cambridge (bl); 267: RSPCA/Tim Woodcock (tr); 271: Science Photo Library/BSIP (bl); 273: RSPCA/Angela Hampton (tr); 275: Getty Images/Jeffrey Sylvester (tl).

All other images © Dorling Kindersley
For further information see:
www.dkimages.com